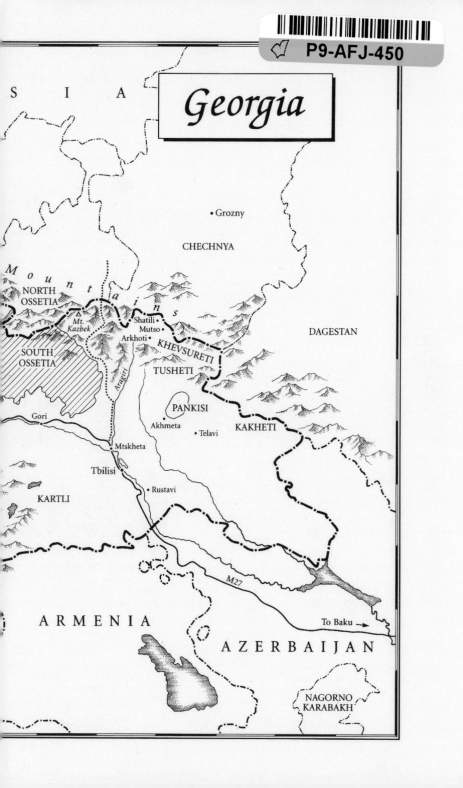

Georgia

S I A

• Grozny

CHECHNYA

Mountains

NORTH
OSSETIA

Mt.
Kazbek

Shatili
Mutso •
Arkhoti •

KHEVSURETI

DAGESTAN

SOUTH
OSSETIA

TUSHETI

Aragvi

PANKISI

Gori

Akhmeta

• Telavi

KAKHETI

Mtskheta

Tbilisi

• Rustavi

KARTLI

M27

To Baku →

A R M E N I A

A Z E R B A I J A N

NAGORNO
KARABAKH

STORIES I STOLE

STORIES I STOLE
From Georgia

✳

WENDELL STEAVENSON

GROVE PRESS
New York

First published in Great Britain in 2002 by
Atlantic Books, an imprint of Grove Atlantic Ltd.

Published simultaneously in Canada
Printed in the United States of America

The following publishers and estates have generously given permission to use extracts from the following copyright works: Gillon Aitken Associates for Bruce Chatwin's introduction to *Journey to Armenia* by Osip Mandelstam, 1980. Random House Group Ltd. for *Letters to Georgian Friends* by Boris Pasternak, translated by Avrahm Yarmolinsky. Random House Inc. for *A Hero of Our Time* by Mikhail Lermontov, translated by Vladimir Nabokov and Dmitri Nabokov, 1958; *Sandro of Chegem* by Fazil Iskander, 1979, translated by Susan Brownsberger, 1983. Random House Inc. and Granta Books for *Imperium* by Ryszard Kapucinski, 1993, translated by Klara Glowczewska, 1994. Random House Inc. and Harvill Press, a division of Random House Group Ltd., for *The Leopard* by Giuseppe di Lampedusa, 1958, translated by Archibald Colquhoun, 1960, 1988. Random House Inc. and Random House Group Ltd. for *Ali and Nino* by Kurban Said, translated by Jenia Graham, 1970.

FIRST AMERICAN EDITION

Library of Congress Cataloging-in-Publication Data

Steavenson, Wendell, 1970–
    Stories I stole / Wendell Steavenson.
      p. cm.
    ISBN 0-8021-1737-6
    1. Georgia (Republic)—Social life and customs—Fiction. I. Title.

PS3619.T4756 S7 2003
813'.6—dc21   2002033864

Grove Press
841 Broadway
New York, NY 10003

For Mum and Pa

... the Caucasus, that is, beauty that is always unfathomable and everywhere overwhelming... it is in more senses than one a country which has most astonishingly never experienced a break in its existence, a country which has remained down to earth even now and has not been carried off into a sphere of abstraction, a country of amaranthine colour and of everyday reality, however great its present hardships may be.

It was just in this light that we now began to see Georgia and we could not help being amazed at the things we experienced with you, as though it were something inconceivable and a legend.

– Boris Pasternak in a letter to the Georgian poet Paolo Yashvili,
July 1932. Yashvili committed suicide during the 1937 purges.

Contents

Author's Note

Some details of character, incident and place have been changed, although not the ones pertaining to real political people or specific news events. Despite this, the facts remain true and nothing has been exaggerated or wholly invented.

Pronunciation: *kh* should be pronounced as a guttural *h* sound. The Russian *h* is pretty guttural and the Georgians have five separate *k* sounds all of which sound like someone being stabbed in the throat. For example:

Kakha is pronounced *Ka-ha*

Khevsureti is pronounced *Hev-soor-et-i*

IN THE UNREMARKABLE VILLAGE of Alkhal Sopeli outside of Tbilisi, there was a gate with a small gold head of Stalin stuck on to it. Unremarkable. Past the gate into a courtyard where an old Lada was parked with another Stalin head fixed to the radiator grille. My eyes moved up; the courtyard was wide and paved, a hedge ran along one side and at the end was a large full-length, silver-painted concrete statue of Stalin. This was Temuri Kunelauri's private confection; his garden, his place; the statue was the beginning of a Stalin theme park.

It had taken him twenty-three years to build it out of the favourite materials of communist nostalgia: mosaic chips, concrete caulking and red paint. A series of interconnecting secret gardens, each swathe of hedge was hung with old bas-reliefs of Stalin, hammered metal portraits of Stalin. Crude painted slogans gave way to a gate which gave way to something else and more incredible. In one garden a gold statue of Stalin stood on a plinth surrounded by light bulbs. Apparently when there had been electricity the statue used to rise with the sun in the morning and then descend at night inside its plinth, to sleep, and the lights used to flash. In another alcove there was a Stalin fountain (not working) that fed into a small rank pond next to a small kiddie Ferris wheel (not working), rusted, pastel-coloured. There was a traditional Georgian hut made from woven branches, full of antlers, desiccated bearskins and moulting stuffed birds of prey in various violent poses. There was a grand multicoloured tile monument to friendship between the different Caucasian nations. There were paintings and placards and artillery rounds wedged into a plaster frieze surrounding gold bas-reliefs of fighting Soviet soldiers, missiles and cartridge belts. There were benches to sit on and admire the stage-set scenery. Strangely, the air was filled with the buzz-hum of worker bees.

In the museum room, where it was damp, cold and dark, the walls were covered with oil paintings and pencil drawings and marquetry portraits and photographs of Stalin. These had been brought by veterans and old Soviet heroes. Plaster busts of Stalin, images of Stalin and Lenin conferring, Stalin visiting the wounded during the war, Stalin kissing Asiatic children, Koba the bank robber. Temuri also had a large collection of phonographs of Stalin's speeches and piles of yellow crumbly newspaper clippings about Stalin.

I was with Thomas. We made noises of impression; we were impressed. Stalin repeated, always the same old Stalin, with the moustache and the thick brushed-back hair and the eyes in which we tried to catch malevolence but which were just eyes in a picture and unremarkable except for their repetition, which followed us around the room.

Thomas and I fell silent as Temuri led us through another series of Stalin grottoes. At the bottom of the garden was a doorway hung with a length of non-colour-rotting felt. Inside it was dark and we could not see anything; it smelled of must, attics, dead flowers and rain.

'Have you got a torch?' Temuri asked in a whisper, adding, apologetically, the single word, '*shuki*,' as explanation.

Thomas handed him a small pencil torch. 'The battery is low,' he apologized. A faint narrow beam illuminated the wall which was encrusted with something brown and friable. I held Thomas's hand.

Through the gloom came a small patch of wobbling glow; it came into slow focus. Stalin's head, pale, waxen, recumbent, shone out. The hairs on the back of my neck bristled. Thomas curled his fingers around mine. Stalin's features were slightly misshapen in death, his nose misaligned, his moustache touched up with mascara, his lips too red. He was horrible; the torch beam moved down to reveal him, laid out in an open coffin, his chest heaped with dusty plastic carnations.

'All religions are weird,' I told Thomas, as we came out into the daylight and blinked at each other with a strange expression on our faces. 'It's their job to make the hair on the back of your neck stand up. We should go home and drink a glass of wine and make love and realize that corporeal is more important.'

Shashlik, Tamada, Supra

THERE WAS A MAP of the world on the wall in my office and for some reason I had stuck a pin in Tbilisi. Nina had stuck one in Pamplona – she wanted to go and see the running of the bulls. We used to lounge under our escape fantasies, chatting instead of working. Nina would halt her reverie of tapas, sherry and Hemingway and shake her head at me and say, 'Yeah Wendell, but why the hell Georgia?'

I could only offer scattered answers. A lonely epiphany watching the Vltava, black ink at night, flow beneath me, a strange affection for concrete Khrushchev housing blocks, rumours of wine and orange trees, milk and honey; Lermontov, a breakfast meeting with Shevardnadze in New York in 1994, a snowy happy winter in Moscow curled up in a garret writing my first great unpublishable novel. These triggers were half-identifiable (Nina would nod, nonplussed but kindly), but they belied a reservoir sunk deep out of explanation. To be honest, this was my own sinkwell. Who knows from where it sprang; spirit, soul or only runaway.

In any case, I got on a plane.

In the beginning all I did was walk. Past faded grandeur and cracked façades, crumbling swags and cherubs and dilapidated marble entrance halls, wooden gingerbread balconies, old apricot-coloured paint daubed with bits of graffiti, rusted tin roofs and filigree tin gutters housing small shrubs. Little basement shops selling stacks of bread and piles of tomatoes, newspaper twists of sunflower seeds, left-over rubble of bomb damage around the Parliament building, hexagonal Orthodox church steeples, the rusted-out funicular that went up the mountain. I walked up the steep cobbled streets and around the dusty squares; I walked past the carpet-seller's shop and up to the Narikala Fortress. I drank Turkish coffee in the shabby cafés. The sky was blue above; the river flowed in a swathe underneath the city's bridges, below the Metechi cliffs overhung with sagging houses, towards the ancient capital of Mtskheta.

I was a guest, an honourable occupation in Georgia. I reflected in those very first days, October 1998, when I woke up in the morning and found that the electricity was off which meant that there was no hot water, how very lucky I was to have fallen so randomly into Tbilisi's warm and easy embrace.

To celebrate my arrival, Dato the First, my first friend in Tbilisi, but not the last to bear that name, decided that we should go to Kakheti for the day. Lela and Kakha came too. It was perfect autumn weather, the sun was hot on our backs but our faces were cooled by the breeze. It was as if the earth was still warm from the baked summer and the air was soft and sunlit. The vineyards striped away from the hills along a rolling plain. We sat in the car driving through villages and ate the last summer raspberries out of a wicker basket.

Dato had an old friend from the town of Telavi who had arranged a barbecue in the woods. There was a table in a clearing – a piece of lopsided battered metal which we covered in paper; someone took the long seat out of the back of a Lada and rested it on the ground for us to sit on. Dato's friend had brought his friends and there were about ten of us. A fire was built out of dry logs, which burned down in a burst of flame into embers. Four skewers laden with well-salted pork, the shashlik, were balanced over the embers on stones and the table spread with rough-hewn tomatoes, green chillies, mustard greens, thin white onions, sheep's cheese, flat *lavash* bread, fiery red chilli sauce, pomegranates, pears, grape–resin walnut sweets. The cook, the acclaimed shashlik king of Telavi called Omari, squeezed pomegranate juice on to the pork as it fired crusted fat into sharp burned edges. The tomatoes burst with tang and fruit and salt. We drank young rough red wine decanted from a petrol can that scraped the roof of our mouths dry. Pomegranate seeds spilled on the table gleamed like rubies.

Lela and Kakha and I were polite as guests, gave our compliments to Omari with our mouths full, ate his shashlik with our fingers and teeth, rubbed torn pieces of *lavash* around our plates to absorb the residual mulch of tomato water, gravy and flecks of chilli.

And then the toasts began, as they had for centuries. The largest man, rotund with a beaming red face and a mayoral disposition, rose with his glass in his hand and began to speak.

'Today we are here to welcome new friends and old friends. I have known Dato since he used to come and visit his grandmother here when he was a child. We've had a lot of good times! A lot of wine! And a lot of love has flowed between us. And so I was very happy when he told me that he would be bringing his friends to Kakheti today. Kakha –' and our master of ceremonies, *tamada*, raised his glass to Kakha, 'is someone I have always admired. I know he is a very close friend of Dato's and I am honoured to welcome him here. I feel –' the *tamada* put his hand on his heart, 'that we are very good friends now that he has come to visit me in my own village, here in the woods where Dato and I have spent long hours –'

'Drinking!' cried out one heckler.

'Drinking sometimes!' replied the *tamada*, laughing. 'Drinking often! And always happy.' Then he paused while he shifted his subject to me and Lela. 'I should also welcome Lela and Wendell. Lela I know is very talented, a journalist for Radio Liberty! That means she can say whatever she likes! And our guest from England or America – I don't know which – or both places – Wendell – has come to Georgia to write about us. She tells me she is looking for stories. Well we have many stories in Georgia, old ones, good ones, stories about friendship. She is welcome! We may not have luxury, we may not have electricity, but we are friends and friendship begins with a glass of wine, a toast – conversation comes later; interviews we leave to the experts. Here we have a few things, we have wine, we have our stories and these things we would like to share.'

Our glasses were held poised. The dry rasping young wine made us thirsty but we were unable, as procedure dictated, either to drink or put the glass down on the table while the *tamada* was still speaking. And he was still speaking.

'We are here together,' said Otari, circling his hands wide in munificent gesture. 'A special day,' he touched his heart, 'that my very good and old friend Dato has honoured me by bringing his friends to our village, to our woods, to share with us our wine and our hospitality, and to bless us with their company. *Gamarjos!*'

We drank our full glasses and thumped them empty on to the table. Dato the First inclined his head in a little bow to me and drank another glass of wine in one ceremonial gulp. The trees around us shook down their dry leaves. Dato the First stood up and we quietened.

'Otari is a very good friend and a fine *tamada* –' Dato held his glass outstretched; around the table the refilling ritual went on, puddles of wine forming under glasses that were filled to overflow –

Dato spoke, intoning Otari's virtues. Otari's grin was filled with a piece of *lavash* held in two fingers, as the compliments were returned.

Then another man got up to speak, to propose a toast to the sacred grape that he was drinking, 'I want to drink for wine, for the fruit that grows here in Kakheti and for which the whole of Georgia is grateful! Our wine, our country. The things that grow friendships and foster peace: we should remember to respect these things always. Drink! Be merry! Wine is a thing to be shared, like the bread of sacrament. As a gift, as a gift that we give each other.'

We drank. The wine was passed around and glasses replenished, cigarettes lit and we leaned back from the table, looking at each other's content and smiling faces. Kakha was leaning with his arm around me –

'Another glass, another toast!' he groaned. 'You should eat the peaches. They'll be the last of the year – they are wonderful from Kakheti!'

Lela had her arm linked in mine, 'And now they'll drink all night – you watch! Pass me some more wine, for God's sake! And a cigarette. I can't eat any more – that's probably the best shashlik I've ever tasted.'

Otari the *tamada* regained the floor and began an elegy to women, benediction, dedication, acknowledgement. After women, Otari elaborated his toasts into a series on the family, on children, on wives (everyone laughed – wives were, after all, a necessary evil), grandparents (one of his daughters had recently given birth to a boy), to sons (to grow up strong and take your place in the future), on love, on happiness (which does not depend on money but only on the things that had been previously drunk to).

One of the men fetched another petrol can from the car and decanted it into an old plastic Coke bottle. Otari continued to honour life with his glass of wine. He rested his glass on the great belly curve of his stomach. My eyes blurred; I focused on fleeting vignettes: the edge of Kakha's smile, a blonde curl of Lela's hair, a half-full glass of wine, a bowl of grapes, the perfect interior blush of a peach segment. Time distended and hung about us in a premonition of memory.

The fire burned brightly when we tossed dry leaves on to it, the beech trees swayed like a living cathedral above us. At first their leaves were yellow against a blue sky, then leaden against grey as evening fell, and finally black against a deep purple night. The moon came up very clear and lit shards of clouds silver. Each person was toasted and included: to friends, to friendship, to marriage, to children, to women, to parents, to our teachers and mentors, to our country, to Stalin, to the Queen, to love, to understanding, to remembrance, to dead people. We shared the satisfied smile of well-being. My stomach gurgled, sloshing full of shashlik and sharp red wine and friendship. I was happy; charmed, drunk and beguiled, like thousands of guests and invaders before me, in the land of hospitality.

'It doesn't mean anything,' Kakha told me months later when we were sitting around at a birthday party, bored by the rigmarole of the banquet, the well-laden table, the inimitable Georgian feast, the *supra*. 'Thirty years the same idiots sit around a table and repeat the same toasts. They are only words and insincere.'

The *tamada* culture was honour; it was Georgian, old and entwined; it enshrined wine and poetry. But it served another purpose too, this exaggerated hospitality; a point-of-honour hospitality. Always the raised glass, the exhortation, 'Drink!' In the mountains in Svaneti once I stood on the table and drank *chacha*, distilled grape, from the hollow of an elkhorn, cheered by twenty local men with faces rubbed red with sun and alcohol. High up in Khevsureti an old woman with a deep-creased face held my chin to force vodka down my throat and followed it with a glass of molten butter. And on a festival day one summer Zaliko and I drove out of a village with several inhabitants running after us brandishing bottles of clear liquid. 'God they are all madness,' said Zaliko, looking over his shoulder and accelerating, 'if we stop we'll never be allowed to get away.'

It was a kind of aggression. When they did not know you well, they filled your glass and filled it again and carefully watched how you drank it. This was their measure of you; this was done to disarm you. Georgian to Georgian, between friends and family, at funerals and birthdays, for meeting and for parting, the toasting was less belligerent. The quantities, however, were still fairly large and could provoke either love or violence. This was the Georgian way, friend or enemy with nothing in between. History was lost in tradition, drinking a way of remembering and forgetting at the same time.

Shuki

I RENTED AN APARTMENT just off Perovskaya Street. It belonged to an artist and was filled with collected generations of remembered things like brass ashtrays and butterfly collections and thick glossy art books from St Petersburg, the Royal Academy, the Vatican and the Prado. The past was all around; seventy years of intervening communist taste (beige, nylon, cheap veneer) had been ignored. Throughout the apartment there was a dim patina of hand-worn use, a dull shine from softly shuffled feet across the parquet floor. On the wall in the living room there were two Hogarth prints, fragments of tapestry, beaded evening bags from some distant imperial epoch, cubist paintings by friends, sketches and cartoons and an old cavalry sword which I thought I could probably reach in an emergency.

The hall was hung with black-and-white photographs: smiling portraits of dead ancestors, stiff couples in high-necked Victorian dress, highlanders in woolly sheep hats gripping *kinzhals*, daggers, at their waist, rifles propped against the wall, groups of friends at picnics, lace around the collars of high-necked dresses and parasols. The long and aristocratic profile of one woman appeared in several pictures. Her eyes were large and dark, her nose thick and prominent, her hair was swept up in a voluptuous chignon. This was a great-aunt, revered as a great beauty of the day. In one photograph, sepia and blurred, she sat next to A Famous Georgian Poet under a peach tree. He was looking at her adoringly while she smiled at the camera in the midst of a languid summer meadow. Both of them were killed in the purges of 1937.

The house had belonged to a rich merchant before the Revolution; the entrance hall was marble but the walls which the communists had put up to partition the floors into apartments were thin. A family of seven lived on the other side of my bedroom wall: an old father dressed in a dirty singlet and a pair of grey greasy trousers, slopping about in house slippers, a stout woman of about fifty who was perhaps a cousin, three sisters and two babies, one of whom yelled continuously. They were telescoped into three narrow interconnecting rooms with a bed in every corner. Apart from a television, they had no other furniture. Plaster had fallen down from the ceiling exposing wooden slats and the whitewashed walls were spotted with damp. It was very bare.

In the evenings I could hear the father belch at the TV, the baby cried, pots clanged in the corridor-kitchen. One time there was a God-awful racket of clattering and smashing outside my back door which led on to our communal wooden balcony. A man was shouting and banging on the door and entangling himself in our washing as two of the household screeched insults at him until he went away.

Venera, the older woman, was an indefatigable borrower: my telephone was her telephone and whether it was kerosene or a bit of garlic or an extra blanket or some coffee or a couple of cigarettes or a few balls of naphthalene or three eggs, I surrendered them to her. In return she knocked on my door at all hours and exhorted me to come and drink vodka with her and eat home-made raspberry jam. I usually went; I was very fond of vodka and home-made raspberry jam.

'You are too thin,' she would tell me, despairing of my lack of husband, pinching my cheeks and slapping my arms, 'no man, no children –' And then she would pause for a second before asking, 'You don't have any extra candles? We're down to one old stub until I go to the market tomorrow –'

My apartment was merely the extension of hers. She banged on my door, drank my tea, complained about her headache which was constant:

'You have your foreign medicines. Your very good pills. Please, just give one to me because my head is swollen like a water melon and I can hardly breathe with the pressure of it!'

My medicine cabinet was her medicine cabinet. By the middle of December I was left with half a packet of indigestion tablets and twelve Valium which I was hoarding in case hibernation became necessary.

In the autumn it was fine to stand out on my balcony and watch what was going on below: the precise, tinny sound the loose flap of metal roof on the house opposite made when it twisted and banged in the wind; the workmen with permanent cigarettes between their lips installing a satellite dish on the balcony of the apartment downstairs ('He works for the customs! He can afford it!' snorted Venera). There were plenty of colourful melancholy details of the neighbourhood. Perovskaya was Tbilisi's bar district, lined with neon signs and advertisements for the usual global brands of Western vanguard: Marlboro, Camel, Guinness, Lucky Strike, and 'Coming Soon to Tbilisi!' McDonald's which I inevitably patronized when I had a hangover. The bars too were lit up with fluorescent signs: Manhattan, NorthWest, Nostalgia which aptly hosted later scenes of love and break-up, Wheels, The Nali, The Toucan, and the Admiral Benbow before it closed because its seven female owners sat at the corner table every night and drank the place dry.

There was the Beatles Club with a fab four theme, pretensions of swank and a strange atmosphere. The clientele was mixed: middle-aged World Bank mission chiefs with their technocrat colleagues, all straight-from-the-office, still wearing ties, dancing with their inter-preters amid mid-rank Mafia boys who occasionally stabbed each other over drugged-out prostitutes.

On the corner was a Mexican restaurant which was nouveau-flash, full of brass fittings and potted plants, linen tablecloths and super-cilious waiters with bow ties. The place was popular with rich parliamentarians and their mistresses. On election night I sat in there with Zviad who narrowly missed getting a seat, Lawyer Dato who had been successfully elected and the president of the Georgian National Bank, Irakle Managadze, who was cynical and intelligent, and who had upended a bottle of whisky down his throat and was railing at all of them, 'You morons have no idea! It's all bullshit. Now you'll begin to learn about politics! You'll begin to see how you have sold your souls! Ha!'

Outside, the black Mercedes with AAA government plates cruised among the prostitutes and the street kids selling roses and the deaf man selling pocket torches. Some of the bars were empty, some were full. As soon as one closed a new one opened. It was the paradox of Perovskaya that it could appear popular and prosperous, full of happy rich drunken people, and at the same time pathetically bereft, a grave-yard of hopeful businesses with loan-shark loans and empty tables.

In the third week of November, it became winter and such obser-
vational dilettantism was impossible; every unit of time and energy
was taken up with waiting for the electricity to come on and trying to
get warm.

It would take too long to explain why there was very little
electricity and no heat in Tbilisi during the winter months. The
municipal heat had been turned off in 1994; the electricity had begun
to go off earlier than that. The reasons were so intertwined with
Georgian networks of 'patronage', black hole, patchwork and jerry-rig
that it was impossible to separate sabotage (a strange and sudden
fire at Gadarbani, the country's only thermal power station) from
corruption (the bungling greedy idiots at SakEnergo, the state
energy concern) from non-payment (less than 30 per cent of the population in Tbilisi paid their electricity bills; Georgia owed Russia
millions in electricity back debts) from theft (part of the copper trans-
mission line between Armenia and Georgia was nicked one winter),
from black clan economics (Someone had the kerosene trade sewn
up; it was in Someone's interest to make sure there was no cheap,
clean alternative) from incompetence (the next winter the pride of
Gadarbani, brand-new gleaming Unit 10, repaired with sackfuls of
German money, broke down because the engineer on duty didn't know
what to do when a red light on the computerized display panel started
to blink unexpectedly) from infrastructure deterioration (once the
whole of eastern Georgia went black as the 500kW line from the
Enguri hydro plant collapsed under the weight of what one com-
mentator described as 'pre-election abuse') from the oft-repeated
worn excuse: 'The Soviet Union collapsed; there was a civil war.'
Which was true. But if the Armenians could sort out a meagre
supply –

'Ah, true,' replied Lawyer Dato, glibly. 'But the Armenians have their own nuclear power plant.' There was always an excuse.

The lights went out all day and they were supposed to come back on, according to the ration, at around six for four or five hours. But the winter weeks went by and the ration decreased and became more random. The sky darkened, the room darkened. I lit candles which spilled small pools of illumination and wax. I bought kerosene from a man in a tin hut hovering over his barrel of fuel with a wirewrap-handled jug and a cigarette between his teeth. I played solitaire and listened to the chugging generators of the bars in the street below. I sat in my coat next to the gas heater, which ran off a red gas canister. I drank half a bottle of whisky a day.

In a sense there was nothing I could not do with the lights off; but dark and cold was so miserable that it became impossible to summon the will to do anything. Tbilisi went to bed like Oblomov in the winter, grumbled, sank quietly out of sight, conserved, endured. After a while you got used to it. Every three days the gas canister for the heater ran out, every two weeks the gas canister for the stove and the hot water ran out and I called Ramaz, the gas canister man, who came to the door hefting the monstrous thing up the stairs. In my first winter the price went from seven lari to ten to fourteen. Winter was expensive.

But, as Kakha used to say, without any mirth, 'In England you have electricity. But you do not have the *happiness* that comes when the electricity comes!' Kakha lived on the fourteenth floor of a block. Sometimes he said he couldn't come out, 'because I'm tired and I just can't face walking back up again.' But the happiness was true. When there was hot water I bathed in a windowless frigid bathroom by candlelight. I never saw my face in the mirror. One day, unexpectedly, in the middle of the morning, (when there was never electricity, never) the bulb flashed bright yellow: I was so amazed that I danced. I actually danced. I twirled like a strange sprite, grinning with delight and then wrote, with glee and relish, in fingertip across the condensation on the mirror, the Georgian word for light: *Shuki!*

In the winter evenings Kakha and Lela, different men called Dato and assorted others sat in my apartment drinking tea and whisky, putting a log on the fire and watching carefully when it had almost burned down before throwing on another one; logs were very heavy when you had to carry them up three flights of stairs. In the same way that the English talk about the weather and the Americans about e-commerce, we talked about Tbilisi's perennial preoccupation, electricity. We were experts; the whole city was. We knew which units at Gadarbani were functioning that week, we knew the status of the negotiations between SakEnergo and the Russians about importing electricity, we knew about the investments and new re-metering programmes of the American company, AES, that had recently bought Telasi, Tbilisi's groaning electrical distribution company. We knew how much it cost to get a corrupt Telasi engineer to run a cable to the nearest hospital, metro, casino, minister's house – places that were guaranteed a virtual twenty-four-hour supply. We saw Mike Scholey, the British head of AES, miserably trying to explain why privatization had brought no improvement every night on the news.

Scholey was a bluff laconic Yorkshireman, intelligent and tough, with one eyebrow that went up and one that went down. He was perpetually tired, he overworked because there was so much work to do, he chain-smoked. When I first met him he was laughing about the size of the rats in the toilets at Telasi and how bringing electricity to

Georgia was a challenge like climbing mountains and exploring deep Africa was a challenge a hundred years before. Two years later I bumped into him in a bar; he was haggard and thin with yellow eyes, smoking forty a day, and talking into his mobile:

'Bloody hell, Derek, there's a rumour the United Bank of Georgia is about to go belly-up. One of the directors just shot himself because he had been caught siphoning off a million lari of deposits,' he looked up and saw me, 'Wendell, hi, catch you in a minute, I'm just having a crisis,' and he turned back to the phone, 'No, that's just it. It's not funny. That's the bank *we* bank at.'

When Scholey first came to Tbilisi there was the hope that privatization would bring light, but this was Georgia so it didn't.

'Did you have *shuki* this morning?'

'Only half an hour. My neighbour told me; I slept through it.'

'Parts of Vake were black all last night.'

'That's nothing, I heard that a transformer has blown up in Gldani and they haven't had any light at all for a week.'

'They've cut my second line.'

'Who?'

'Telasi bastards. Scholey is clamping down. It's annoying. It was a good second line too, I had it rigged to the Ministry of Finance.'

'Scholey looks ill, I saw him at the Beatles Club –'

'Scholey is ill, they've turned off the gas in his part of the city and he's got no heat and he told me that he had to spend all last week in midnight meetings at the Energy Ministry.'

'Haven't they sacked the Energy Minister?'

'No, that was the other one.'

*

When you looked up at the sky all you could see was a network web of black cables; inside stairwells wires ran, spliced, cut, re-fused, stapled to the wall or stuck there with putty and masking tape: everyone had their supply rigged to somewhere else. I had an illegal second line running out of my bedroom window to the street lamp; this was, however, only effective when the street lamp was on, which wasn't often. Out of pique I never paid my electricity bill and when I got a final demand for $200 I simply paid a man to come and run the meter back so that it showed I only owed $20. Scholey laughed when I told him this and rolled his eyes at the ceiling.

'You are awful, Wendell,' he said, 'but frankly I have other things to think about.'

Kakha's aunt was the funniest: by some strange quirk of fate, her building – a perfectly ordinary block in Saburtalo – had a permanent twenty-four-hour supply of electricity. This was wonderful; except that everyone had to keep their curtains closed in case the neighbours saw the light in the windows and demanded to know why they had electricity when no one else did.

There were a million *shuki* anecdotes. I got to know an engineer who was in charge of the electrical substation in the central Tbilisi region of Vake. He used to tell me stories about citizens coming with clubs, threatening to make him turn the lights back on, and beating up his colleagues. Scholey told me stories about SakEnergo that were so complicated and enmeshed in some deal with the Russians to sell electricity to the Turks... that I could never follow them. My Russian teacher opened her front door one twilight afternoon, gloom inside and out. It was the man from Telasi come to collect her electricity payment. Neither of them had a torch and they couldn't read numbers off the form so he had to come back the next morning, in daylight. Children would point at the long-cold radiators and ask what they were for; they were absolutely incredulous when told that once upon a time heat had come out of these strange things.

Waiting for the *shuki*. Black streets, absolutely black: the dark ages. Without lighted windows or street lamps or traffic lights. At night, before the electricity came on, it was eerie driving down avenues with vast housing blocks on either side, unlit and sightless. Only the veering bright white of car headlamps illuminated grey bundled figures crossing the road. Lots of times people got hit because a driver couldn't see there was someone there. Then when the electricity came on, and we blinked in wonder at civilization, everyone would turn all their switches on, stereos, ovens, mobile phone chargers, and within five minutes the voltage coming through the wall was down below 100V and the lights dimmed brown.

At night I lay fully clothed under three padded quilts with the winter moonlight on my face, a solid circle of otherworld bright. It fell through my window, just above the taped-over crack in the glass. Candlelight lifted the type from the pages of books and made them shine in three dimensions like oil. The ceilings in the apartment were spread with tea-coloured water stains with ruffled edges. I was particularly fond of the one above my bed; when I looked up at it, I pretended it was a cloud. My boxspring had a large dip in it. I stuffed extra pillows in it and bought several mattresses ($5 each for ticking stuffed with washed, uncarded wool) and lay them one on top of each other so that I slept like the Princess and the Pea.

The stars watched me read in bed and I suspended myself above them and watched me too. One hand, sacrificed to frigid discomfort, was left outside in the air to hold the book; I tried gloves but then I couldn't turn the pages. At night the bathroom was so dank and far away across two rooms of cold flooring that I took to using a chamber-pot. I learned not to be afraid of the dark, it was not sinister; sometimes it felt like a soft blanket wrapped around my soul. During the first winter there were even times when I thought candlelight was romantic. I curled up, insulated in my own body heat, the slumbering city all around me. I could feel the old carved wooden balconies, over-hanging twisted spiral staircases and leaning balustrades sighing gently, run over by the padded tread of cats and hung with ghostly washing.

Generosity of spirit, generosity of cheap vodka, generosity of crumbling faded architecture, the generosity of time, which hung about meaninglessly, all this, and friendship, yes, but no material generosity; Tbilisi was mean with its comfort. Luxury was my bottle of single malt and the level was falling.

When I had accumulated three or four days of cold hunched in my shoulders and my feet were damp and there was nowhere 'inside' to get warm because there was no heat anywhere except for fireplaces and kerosene heaters which you had to crouch next to, blazing one side, blue the other, I went to the *banya*, to the hot baths. The first time I was directed to the communal *banya* in the Old Town. It cost one lari and, such were the vagaries of Tbilisi's supply of hot water, it was usually full in the early evenings. The babushkas overseeing the process of undressing and dressing, clad in flesh and underwear under white housecoats, were directive: they pointed to a locker, pointed to my towel, pointed to a pair of plastic slippers, pointed to a metal door through the casement of which wispy strands of steam were escaping –

From a large vaulted room dimly decorated and lined in marble. In one corner was a pool with a submerged sitting ledge. The floor was polished by bare feet, soft, slick marble that sloped towards a central drain. Maybe forty women were washing underneath a pipe interspersed with twenty taps. The steam was immense, it rose in columns. The warmth, all round, permeated like a womb. It smelled of sulphur and soap and a drain smell, underneath, of faecal matter. Above the hiss of steam, splatter of water, the slosh of feet on wet tile, was the gossiping chatter of the bathhouse which echoed, mellifluous, up into the vaulted ceiling. All around lay bags of necessaries, rough flannel pads, cakes of soap, sponges, bottles of shampoo, shower gels, hair oil, henna, moisturizer, exfoliants, perfume. Aha! The business of cleaning! And I subjected myself to having my skin sloughed off with a pair of wire mittens and vinegar. Zoya, mistress of the *banya*, laughed a great heavy laugh, noticing the quantity of black dead skin peeling off my body,

'Is this the first time you have had a bath?' she asked, slapping me around until I was covered in red tingle-stretched new skin that stung like witch hazel.

After being scrubbed, I lay in the pool full of hot slimy water and exhaled. Submerged like a crocodile, I spied a thing of pure poetry: a girl, perhaps ten years old, perhaps the most beautiful thing I ever saw, leaned over the drinking fountain in the corner, standing on her tiptoes, arching her body, naked, purely fluid, like a statue of a water-nymph. Cold water hit her lips; her body shivered involuntarily with brown, gentle curves – not curves, exactly, not yet, but lines, lines of ellipses.

I tried all the *banyas* in the Old Town. Tbilisi was founded on its natural hot springs and they had survived all of its history. The famous Pushkin Baths had the nicest décor, housed in an oriental building covered in blue Islamic tiles, but the baths were small and the water not quite hot enough. There was a modern *banya* fitted out with Western bathrooms and jacuzzis, but it turned out to be a brothel and their water wasn't hot enough either. My favourite was called simply 'Sulphur Baths' and it had four private rooms, each fairly large with a domed ceiling, marble plinths for washing and massage and lying about on and a properly deep, properly hot, hot pool of water.

Something about the heat, something about the sulphur, something about feeling the swoosh of water against my legs as I floated belly-up, something about lying numb with heat on the marble slab, my skin panting slightly, and vaguely wondering if the management had drilled spyholes in the walls, something about the steam that flurried off the surface of the water like mist rolling on the sea, something about the navy blue colour of the deep water contrasting with my pale skin...

In the summer we went to the *banya* straight from the Khevsur mountains, filthy, exhausted after three days of walking and tents and clear firewater *chacha* and eight hours of sitting in Zaliko's army jeep being battered against the rocks and the potholes. It was midnight, we were exhausted and sore. The *banya* permeated; the three of us lay faint with relief, rubbing each other's feet, a pile of muddy clothes thrown in the corner. It felt almost like a resurrection; ethereal and yet corporeal, renewed.

The *banya* was sultry, but it wasn't sexy. It made you want to smooth and slither and stroke, but the energy necessary for sex – in that delicious supine, horizontal, indulgent state – well, it seemed unnecessary. Naked didn't seem to matter; strangers and lovers were almost the same in the *banya*; an hour or two to lie and feel and not think; conversation boomed around the dome and blurred words, we stole small glances at each other and felt good and warm and benevolent. Lungs expanded, head relaxed, limbs stretched out, washed and supple. Even afterwards for an hour or two wandering through the little streets in the Old Town, the tumbledown jumble of the Jewish quarter which was right next to the old Armenian corner, twisted around the goldsmiths' alley and a couple of carpet shops, I felt a warm core glow from the sulphur. It was a miracle of comfort; in the winter I went four times a week.

In general, the trials of comfort were petty and it would have been impossible to complain; I saw in the streets people all around with greater worries than me, tired and poor. A tailor looked out from under his sewing machine in the window of his shop. His face was lined. An unshaven man hung out over his window-sill watching the street as if it had something new to tell him. An old man sold tightly bound violets stolen from the woods; once I bought some out of pity. They were beautiful, like purple velvet. The old men hurt me the most, it was hard to see them begging, cap in hand; war veterans with no legs, ragged and dirty, begging.

The old women, the crones, were more enterprising. They were mainly found in the big central market, selling plastic bags and cigarettes, holding up a single greeting card or a packet of tissues: please, buy this, so that I can eat. They had less compunction about tugging your elbow, beseeching, following you about, short-changing you. They were part of the inclusive cacophony of the market; the men still had pride and for this reason it was more awful to see them so reduced.

The central market in Tbilisi was enormous, it elbowed pride and pity aside; it was crowded and densely sprawled over a big area. Hundreds of people lined the streets selling potatoes, onions, herbs, pomegranates, spinach, beetroots, carrots, garlic, turnips, radishes, buckets of frozen chicken legs, late-season strawberries, mandarin oranges. There were separate women who walked around with handfuls of lemons or tarragon. There was the whole cigarette part of the market, the clothing section, leather jackets from Turkey, Babygros, huge pairs of ladies' underpants. There was a row of stalls selling hardware, batteries and glass hoods for kerosene lamps, bath plugs, light bulbs, washing powder, scouring pads (sold individually); there was a row of money-changers, pink sausages lined up on a sheet of cardboard laid on the ground, sacks of flour and sugar, a barrel of tiny frozen Black Sea anchovies defrosting into mulch. Upstairs in the covered market there were the fish men with small packets of boiled river fish and gasping carp at the far end. Then came the butchers with carcasses hung on hooks, piles of brains, piles of tongues, piles of beef jawbones; there were ham sellers and rows of cheese sellers among whom you could sometimes find fresh milk next to the chicken women and the egg women just beyond the honey sellers, counters full of walnuts, hazelnuts, almonds, bottles of *tkemali*, *adjika*, fruit leather, strings of dried apricots and apples, bunches of camomile, pots of cinnamon and saltpetre, dried peppers, vine leaves, rosehips...

Outside there were hundreds of cars jostling, old Ladas driven from the provinces full of tomatoes or peaches or plums or grapes and taxis and *marshrutkas*, small buses, honking like hell. It often seemed that there were more sellers than buyers. Like the Dry Bridge at the weekends when a crowd of householders stood with their details on scrappy pieces of paper pinned to their jackets, trying to sell their flats for a few thousand dollars. Like the car-parts market where there was a whole section of second-hand bits of sprocket and screws and gears to patch up ancient broken-down cars, or the flea market where they sold a jumble of tiny electronic components to fix alarm clocks and radios with. Near the hardware market where I bought my gas heater (Turkish $100) workmen stood along the road waiting to be hired as day labour.

Times were difficult; people had very little money. A lot of men were unemployed and all the old good professional jobs, teachers, nurses, police, engineers, were state jobs and paid less than $50 a month and their salaries were in constant arrears. Very very few people had bank accounts and there was no easy credit. It was hard to know how families survived. Heat cost money, food cost money, children's clothes cost money. A family needed at least $100 a month to eat; more to keep warm because kerosene was expensive and the electricity company Telasi was beginning to make people pay for electricity; more if someone died and had to be buried or if someone got sick and medicines had to be bought. Cash in hand; maybe a hundred dollars this week and nothing the next, sell something, rent your apartment, a relative in Moscow sending money, borrowing.

This was the city; it lived on kindnesses. Nurses often bought medicine for their patients with their own money, neighbours bought bread for neighbours, people pooled resources. A man who was earning well, a customs official, a policeman who stopped people for a few spurious lari every day, a bureaucrat, a driver for a Western NGO (non-governmental organization), supported an extended family of several families. Friends gave friends overcoats or clothes for their children. If you had some money, there was someone who needed to borrow it. Half Tbilisi owed the other half money.

*

On Saturday nights we congregated in someone's kitchen or in Levan's Magic Room. Levan was a film-maker and his family lived in the same block as Kakha's. His room was on the ground floor and when people came back at night they looked to see whether the light was on and if it was they would often stop by for a cup of coffee, a glass of vodka, a couple of cigarettes. Kakha told me that during the bad time of the civil war and Mekhedrioni gunmen in the early nineties, when it was impossible to go anywhere at night, all the younger people from the block used to assemble there. It was called Levan's Magic Room because it had the magical effect of making people fall in love. Lela had fallen in love in it, I fell in love with Thomas in that room, Kakha well... another story; and there were many other examples. Levan, however, strangely, had never fallen in love in his own bedroom.

The room was an interesting mess. The walls were entirely covered with posters for films, notices, old watercolours, portraits cut out from magazines: Stalin, Hemingway, Jimi Hendrix; there were small oil paintings given by artist friends, photographs of Levan when he was a boy, old photographs of Georgian highlanders in shaggy wool hats, doodles, monographs, bits of poems. There were scripts lying about on the desk amid the detritus of kerosene lamps, tiny overflowing ashtrays, a candlestick, a toy car. Stacked up in book-shelves were biographies and collections: the entire works of Jack London, an old, inexplicable Soviet favourite, Shakespeare, pamphlets and art books. Every time I sat there I saw something I hadn't seen before and I had a new thought connected to it which connected with something else. There was a torn portrait of the medieval Queen Tamara, for example – didn't the famous Armenian director Parajanov make a shadow-box collage about Queen Tamara? – didn't Sophiko Chiaureli star in the Parajanov film *The Colour of Pomegranates?* And the conversation would swirl about with the vodka and we would wriggle inside our coats to feel warm amid the fragments of Tbilisi intelligentsia life, the bright yellow pool of kerosene lamplight and something Lela was saying...

Zaliko's Theory

I THINK ZALIKO LIKED me because I liked to listen to his stories. The detours were often better than the destination and when I listened I felt my way through Georgia by vicarious osmosis. In the winter my favourite place to sit was by the fire in Zaliko's family's apartment. There was a chair made out of rough pine and carved with tessellating triangles and everlasting-life spirals. Zaliko called it the throne and a carpenter in Svaneti had made it for his father. When his father was away at their farm in Karsani I was allowed to sit on it. It was the best chair in the room and padded with cushions and half an old *burka* cloak; the arms were wide enough to rest a cup of tea, an ashtray and a small saucer of walnut jam on.

Zaliko was a Stone Age archaeologist by profession and a mountaineer by passion. He was in his fifties; he had a bushy whitish beard that made him look like a grandfather (he did have two small grandchildren), he smoked filthy Viceroys, was fond of 'getting some alcohol' as he called it, and telling stories that wound around each other and went off at tangents into dead ends before double-backing through a bit of history via some gossip about the parliamentarian Guram Sharadze that usually involved the KGB and was unrepeatably scurrilous.

29

The room was dishevelled, familiar, comfortable. The floorboards were bare; the wallpaper ancient; there was a big dining table scattered with paper and copies of *National Geographic* and photographs of mountains. Covering one wall was an enormous large-scale map of Georgia that included every village and hill and rivulet. It was soft and creased with age and use; there were patches worn with finger grease and fragments torn and missing; Mount Kazbegi had been completely rubbed away. Next to the fire was a bookcase with family photographs propped in between the books. The photographs were snaps: grandchildren, children, weddings, but there were also three black-and-white portraits in a row that I loved: Zaliko, Zaliko's father, Kuchuk, and Zaliko's grandfather. The pictures had all been taken at the same age, mid fifties perhaps (Zaliko's was recent) and they showed the same man. Each was the same long face half covered by thick mountain beard, the same long nose and small dark eyes wrinkled with smile-lines.

In the opposite corner was a bookcase with glass doors stuffed with Zaliko's manuscripts, books, dust, bits of ancient pottery shards and a small collection of hand axes.

'But how do you know that man, a man, did this twenty thousand years ago?' I would ask. 'It's chipped; there is a ridge: but there are no patterns to the chips, it could be abrasion, it could be a bored shepherd, whittling sixty years ago. How do you know?'

'Pah, Wendell! Too many questions. It is very complicated. Shut up and have some wine.'

Zaliko was a humanitarian, which is an overused corny word, but I can think of no other for someone who had volunteered to dig out corpses after the 1988 Armenian earthquake and who had carried refugees out from Abkhazia across the mountains on his back. Zaliko had organized aid programmes in South Ossetia, and in Tbilisi during the civil war he had been a stretcher-bearer.

'One time – it was during the bad time of it – they were fighting all the time, they were shooting. I was by the Opera, they were firing on the Parliament. We were expecting more casualties. I looked up and saw Father! Walking with his head up, walking with his basket in one hand down Rustaveli Avenue. He was going to buy bread. "Old man!" I called to him. "What are you doing? Go home! It's dangerous! Can't you see there is a war here?" He saw me and gave me a wave with his hand; he said, "Pah! What are you calling a war? This is not a war. This is just boys." He was in the Great Patriotic War. He went to Berlin with the Red Army. And he was right. It was only a stupid fight between boys.'

Zaliko was a good man not just because he did good things, not because he loved people, not because there were always people sleeping on his floors, sitting around his table, fed and poured wine: old friends, NGO workers, visiting foreign professors, Chechen refugees, students from Kutaisi or Boston, young Englishmen come to climb the high peaks in Svaneti. Not because he cared about us all and took care of us all and showered kindnesses – all of this he loved and we loved in return. Zaliko was good because he had held himself true through all the insanity. He was independent and his independence shone through everything. His favourite expression was 'It's all a bullshit' and, to be honest, in Georgia, it was widely applicable.

Everyone knew that it was all bullshit – *now* it was obvious. Mercedes, SakEnergo, Shevardnadze, dacha, businessman, fuel oil, VAT, privatization, government, dollar: all these words were pronounced with an unexasperated knowing tone. When *everything* was

31

bad, cynicism went beyond the cynical; cynicism was moot. It was not about feeling superior to something any more since the bad was everywhere and everyday. Commenting on it was only letting off steam – there wasn't anything you could do about it –

But it hadn't always been this clear. The last decade of the twentieth century had been filled with excitement, ideals and violence; people had been carried along in all directions. Briefly: the Soviet Union collapsed into a vacuum, the Georgians elected a president, Zviad Gamsakhurdia, who was a disaster, civil war ensued along with bandit rule and a warlord cabal, and, simultaneously, two separatist wars, one in Abkhazia, one in South Ossetia. Both of these the Georgians lost. During this time Gamsakhurdia fled (he died later and was buried in Grozny) and Shevardnadze came back from Moscow to take over. Lawlessness was everywhere. Paramilitary bandits called Mekhedrioni roamed the streets. People were afraid to leave their homes; there were shootings and car-jackings, robbery, arson. There were hundreds of thousands of refugees fled and ethnically cleansed from Abkhazia and South Ossetia. Sometimes I loved the Georgians for doggedly believing that Georgia was the best country in the world, at other times I despaired of their myopia.

Zaliko kept his head in all this chaos; his moral compass remained constant. He never joined the Communist Party even though he should have done when he worked at the State Museum; he never thought Gamsakhurdia was anything more than a foolish dissident, but he didn't demonstrate with the Kitovani–Jaba opposition that was to become the twin apocalypse of war and banditry, the National Guard and the Mekhedrioni. Zaliko lost his job at the museum – 'The vice-president of the Georgian Academy! Can you believe this man still exists? He has been vice-president of the Georgian Academy since

Stalin! This same idiot.' He forcibly stopped his son from going to Abkhazia to 'fight for the motherland', he defended his home against Mekhedrioni gunmen but he picked their wounded off the street. When things were very difficult he sold cheese from the Karsani cow to make money. Later on he started to work for NGOs, here and there, offering up projects, taking care of visitors. And he had his own business: guiding people who came to walk in the Caucasus in the summer, to climb Mount Kazbegi and Shkhara. He didn't think Shevardnadze was either a demon or a deliverance. He was frustrated with the way things were, but there were many things that made him happy and happiness was in short supply in Georgia. Zaliko was at home in the mountains; by a fire with a glass of home-made *chacha*; a walk up a valley to a house where a poet lived, doing a favour, delivering a sack of flour for a poor family, news of a man he had met from that village years before, a little dancing; bread, cheese and wine: these things made him happy. Not the intelligentsia mêlée in Tbilisi, but the ordinary people who kept their faith and their lives, their songs and their poems.

In early November Zaliko took me up to his family's farm at Karsani for the day, in the hills above Mtskheta.

'You are looking tired. You are either not working or you are working too much!' he told me. 'I have to go and see Father. To take him some bread. And to the neighbours. And I should do some work on the farm. You can lie in the meadow and read your book.'

It was warm and autumn, the trees were gold. We drove in Zaliko's ancient Soviet Army jeep.

'Who's that?' I asked as we passed a statue of a man on a massive socialist horse with great musculature. The man was wearing armour and a helmet and was in the process of unsheathing an enormous sword.

'Ah, Wendell, that is Giorgi Saakadze.'

'Who was Giorgi Saakadze?'

'I have a good story about this, actually a long story, but it will have to wait until we are in Karsani.'

The farm at Karsani was tucked under a forested ridge. Zaliko's father, Kuchuk, had metal teeth and strong hands. He looked exactly like Zaliko only a little more wizened. He lived at Karsani most of the time, in one room on the ground floor of the unfinished house. He fed the cow and tilled the land; he fetched water from a well at the bottom of the garden. When he had finished his work for the day Kuchuk liked to sit on the edge of his bed and carve crosses and spirals on to small wooden bowls with a blunt awl, scraping the wood smooth with a piece of broken glass. He had remarkably large strong hands; they looked like the hands of a young Stakhanovite. His palms were calloused, but not roughly; they were worn smooth, polished by the smooth wooden handle of the hoe and the scythe. His wrists were thick with knots of muscle; the tendons stood out taut and stretched like ropes; his fingernails were clear, pink and filled with dirt.

I lay on a pile of a million dead leaves and read Tolstoy's *The Cossacks* earnestly. The dogs tried to lick me and the cow wandered about, benevolently nosing. Zaliko and his father harvested the grapes into baskets and then cut back the vines and stacked the wood. The vines, Zaliko told me, made the best fire temperature for shashlik.

Dry leaves are very comfortable; perhaps I fell asleep. In the afternoon Zaliko brought me a glass of water and some bread and cheese.

'Now you are too lazy – we're going for a walk.'

We walked along a path through the woods. Beech trees grew on opposing slopes; their trunks were dark black from the damp and their leaves were half green and half yellow. There was no undergrowth, just an even carpet of yellow leaves and a very occasional blue crocus out of season. The light was dappled. After a while we came out into a small patch of meadow, the grass cropped short by the village cows. There was a view over the edge of the hills, into the next valley, creases of forested ridges and slopes. The forest was thick and when the wind blew through it sounded like a river rushing. Zaliko let me rest in the meadow, the sky was high up and blue. The path beyond was steep enough, a tiny track that wound up around a contour until we came to an old fortification, a shelf of stones, a ruined wall, a swathe of grass and bushy trees, clumps of rock and then a small stone chapel right on the edge of the ridge of cliffs that overlooked the ancient capital Mtskheta, abandoned in the sixth century when King Vakhtang founded Tbilisi on its natural hot springs.

Zaliko and I sat on an outcrop at the base of the chapel and looked down. Mtskheta lay at the confluence of the Mtkvari and the Aragvi rivers; we could see the great basilica of the eleventh-century cathedral of Sveti-Tskhoveli. Far on an opposite mountain, we could see Jvari church and below it cars on the M27, the white tower blocks of Tbilisi's outskirts beyond. Zaliko pointed out Roman digs, the caves at the base of the Mtskheta mountain, old burial sites and a swanky new house with a swimming pool that some minister had just built.

'Why did they always build their churches on top of hills?' I asked.

'So everyone could see them.'

'Domination.'

'Maybe. There are other theories. But I think this one is correct.

Christianity was a new religion and they wanted people to be able to see that it was higher than everything that had gone before.'

'Giorgi Saakadze,' I prompted.

'Ah yes, Giorgi Saakadze.'

'When did he live?'

'Seventeenth century.'

'Was he a king?'

'No, but they called him great, *Didi Moravi*.'

'Was he great?'

'Well, Wendell – that's an interesting question.'

Giorgi Saakadze was born in the waning years of the sixteenth century into a good family. There were many minor nobles of Kartli and his family was not exceptional or exceptionally wealthy. But Saakadze was a formidable warrior in times where warriors were called for. His career accelerated through victories and he became an important man, prefect of Tiflis, Krtzkhilvani and Dvaleti.

The turn of the seventeenth century was much like the turn of previous centuries in Georgia and was much like the turn of centuries to come – the region was torn and crushed and trampled between the interests of competing empires and fragmented between its own different kingdoms; autonomous nobles, each with their own weaknesses and allegiances. *'Spoilt lions,'* the historian W. E. D. Allen called the Ottomans and the Persians, *'clumsy, lumbering mechanisms of the two Mussulman Empires went slowly grinding on, chipping off and granulating one by one the little easy-going, anarchical feudalities along the Caucasian borderlands.'* This was the violent to-and-fro of things.

At this time the King of Kartli in central Georgia was Luarsab II, young and feckless. In the eastern province of Kakheti there had been a revolt of nobles against the king who had killed his father to take the crown. In his place Teimuraz I was elevated to the throne, a boy of only sixteen, who had been raised at the Persian court.

Giorgi Saakadze was ambitious. Sir John Chardin, travelling in Georgia a few decades later, described him as *'a man, brave and strong, who united tremendous energy with audacious courage, but who was cunning, cavilling, distrustful, whispering always and ceaselessly interfering in the affairs of his neighbours'*. According to Chardin, Saakadze contrived to have Luarsab of Kartli fall in love with his daughter. According to other sources, Luarsab married Saakadze's sister. In any case, the upstart was considered to be getting ahead of himself. Saakadze's political plotting encouraged counter-plotting. Saakadze, having manoeuvred himself close to the throne, was forced to flee an assassination attempt by a faction of rival nobles.

He fled with his family to Persia, and offered his services to Shah Abbas.

The Persians had replaced the Mongols in eastern Georgia, raiding and forming alliances in Kakheti and Kartli. They did not quite have the extended strength from their capital in Isfahan to rule directly, but they sent regular armies to support their supporters. Many Georgian nobles had converted to Islam, many of their subjects fought in Persian armies; the politics were fluid. Until Abbas ascended the Persian throne. Shah Abbas the Great was truly a great and terrible man. He wanted to vanquish these troublesome provinces once and for all. And Saakadze, eager to inveigle, helped him. He found him Kakhetian nobles to pay off; he wrote letters to Luarsab and Teimuraz trying to drive a wedge between them, playing them off against each other, promising, threatening. And he counselled that an invasion should be made in winter so that the armies of Teimuraz and Luarsab (and, indeed, the general population) should not be able to flee into the mountains and escape.

In 1613 Shah Abbas attacked Kakheti with tens of thousands of men and heavy cavalry.

At the last moment Luarsab and Teimuraz realized they must stand together and Teimuraz was quickly married to Luarsab's sister. But this alliance didn't hold in practical terms. In Kakheti, Teimuraz realized he would be first to the slaughter. He sent his mother, Ketevan, to remonstrate with Shah Abbas in Isfahan and with her, two of his sons as hostages. This cut little ice with the dread Shah. Ketevan refused to surrender her Christianity as demanded and was eventually martyred: a euphemistic term for the nasty details of knives, racks and burning coals. Abbas overran Kakheti without much difficulty and, angered by Teimuraz's escape, had his sons castrated.

In Kartli, Luarsab initially tried to hold out, but the Persians burned the silk-bearing mulberry trees and Luarsab surrendered in favour of being showered with Persian bribes. Unfortunately he was later thrown into a pond, having not outlived his usefulness.

Teimuraz meanwhile regrouped and in the summer of 1615, no doubt with some Ottoman help, he defeated several Persian garrisons that had been left behind. Abbas was incensed. He sent an army of north Caucasian Lesghians to Kakheti and announced his intention to wipe out these revolting provincials for good. Kakheti was laid waste. Tens of thousands of Kakhetians were killed. Churches were burned. Some people managed to escape into the mountains, but they were few. Those that survived the massacres were deported to islands in the Caspian Sea and Kakheti came under a severe Persian military occupation. As Monshi, Abbas's official hagiographer, records: *'It had been the Shah's policy to devastate the Kakheti region of Georgia, to subjugate the infidels there, and to convert them to Islam and more than one hundred thousand women and children had already been taken captive in the course of his previous campaigns.'*

For ten years Giorgi Saakadze served his new master, Shah Abbas (the Great), fighting as his general against the Afghans and in other margins of Persian ambition. He and his family converted to Islam and grew rich on rewards of land and money. Saakadze became a trusted dinner companion to the Shah.

All that had happened was merely prelude.

No Persian army could quell the rebellious nobles in Kakheti. They schemed and talked and nodded at Persian suzerainty while supporting the exiled Teimuraz. There was an increasing danger of revolt. In 1623 Shah Abbas decided to send an armed embassy. The leader of the embassy was to be the Commander-in-Chief of Iran. Giorgi Saakadze was sent as loyal adviser.

At first Saakadze seems to have fulfilled his task. Ten thousand Georgians under arms were gathered together by the Persians and then killed, 'just in case'. But then Saakadze began to conspire. He was back in the land of the nefarious nobles. Probably they drank together, probably they drank the red wine of Kakheti with their heads back and their hands on their hearts pronouncing, *'Sakartvelos Gamarjos!'*, the favourite toast, 'Victory to Georgia!'

Saakadze encouraged the Persian commanders to go off on scouting and clean-up operations and while they were away, he killed the Commander-in-Chief of Iran, other Persian officials and their families. The Georgians had risen up! (Again.)

Saakadze united the Georgians for a brief moment of heady blood-soaked triumph. Teimuraz came out of exile and threw his support behind him. Kakheti was retaken, Tiflis was besieged, the Georgians pressed into Ganja, into the lands to the east of Kakheti, and plundered it, killing Muslims, carting off women for slaves.

For six years there was vicious fighting but the Persians could not destroy the armies of Giorgi Saakadze. Even remote Ossetian districts were burned with the ravages of war. The Ottoman Sultan issued letters declaring Saakadze Governor of Kartli and Teimuraz Governor of Kakheti; there were emissaries, negotiations, letters, messengers. Shah Abbas sent armies raised from Iran, Shirvan and Azerbaijan under the generalship of Armenian Christians. And even though the Persians could win a battle, somehow the Georgians always managed to make off with all the gold in the baggage train. Even though Tiflis never fell to the rebels, somehow the Georgians ransacked and ravished as if it didn't matter. Burning bridges, ambushes, kidnapping governors loyal to the Shah; the roads were always bad and full of mud and the Persians were always vulnerable when they marched along them.

But there were the old shadows and enmities to dodge. The King of Kartli died without issue. Saakadze wanted to claim the throne; Teimuraz wanted to claim the throne; Kartli was a richer prize than Kakheti devastated by decades of war. The Kartli nobles conspired to put the royal-blooded Teimuraz on the throne. Saakadze conspired to assassinate Teimuraz. Teimuraz escaped the plot and went after Saakadze with an army. Saakadze's time was done. His faithful support had dwindled to a diehard few. They were defeated and Saakadze fled to Anatolia, broken and treacherous, offering his services, this time, to the Ottomans.

Shah Abbas and Giorgi Saakadze died in the same year, 1629. Shah Abbas died stuffed after a large dinner. An officious Ottoman officer sentenced Saakadze to death because the Georgian soldiers under his command had got drunk and started a fight.

'He was an old man of an extraordinary stature,' recalled a witness to this end, 'and so full of strength that they called him the Bull. Without regard for his past services, he was given over to the executioner.'

This was all an old story, but Stalin remembered it. When the Germans invaded the Soviet Union he called upon a Georgian director, Misha Chiaureli, to make a film of Giorgi Saakadze's life. 'You have an apparent talent,' Stalin told Chiaureli, 'and I want you to make films about Georgian national heroes.'

Misha Chiaureli had been born poor. He started off as an actor, organizing the first theatre in Tbilisi where workers performed. The Workers' Theatre became very successful and he went on to establish the Theatre of Comedy and from there, in the 1930s, he went into films.

All this was explained to me by his daughter, Sophiko Chiaureli, who received me in a grand salon of apparatchik luxe. There was a chiming grandfather clock in the corner, vitrines full of fancy china, gilt-edged imperial chairs and several original paintings by Pirosmani. In her youth, Sophiko had been an indelibly beautiful actress; on the wall was a picture still of her from Parajanov's *The Colour of Pomegranates*; a perfect face with kohl-lined eyes beneath a medieval headdress. In black-gloved hands she was holding up a piece of red lace; her expression was clear and distant. Georgian cinema: exquisite, but utterly impenetrable.

Sophiko Chiaureli was now superannuated, the doyenne of Tbilisi's film community. A lofty position, Tbilisi's film community prided itself on being the cream of the intelligentsia. Once they had made some of the best films of the Soviet era; once their films had won prizes all over Europe; once a Georgian film called *Redemption* had opened the Pandora's box of glasnost. *Dom Kino*, Tbilisi's House of Cinema, was almost as large and prominent a building as the Parliament. But no one made films any more, except Ioseliani who worked in Paris – there wasn't any money and Tbilisi only had one cinema.

Sophiko had filled out somewhat since her heyday; sitting opposite me she wore a voluminous green velvet tent and played with her Pekinese called Ciao. She had the authority and grace of a duchess and was quite terrifying.

We were talking about her father; I had been allotted thirty minutes.

'Misha himself was a great dancer and singer although he was entirely self-taught. But it was still not enough for him,' she told me, twirling a length of pearls around her left bosom. 'He wanted to combine everything, and so he decided to become a film director.'

Misha Chiaureli made the film *Giorgi Saakadze* between 1941 and 1943. It was an expensive undertaking, particularly in the middle of a war effort that was total. Costumes, brocade, plumed turbans, pearls; things that would impress and flash and glitter on a black-and-white screen more than the bombarded sky outside: curved daggers, jewelled epaulettes, the opulent oriental replicated court of Shah Abbas, embroidered tents and chainmail, horses, wagons, and a cast of thousands wearing incredible moustaches. The final film ran over three hours long.

'Giorgi Saakadze was the right person at that time to illustrate to the Georgian people that they could not betray their motherland,' explained Sophiko. Apparently the film was often left behind in captured towns so that the Germans could see that even in such difficult times the Soviets could produce a blockbuster.

In the film Giorgi Saakadze looks like Errol Flynn, rushing from horseback to banquet to battle, brilliant intensity burning in his eyes and a determined mouth set beneath a wondrous rakish moustache.

'Of course you are right,' Sophiko said to me. 'The real Giorgi Saakadze is far from his portrayal in this film. But it was Stalin's request to Chiaureli that the Georgian people needed a kind of hero, a person they could follow as an example.'

Stalin was very pleased with the film. It was awarded the Stalin Prize, which came with a hundred thousand roubles, twice. Sophiko's mother, Veriko, who played Giorgi Saakadze's wife, also received the Stalin Prize for her role, and Stalin maintained that Haraba, who played Giorgi Saakadze, was the greatest actor in the world.

After the Soviet Union won the war, Stalin was even more popular and Misha Chiaureli announced that he respected the leader so much he had decided to dedicate the rest of his films to him, beginning with his classic, *The Fall of Berlin*, which he made in 1945. Chiaureli seems to have been a favourite of Stalin's. He was quite often *tamada*, toastmaker, at Stalin's famous dacha evenings, those interminable, agonizing dinners, as Khrushchev remembered them. Sophiko said he had a singing voice that was compared to Caruso's.

'But when Khrushchev became leader those responsible for establishing the cult of Stalin were repressed,' Sophiko lamented. 'Of course Chiaureli was affected. He was sent into exile for three years in Sverdlovsk and when he came back he was forbidden to work as a fictional film-maker. He was only allowed to make animated films. But even though he was not given the opportunity to show his love for Stalin he managed a kind of subversive Stalinism in a film called *How the Mice Buried the Cat*.'

It was not clear to me whether Sophiko approved of this or not. But towards the end of our interview she allowed a smile.

'Chiaureli worshipped Stalin, he was almost like his slave,' she said, remembering. 'My brother and I would joke that if Stalin asked our father to send him our heads he would not even hesitate.'

The emotional crescendo of the film is the scene where Giorgi Saakadze, venerated, feasting, glorious after the armies of Georgia have defeated the Persians, receives a box from a messenger. Dread is already writ on his face as he begins to open it. The portent is shame: the messenger, having delivered his miserable parcel, darts away before Saakadze can ask him from whence the gift has been sent or take revenge upon the deliverer. All triumph gone, Saakadze fumbles with the clasp and opens the box. Inside is the head of his eldest son, left hostage at Abbas's court in Isfahan.

'Pa-ata!' he cries, uttering a death-like gasp. The syllables of his son's name intone a lament and a heartbeat. The price of victory had been very high.

In 1943 Senior Lieutenant Yakov Iosifovich Dzhugashvili was captured on the Belorussian front. An unremarkable incident apart from the fact that he was Stalin's eldest son.

When the Germans realized who they had, they tried to arrange a prisoner swap through diplomatic intermediaries. The Germans had just been defeated at Stalingrad. It is said that Hitler wanted the captured commander of the Sixth Army, General Field Marshal Paulus, in return for Stalin's son. The story went that Stalin thumped his fist on the table and said, 'No! I will never agree to exchange a private for a general!'

Yakov was killed in a prison camp. It was always said that he died trying to escape, more likely he was simply shot.

I went to see Yakov's grandson, Stalin's great-grandson, Vissarion

Dzhugashvili, who agreed, 'There are of course some parallels between Yakov and the story of Giorgi Saakadze. At different periods the perception of this coincidence was different depending on the different political atmosphere. For example during the Brezhnev era when there was an attempt to rehabilitate Stalin, the parallel was understood as a parallel rather than a coincidence. There was a feeling that Yakov was sacrificed, as Paata was, for the sake of his homeland.'

Vissarion was a friendly, jolly fellow in his late thirties. He lived in an ordinary block of flats on Chavchavadze Avenue. On the walls there were three portraits of Stalin; but they were of the normal mass-produced kind and such pictures were not uncommon. He spoke Georgian very fast with Russian words mixed in. He had married a Georgian, his mother was Georgian. His brother, Yasha, named after his grandfather, ran an Internet company in Tbilisi.

Vissarion had trained as a film-maker. His student film was a six-minute short called *The Stone*, about a young man tending a grave, intercut with ordinary images: old people sitting in the park, children playing. Vissarion explained that he wanted to convey the idea that there are some young people interested in the past, some less so, but still the past exists. Maybe the man in the grave was good, maybe he had been bad, but he had at least inspired someone, perhaps a relative, to take care of his resting place.

When I talked to him he was in the process of finishing a documentary he had made about Yakov with a German production company.

'When I was growing up Yakov was a kind of hero,' he told me, 'there was a cult around him, but later this changed.'

Yakov was born in Racha in the mountains next to Svaneti in 1907. It was a rural area where nothing had changed in a hundred years. He grew up as an orphan because his mother died when he was a baby and he did not see his father until he was sixteen. In 1921, the year that Independent Georgia was annexed by the Soviets, Yakov was sent to his father in Moscow.

'Everyone we talked to who knew him used the same three words to describe him. They said he was quiet, shy, and not-very-tall. They said nothing more about him. I was annoyed that these people who knew him – sometimes for ten years – could not think of anything else to say about him.'

Yakov was apart from the Stalin family. He used the surname Dzhugashvili, while his half-brother, Vasily, used the imperious name of Stalin and swanned about in limousines, a vodka playboy. He did not seem to have been very happy; as a young man he tried to commit suicide and shot himself through the shoulder. After graduating as an engineer, Yakov went to work at the Stalin Car Factory in Moscow where he supervised thirty or forty workers. He was so unassuming no one seemed to realize he was the son of the leader.

'I think that Yakov was a closed person,' said his grandson, 'his inner persona was very fragile and he was unable to show his emotions, not necessarily because he was Stalin's son – maybe the Kremlin atmosphere contributed to his diffidence.'

There is no documentation that a swap with Paulus was ever discussed. The famous quote, 'I will never agree to exchange a private for a general!', actually belonged to a line from a Russian TV serial, *The Battle for Berlin*, which was shown in the early seventies. 'But my father and Molotov knew each other and my father used to say that such a proposal existed,' said Vissarion. 'According to Molotov, Stalin said, "No, we will not do this: what would other fathers say? If Hitler wants his generals back we will ask for one person only in return,

Ernst Telmann"' [the leader of the German Communists]. In a conversation with a journalist in 1979, Molotov remembers Stalin as quashing the possibility of an exchange, saying of Soviet prisoners of war, 'All of them are my sons.'

I asked Vissarion if he minded. If, for him, this episode was history or something personal.

'I think the question is not relevant. It doesn't matter to me what Stalin thought or said,' he replied, a little defensively, with his arms crossed across his chest. 'It is clear after understanding Stalin's personality that he could not save his son, even theoretically.'

'It's just a story,' Zaliko told me, months later, as I sat through another winter next to his fire. We were trying to decide whether Giorgi Saakadze was a hero, a nationalist chameleon, an adventurer or only apostate – or, perhaps, the ultimate Georgian: all of these combined. There was a litre Coke bottle filled with Karsani wine on the table. Zaza Abashidze was there too, a friend of Zaliko's, a historian.

'There was always an internal struggle for power in Georgia,' said Zaza, 'they were always looking to their neighbours for an edge in that struggle. The problem of Giorgi Saakadze is the problem of Georgia,' he continued. 'Very painfully Georgians will admit that Giorgi Saakadze was not a good guy. People tried national mythology to make him a hero; it was during Stalin's time that Saakadze was given a completely positive assessment. And even now, everyone who tries to revise and investigate always tends to maintain that he was still good. The consensus is that we don't want to have bad guys in our history – there are already too many traitors.'

Zaliko 'got a bit more alcohol'. He poured wine, we toasted Saakadze as '*Grozny*', which in Russian means either great or terrible or dreadful, the moniker given to the Tsar Ivan, the name the Russians gave to their biggest fort in Chechnya during the Murid Wars of the mid-nineteenth century.

'There is another part to this –' said Zaliko, lighting a Viceroy and gesticulating with the glowing tip; the lights were off and it made red circles in the firelight gloom. 'Before Chiaureli's film, the name Paata was not so common. And after this film there are many Paatas. What kind of father would name their son Paata? But now it's normal. For example Shevardnadze's son is Paata.'

Zaliko heaved his final theory out into the open. 'I see absolutely one line between Saakadze and Shevardnadze. You don't believe me? I am a scientist.' Zaliko twinkled, 'I started to check out all the Paatas I know, one by one. And it turned out, categorically, all their fathers are idiots!' Zaliko was laughing; he had a lot of crazy theories that turned out to be more prescient than you thought.

'Pah! It's all a bullshit.' Zaliko was never swayed by theory, even his own. 'It's nothing. But the name Paata! Specifically Paata. It is a strange name to call your son – internally, unconsciously, it is like Shevardnadze saying he is ready to betray anything, perhaps even his son, to preserve his authority.'

From time to time I came across Paatas in Georgia. A bartender, a friend of a friend in London who I once delivered a letter to, an officer in the border guards on the Armenian border. Each time I would learn their name I would say,

'Ah! Paata! Interesting name! But perhaps a little strange because of the historical connotations, no?' And Paata would smile at my analogy, agreeing that sacrifice was an unusual label, and shrug his shoulders gently; perhaps it was a bit odd, but it didn't mean much these days –

'Anyway,' said Paata the border guard who remembered me from the last time I'd been through the Armenian border because I'd had a flat tyre and three of his soldiers had helped me change it, 'you can call me Patiko.'

Ethnic Cleansing

ONE NIGHT IN TBILISI, at Zaliko's, I met a Georgian refugee from Abkhazia. Irakle was middle-aged; he had been a history professor at the university in Sukhumi. He had fled Sukhumi when it fell to the Abkhaz in 1993 and Zaliko had found him and his wife and teenage daughter on the outskirts of Zugdidi, on the far side of what was to become the cease-fire line, sitting under a tree, cradling their grandmother who had just died because her heart was weak and she could not walk any further. 'I fed them lemon slices and sugar,' Zaliko told me, 'it has a lot of energy and a good taste and you can carry it in a plastic bag in your pocket. It was a difficult day, I remember. There were many people walking out, some in cars, ten people in a Lada, tractors, people walking if the cars had broken down, abandoned buses that had run out of fuel. The roads were full of refugees and retreating Georgian soldiers – not soldiers exactly; just those idiots with guns, bandits mixed up with them – nobody knew where they were trying to get to; chaos. I found one boy who had lost his family, about eight or nine years old, walking around holding a grenade. I took it from him. But very gently!'

Irakle and his wife and daughter lived in a room at the Iveria Hotel and I teased him because the Iveria had the best views of Tbilisi and some of the best electricity. All the big Soviet hotels in Tbilisi were full of refugees from Abkhazia. They built extra rooms on their balconies with plywood and blue plastic UNHCR tarpaulin and strung up TV aerials and washing.

'It's true – I am always reminding my wife that we live in the most prestigious building in Tbilisi.' He took up my teasing with good humour. There were plenty of families who had fared worse, plenty of refugees from Abkhazia camped in abandoned hospitals and sanitoria. He was very grateful to Zaliko; he had a job as a driver for the Soros Foundation and Zaliko had arranged this. Zaliko poured us more *chacha*, Irakle made several warm and grateful toasts. And Zaliko was pleased because Irakle was a good man.

I told Irakle that I was planning to go to Sukhumi and he became very excited about this. His eyes filled with nostalgia and he talked about the seaside and the town, his town, and how beautiful it had been; what a good life they had had there, and then a terrible curiosity overcame him, and he paused. Please could I try to find his old apartment, his old address, try to see if it was still there –

Two weeks later I set off to find 44A Leninsky Prospect, entrance 2, apartment 17 on the third floor. It turned out to be a new block in the north of the city near the front line where Abkhaz shelling had been bad as they tried to retake the city. Half the building had been hit by a bomb which had torn off the exterior wall. The other half had taken a hit through the roof that had blown open the top two floors to the sky. On the lower floors, however, there was some sign of habitation: red curtains and a line of washing strung out over a pock-marked balcony. Across the entrance, No. 2 was an arc of bullet holes. I walked up inside and found the third floor and, as

Irakle had described it, a black metal door on the left and knocked on it.

A woman answered. She was in her late thirties, no longer pretty, fleshy, but her face was still strong and it was a good smiling face and her hair was thick black with only a few strands of grey through it. She self-consciously smoothed it behind her ears and invited me to sit down on the sofa. Her sense of hospitality was absolute; I had not explained why I was there.

'I am sorry to bother you,' I told her, wanting to be very polite and friendly, 'I am a writer. I am just in Sukhumi for a few days to do some research. Really, I wanted to come here because I have a friend, I know a man, a Georgian, a refugee from Sukhumi, and he wanted me to come and see his old apartment – I think it is this one – just to check –' I tried to reassure her, 'just to see how it was.'

'Oh.'

I tried to look as mild as possible, I didn't want to frighten her. She looked worried. Her name was Larissa, she was a little hesitant and she looked at me as if she wanted to ask me something but was slightly afraid to...

'Honestly, I don't want to get anyone in trouble, I understand it's a strange situation, but I don't mean any harm, I just came to look, that's all.' Things were difficult to explain, to articulate, but eventually the niceties were understood. I smiled at Larissa and repeated what I had said, 'Really, it is nothing; nothing will happen.' She relaxed a little, I leaned back into the sofa and made a comment about the weather. Presently the teenage daughter put two small cups of muddy coffee on the table and unwrapped a box of chocolates. Encouraged, Larissa began to tell me what had happened.

She had three children and she came originally from

Omchamchire. In the war there was fighting and her house had been burned. She only found this out later; neighbours told her. During the war she fled Omchamchire because her husband was fighting with the Abkhaz and she was afraid. She had gone to stay with her sister in Gudauta, the Abkhaz capital for the duration, for several months. It had been difficult there, there was very little space, there were aircraft throwing bombs down, her sister's apartment was bombed and they had to find another place to live.

'My husband left me,' Larissa said simply, 'he left me, three children! For another woman. I was alone with three children and my sister – they also had nothing, it was very difficult to ask them for help.'

After Sukhumi fell to the Abkhaz she came with her children and they had told her that she could live in this apartment.

'It was the only one that survived in this block!' she said proudly. 'And when I walked in, it was perfect. There was not even dust on the floor, the floor was clean; the electricity was off, but there were still a few eggs and some cheese in the fridge and there were sheets on the beds. Someone had left recently I knew. But I also felt that after everything that had happened, it was as if it was waiting for us to come and live here. I had a good feeling here from the moment I arrived.'

The apartment was well kept. Irakle's piano was dusted in the corner and some photographs of Larissa's daughter were stacked on top of it. On one wall was an autumnal diorama, birch trees shedding leaves into a mountain stream with a high snowy peak in the background.

'And the furniture?'

'It was all here. Everything was in its place, there were even plates and cutlery in the kitchen, there was *varenie*, jam, out on the balcony. It was as if God had smiled again –'

Larissa had lost some of her fear, but at the same time she knew that she was living in someone else's home. A cloud passed over her face. She was very happy here, she said; she had done nothing wrong, she said, they had told her that she should come and live here.

'I know, don't worry, nothing will happen. No one will come and take it away from you, too much time has passed, it's quite safe,' I told her.

'Please tell him that I have tried to keep things perfect, that I am a good housekeeper, I have tried to take care of it.'

'I can see; it is very well kept.'

'Look here,' Larissa pointed to the diorama, to a patch on the edge, 'it was torn here and I repaired it.' When I looked closely I could see that, indeed, someone had gone over the torn part with coloured pencils, shading in a birch trunk and colouring leaves around it so that it blended in perfectly with the whole picture.

'That's impressive,' I told her and she began to smile again.

'And there was a garden in the yard.' We went outside, Larissa leading, excitedly, to where there was a small allotment patch cut in half by a collapsed crane. 'I am sure that this was his garden,' she said, 'because there was a hose connected to their balcony. Look, I have tried to plant things and keep it growing –' And there, in the shadow of the burnt-out block, was the most perfect garden I had ever seen. Little rows of cabbages, green onion fronds, white-flowering potato plants. The earth was black and clear of weeds. There was a delicate path laid of broken paving stones. 'I have tomatoes and cucumbers in the summer,' Larissa continued, 'I have raspberries, over there, against the fence, and I am trying to grow pumpkins this year also. I am very fond of pumpkins, and flowers – you cannot eat them, but I love flowers.'

The garden was a jewel.

'This is amazing,' I told her and she beamed. 'Do you have a job?' I asked her.

'Oh yes, I work in the municipal administration, I am a secretary.'

'Does it pay OK?'

'Not so much,' she admitted, 'but it's better to have a job. But you know –' she spread her arms around to take in the bomb-site next door and the scrap of weeds and walls on the other side, 'life is difficult.'

Who are the Abkhaz?

SHALVA, MY MINDER, my guide, and I sat on the beach in Sukhumi with a couple of beers and a packet of cigarettes and threw stones into the sea. I had made a large pile of only white stones and Shalva was engaged in hunting out flattened pieces of slate that would skip well. It was late afternoon, May, tender and soft; the rain had stopped and the sun had come out to shine low and gentle on the blue Black Sea. I was tired from interviewing officials in large empty offices off long, dusty-parquet Soviet corridors and being lectured on the integrity and original authority of the Abkhaz nation.

'You're just a Mingrelian.' I told him. 'Your name is Mingrelian – Kiziria. Shalva is a normal Georgian name. I bet you could understand Georgian if someone spoke it to you.'

'I am not a Mingrelian. I am Abkhaz.'

'But your cousin is Georgian.'

'His mother was a Georgian. It goes through the mother.'

'But how do you decide? When everyone was intermarried how did you decide you were Abkhaz and not Georgian?'

'I am Abkhaz,' repeated Shalva doggedly and picked up a large slate stone and threw it into the sea sideways so that it skipped three times before it sank.

The beach at Sukhumi is made up of stones of various different rocks: amid the usual greyish, brownish selection there are stones that are green with a faint stratified stripe, white and snowy quartz that sparkle like crystal when they are wet, smaller round pale pink pebbles, chunky black-fissured fossilized coal, red-brick weights that look like terracotta and are shot through with white spots... There should be some trite analogy because in Abkhazia there used to live several different peoples: Georgians, Mingrelians, Russians, Armenians, Greeks, Jews and even some Abkhaz (although the Abkhaz were less than 20 per cent of the population). Now there are very few people in Abkhazia and certainly none of them are Georgian. During the civil war in the early nineties the Georgians were driven out at gunpoint and everyone else sensible left for Russia.

It was thinking about becoming dusk, there were few people walking along the promenade that was now only cracked concrete and rubble, lined with broken lanterns. Two orthodox priests, in long black cassocks and with long black curly beards, were playing with a dog, a man and a woman swung their tiny child up into the air.

Shalva, I suspected, was Abkhaz KGB, attached to the Foreign Ministry, in charge of 'helping' the odd foreign journalist that ventured up to Sukhumi. Apart from this he was very nice, but because of this I minded my words, or I tried to mind my words; Shalva was being taciturn and I wanted to provoke him by calling him a Mingrelian.

We walked to the end of the concrete pier that ran alongside a rusted fishing boat and a burnt-out restaurant which had once served shashlik and tomato salad to legions of blonde Natashas and their families from the cold north. There were tiny silver fish clustered around the mussels that clung to the pier. We scattered them with our toes, they flashed and darted and then we ambled back again. In front of us was the bombed shell of the Grand Hotel Abkhazia. We squatted down on the edge of the pier.

I started to pick up certain stones from around my feet that caught my fancy.

'You like stones?' Shalva was watching me quizzically.

'Let's play hangman,' I suggested.

'OK. But in English or in Russian?'

'Let's play in English.'

'No, it's impossible for me.'

'OK. We'll play in Russian, but only country names. Then I might have a chance.' I went walking in a circle, crouching down to find a cache of suitable writing slabs and writing rocks. Shalva watched me, bemused.

We sat down side by side on the rough concrete stoop, sipping our beer and lighting our cigarettes from time to time and playing hangman. I could see a tanker out in the harbour, running the blockade up from Turkey; a light on deck was flashing a signal to the shore and there was a faint outline of a rowing boat moving out to meet it.

Shalva had a quiet presence. He held a smile in his eyes while the rest of his face was maintained as serious. He was slim but strong and had long elegant fingers with a few scars across the knuckles.

'I can't see it,' I told him, exasperated.

'It's in Africa,' he prompted.

'Desert or rain forest?' Needless to say, I was losing. I had only won one game and that was because I had given *Shotlandia* too many blank spaces for letters and he couldn't figure it out.

'What are these scars from?' I asked him and touched the back of his hand. He shrugged and drew away from me. 'They look like fights.' I told him.

'They are from different things, different places,' said Shalva, not meeting my eyes. 'This one,' he pointed to a red crescent at the fleshy base of his thumb, 'was from a rifle that pinched me when I was reloading it. This one was from an axe that slipped when I was chopping wood; I was only nine and it bled for hours. These other ones –' and he waved his hand in the direction of the past, 'you know in a war there are a lot of sharp things around so your hands start to look like a battlefield.'

There was a dark light in Shalva's eyes, sometimes it gleamed and sometimes it was clouded like shadow. He kept himself guarded, but from time to time he'd steal a side glance at me and say something very intimate. There was a deeper commentary running alongside his official talk, occasionally it came to the surface. His red crescent rifle scar held a story. I had guessed that he must have fought in the war; he was the right age and his expression displayed a certain grim knowledge mixed with compassion that often comes from witnessing things that cannot be talked about afterwards. *A rifle that pinched me* – a phrase, an insight: a home-made army with its stolen Kalashnikovs, its guns bought from Russian soldiers, hunting rifles unearthed in rusted caches, grenades with bent firing pins and rocket launchers repaired with welded aluminium sheeting. God knows what he had done, this gentle, intelligent man, who was at present torturing me with African republics spelled in Cyrillic.

Shalva was always very uncomfortable when talking about the war, especially to me, because he knew I could not understand it. I said, many times, 'I don't understand it. Decades of living together, neighbours, grandchildren –' Shalva was proud of his war but intelligent enough to realize that there was no way to defend it. It had not been a particularly honourable war, for either side. He liked to think he was a tolerant fellow, 'Oh, yes, there are, even now, Georgians here, a few. I live next to an old Georgian woman. She has a few chickens; sometimes we help her out; in the winter. We can visit her if you like.' But he could not tolerate the Georgians, 'No I don't think the Georgian refugees can come back here. The truth is we don't want them.'

'So do you know yet what you are going to write in your article?' he asked me, as he asked me every day, as he must ask me.

'I don't know yet. The problem is –' I said, trying to think of what the Russian for Bangladesh was, 'there's not much to say. There isn't any peace process and there isn't anything happening.'

'There are some negotiations,' offered Shalva, 'and the Abkhaz and the Georgians will meet in Istanbul in a few weeks.'

'They are always meeting in Istanbul and it's boring.' I rolled my eyes at the sky; at the Great Correspondent in the Sky; 'They never talk about anything. They never agree on anything, they just shuffle their papers about and argue about section three of paragraph four and then they get tired of "negotiating" and go off and get drunk together and drink all the old toasts and reminisce about the old days.'

Shalva allowed himself a small smile, but he would not indulge it:

'You are too cynical; it's not good for a woman to be so cynical. And anyway it's the Georgians' fault; they keep changing their minds and lying. We agreed to everything in 1996 and then they changed their minds and wanted something more and we couldn't sign to what they wanted.'

'It's always the Georgians' fault,' I observed.

'No, we have also made mistakes,' admitted Shalva, although he wasn't going to be so candid as to tell me what they were.

For a couple of days we had been tiptoeing around this issue: who was right and who wrong, whose fault was the whole mess? He probed for my opinion and I for his. Outwardly he presented the implacable face of the Abkhaz line and explained to me with logical reasonableness that it was impossible to trust the Georgians and that they would wait for the international community to recognize Abkhaz independence. And I would nod and ask questions about all the complicating factors: the quarter of a million Georgian refugees living in hotel rooms and barracks in Tbilisi and Zugdidi, the Gali region populated by Mingrelians, the Khodori valley populated by Svans, the twelve hundred Russian peacekeepers (should they stay or should they go? what particular piece of Russian machination policy did their presence represent?), the Georgian blockade.

Like everyone else, like the conferences in Istanbul, we went around in circles stuck on the chicken-and-egg treadmill. If the Georgians lifted the blockade, the Abkhaz would allow the refugees to return; if the Abkhaz allowed the refugees to return, the Georgians would lift the blockade. The Georgians offered autonomy, the Abkhaz wanted confederation; no one else could find any practical difference between the two terms. The Georgians complained that the Russian peacekeepers were only protecting a Russian puppet state; the Georgians used the Russian border guards to impose the blockade. Round and around like the static Ferris wheels left behind in every Soviet city that did not work any more.

I had an urge to shout truths at him. I thought I knew two things. That they were all stupid and that they would never stop being stupid. I wanted to shout at him: 'You won the war. You threw out all the Georgians. You have your homeland to yourselves (apart from the

Armenian villages and the pockets of Russians), and what is this place? It's a black hole. There are barely any cars, barely any petrol, no factories, nothing works, no private businesses, a curfew, no salaries, barely any pensions, a shell of a university, a terrible hospital with an infection problem, and only about three aid agencies dispensing emergency rations, food and antibiotics. What did you think you were fighting for? Because this is no kind of way to live.'

But that afternoon I was tired of the endless futility and all I wanted to do was play with stones. After I had hung myself trying to guess *Yaponia* (Japan), we were bored with hangman and wandered about the beach, picking up pebbles and throwing them into the sea. Our afternoon was companionable and slightly complicit. Shalva could make the stones bounce on the surface of the water two or three times. Mine just went plunk. One of the priests saw us playing and came over to demonstrate how he could flick a flattened piece of sea-washed quartz so that it skipped five times.

'How can you do that?' I asked him, impressed.

'Long hours of practice,' said the priest and winked.

'The priest winked at me!' I exclaimed.

Shalva was not so sure. 'You probably just imagined it,' he said, offended. 'Priests do not usually wink at women.'

I recommenced walking around in small circles looking for the right kind of stones, which I began to assemble in a spiral (smallest to biggest) on the pier. When I was quite satisfied with my handiwork I took out my camera and took a picture of the composition.

'I never saw anyone have so much fun with stones,' said Shalva, almost (I thought) with admiration.

'You're not bored?' I asked him

'No. You are very good company,' he told me, teasing, 'Journalist from England.'

Then we talked about our families. He had one younger brother. His father had died of a heart attack two years before.

'It's more difficult now. I must be the head of the family, I must support my mother. And people do not give us the same respect as they did when my father was alive. He was an important man and we used to have a lot of friends.'

Shalva was twenty-seven and married. I never saw his wife or any evidence of her apart from his wedding band, and he never invited me to his home which I thought was strange because Caucasian hospitality would normally demand it. But then, I thought, watching him watch me rearrange the stones I had collected by colour – reddish, bluish, greenish, whitish, grey – perhaps not so strange. He was rather handsome.

His wife had given him a son. This pleased Shalva very much and his face became animated when he talked about him.

'He's beginning to make noises now as if he wants to say something – it's amazing –'

'Do you talk to him in Russian or Abkhaz?' I asked.

There was a small pause. 'Russian,' Shalva admitted, looking out at the thin blue horizon, 'my wife doesn't speak Abkhaz very well.'

We sat there for a bit longer; we didn't want to leave and there was nowhere particular to go. The shadows from the palm trees along the promenade were as long as the beach itself. The light fell in stripes.

'And you are not married?' he asked me.

'No. Not married,' I replied.

'But you are getting old,' he noticed.

'That,' I told him off, 'is not a nice thing to say,' and we laughed about it.

'Maybe it's not such a bad thing,' he told me, staring into the middle distance. 'Sometimes I have the impression of a death sentence.'

I said nothing. Shalva was thinking honestly, and I did not want to disturb him.

'When we got married there were seven hundred people at our wedding.'

'Seven hundred people? God, what did you feed them?'

'Everybody came. Almost the whole of Abkhazia!' Shalva paused, 'And now we have a son.'

'A son is a great blessing,' I said teasingly, to lighten the sadness that had come over him, 'but obviously daughters are much better.'

His eyes were intent and solemn. He was thinking about his life. He saw the familiar sweep of his horizon; the blue sea was darkening into a glossy opaque mass of little rippling waves, the sun shone gold on its surface. He was imagining what might lie on the other side of it and stirring his imagination with all the myriad jumbled images he had seen on videos and in ancient magazines into a jigsaw picture. I avoided commenting that it was only Romania over there and not worth dreaming about.

'There is some possibility I will go to London after the summer,' said Shalva at length.

'London!'

'The Conflict Resolution Group is going to organize it.'

'And you'll talk to politicians and find out about their position towards Abkhazia.'

'I think something like that. I don't know exactly.'

'London!' I said again, thinking about Shalva in London. 'That would be wonderful. I'll show you everything, The changing of the guard –'

'Where do they change?'

'Outside Buckingham Palace. And food; pizza and spaghetti –'

'Macaroni?'

'And pubs with warm beer. And football matches.' I became quite homesick. 'And my favourite Indian restaurant with spicy beans and the antique market along the Portobello Road, and there's a cheese shop that has four hundred kinds of cheese!'

'Four hundred kinds of cheese?' Shalva was incredulous. 'But how can there be four hundred kinds of cheese? Cheese,' he said firmly, 'is cheese.'

'Of course I have seen the West on television and read books,' said Shalva, after a pause. 'Everybody believes that it is a paradise, but I am not so sure about it.' He bolstered his patriotism. 'Here we have everything we need,' he said. 'The land is fertile.'

I looked beyond the town, beyond the war-torn broken masonry and smoke-blackened cavities where there were once doors and windows and homes, up to the green hills that looked down, and the snowy peaks of the Caucasus behind them. There, on the slopes where the previous day I had inspected the smashed television tower (incoming artillery shell apparently), eucalyptus grew next to banana palms, honeysuckle rampaged over banks. Giant blue succulents with engorged purple barbs, mimosa, magnolia and orange blossom that smelled like jasmine stretched and sprouted. Ivy entwined rose bushes, moss spread itself thick like creeping velvet up the shady side of tree-trunks, wild barley waved at the daisies, buttercups, tiny blue star flowers and clover in the meadow hollows underneath the trees.

There were purple flowers that grew up through cracks in the concrete in archipelago colonies, tiny white starbursts that were no higher than my little toe but spread their petals wide with all their might, bright orange happy daisies. It *was* a kind of paradise.

'Shall we go back now?' he asked.

'Yes, all right.'

When we were sitting in his car, a twenty-year-old BMW without licence plates or headlamps (BMW parts being quite hard to come by in Abkhazia), Shalva put the key in the ignition, but then paused for a moment and turned to me:

'Sometimes you have the impression that life is nothing and you cannot remember what happened yesterday,' he said simply. 'Except with you; then I remember everything.'

I smiled at him, grateful, and wrote it down.

The Duel

IT WAS THE USUAL midwinter crisis in Tbilisi, and Kakha and I slunk to Merab's restaurant on a Sunday morning for fried brains and vodka. We sat with our feet in the fire and our coats on. A meagre supply of generator electricity illuminated the brick walls. The waiter sat in the corner smoking and playing with his abacus. I spooned Mingrelian tomato sauce into my vodka to make a Bloody Mary; Kakha was watching me. We were the only people in the place.

'Can you really drink vodka with that stuff in it?' he asked suspiciously.

Our mood was grey and resigned. Kakha's oldest friend Gio had died. Kakha wearily smoothed his greying hair with his fingers and told me stories about him and Gio. As boys, scratching their names on toilet walls, swimming in the fountain in Vake Park, hoarding precious chewing gum; as teenagers, smoking in the yard, cheating in the physics exam (an ingenious system: formulae disguised as technical safety instructions on a poster hung up in the examination room); as students, taking girls up to the woods, summers in Pitsunda. Later Kakha married and went to St Petersburg, Gio went to prison for stealing a car he had only borrowed. They had less in common, but they still used to get together from time to time and drink vodka and laugh about their first wives and the fact that they were forty and, when they were a little drunker, stumbling over nostalgia: the time Kakha had gone into the extra bedroom in Gio's flat, tired, drunk at the very very end of the night and lain down next to his sleeping unsuspecting grandmother, the time Gio had crashed Kakha's father's car, and all the other times past that had been good.

Gio had fallen down a flight of broken concrete steps coming out of his friend's apartment, late, after the electricity had gone off, and hit his head on the corner of the steel lift cage. He had been drunk; the last few years had not been kind. But as Kakha had reminded me at the wake when we stood in front of his body and looked at his dead face for signs of life, or perhaps even the remembrance of life, the last few years had not been kind to anyone.

'All I ever do is go to funerals,' Kakha said flatly, 'people seem to die often. It's too cold when there's no money.'

'How is advertising?' I asked. 'Is it going OK?'

Kakha continued to gaze through the window outside. He did not particularly want to answer me.

'Jesus what shit weather,' he said thinly. It was snowing wetly, slowly, on to sodden streets. 'And I can't find any cigarettes except for this Business Club,' Kakha complained, sticking one in his mouth, the final straw among many final straws.

The government had finally decided to enforce excise stamps on cigarettes and because the importing cartel-Mafias had failed to foresee such audacity and because everyone smoked three packs a day, within a week it was only possible to buy Business Club which were terrible, but at least possessed a filter, unlike the filthy Astras, which were Russian and the only other available alternative, which some had taken to smoking in desperation.

Miserably we smoked our Business Clubs and ordered another bottle of vodka. Merab, the proprietor, came in from the cold where he had been fiddling with his car, a boat of a Mercedes of indeterminate age with Lithuanian plates, and stamped his feet. Merab lived upstairs.

'Miserable,' he declared and drew up a chair and rested his giant forearms on the table.

'You heard about Dato Toporia?' Kakha asked Merab. Apart from Gio's funeral, apart from the weather, apart from the dearth of decent cigarettes, there was another petty tragedy to discuss.

'Bandit Dato has disappeared,' I said.

'Aleko's still in hospital,' said Kakha.

'Yes, I heard; stupid boys,' said Merab and clicked his fingers at the waiter to bring another glass.

'These stupid boys are always shooting each other,' echoed Kakha.

In the village goldfish bowl of Tbilisi everyone knew what had happened. There was a web of knowledge that was integral, lines crossed and entangling. Aleko was Kakha's neighbour. Merab was related to Aleko's mother in some distant way. Our friend Lela's mother had been Bandit Dato's mother's best friend from university. Kakha and Merab and Lela knew all the old stories, had been at school with all the protagonists, knew the interwoven patterns of family by heart. When we sat up late in each other's kitchens or in Levan's Magic Room, kerosene lamp burning, talking, gossiping, I could feel a comfortable blanket of intimacy. Everyone had known everyone for years, there was a deep easy friendliness; they knew each other's parents and where they lived and all the bygone little incidents – those everyday things: fights, marriages, goings and comings back, broken legs and babies…

Although it was a dreadful thing, and we would never have admitted it, the scandal of Bandit Dato and Aleko had somewhat cheered us with its mock chivalry and real guns. And that first winter I was happy to find enlivenment, even if it was tabloid prurience, in any corner. The weather had dripped frozen and wet for a month and I was tired from inactivity. The streets were damp, rainy, soaked; condensation on the car windows, dank underpasses, dripping pipes and cold feet. It was all I could do to get out of the warm bed in the morning into a frigid bedroom. So I didn't; I tended to lie in bed all day under three quilts wearing a sweater and a kimono and a woollen hat, reading book after book and being interrupted every few hours by the need to go to the toilet.

'It was a dangerous place for a bullet to land,' said Merab, idly picking at a frond of tarragon, 'I heard Aleko might not be able to walk again.'

'A week of the dead and the nearly dead,' said Kakha. 'I've got to get out of this place.'

Merab stretched his frame across two chairs and raised his glass. 'Well, to Gio.'

'Of course to Gio.'

'Gio *Gamarjos!*' We remembered and drank.

But the living are always more interesting than the dead:

'Stupid boys,' resumed Merab, warming to his theme. 'We all had these fights – but not with guns. The guns are since the war, since the Mekhedrioni bandits. It's different now.'

'But there was always the macho bullshit. I remember once,'

began Kakha, leaning back in his chair, 'I was just a kid. I was in Kutaisi for some reason. I had a terrible hangover – I couldn't even smoke, my head was so bad. I'd thrown up twice already and my uncle wanted me to meet his friend – I can't remember why. I didn't want to drink and this friend got angrier and angrier at me. We were sitting in a restaurant and he was doing the whole *tamada* bullshit, raising his glass every three minutes. After two toasts he was furious because I still wasn't drinking and after the next toast, when I just put my hands up in front of my face and said, no really, I can't drink, not today, the stupid drunk bastard pulled a pistol out of his pocket – an ancient thing, wood and steel, from the Patriotic War – and put it against my temple. "Drink you cunt," he told me simply. My uncle was shocked, but there was nothing he could do. I told the guy: "I'm not going to drink so take the gun away from my head." And after that he left me alone.'

'I had something like that once – but it wasn't a gun, it was a *kinzhal*, a dull tourist knife,' said Merab.

'Well this is the kind of thing that happens with these crazy Georgians,' said Kakha and he winked for my benefit.

There were lots of these kinds of stories. Lawyer Dato had a scar on his stomach from where a friend of his had stabbed him. They were young, they had been fighting on the street; an argument Lawyer Dato couldn't even remember the reason for. When the police came, called by some passers-by, they took Lawyer Dato to the police station and gave him a bandage from the first aid kit. Lawyer Dato told them he had fallen over in the street and cut himself on a pile of broken bottles. The police didn't believe him and they locked him up bleeding overnight. But he never told them who had done it.

I thought of Mikho who lived on the black edge of the *vory v zakone*, the mafia clans – a school friend of Kakha's; he turned up at parties from time to time and when he was drunk he was very loud and would instigate hard shouting arguments. Mikho once told me about his first encounter. He had been fourteen. There was a boy who lived on his street called Goga who had achieved a reputation for collecting the leather jackets of other boys. Apparently he had a sartorial habit of leaving a business card with his victims; impressing upon them the logic that if they were so easily intimidated into giving their leather jackets up, they did not deserve to keep them. One day he confronted Mikho, but Mikho refused to hand his jacket over. Goga produced a small pistol. Mikho continued to resist him.

'He wasn't a big boy; but he had arrogance,' Mikho told me, remembering the story almost fondly. 'He said to me, "If you can prove to me your resistance, you can keep your leather jacket," and then he handed me the gun. I took the gun. "I am not going to shoot you," I told him and I put the barrel against my own forehead – like this,' Mikho demonstrated with his finger against his temple, 'and I pulled the trigger. Nothing happened. The barrel was empty. I knew the bastard would never be able to get ammunition for such a relic – Ha! It was funny. After that Goga considered me his great friend.'

'They were up at Turtle Lake?' I asked Kakha and Merab.

'That's where these things are always settled. Around in the woods above Turtle Lake. You can't see much through the trees so it's private – and it's handy for the city centre.' Merab leaned back in his chair and rested his small tumbler of vodka on his grand stomach. 'But from the sound of things, the matter is not yet settled.'

'And Dato has disappeared,' repeated Kakha.

I sat quietly listening. I kept my thoughts inside and said nothing because I knew where he was. ('I had to say yes, where else could he have gone?' Lela told me in a whisper on the telephone.)

When we were getting ready to leave, Kakha asked me if I wanted to come with him to see Aleko in hospital. 'I should go. He's a neighbour. His mother asked me to take him some cigarettes.'

'OK,' I said. 'If it's OK.'

We went to the old apparatchik hospital on Chavchavadze Avenue. It had not been refurbished, but it was relatively clean and there were two or three new pieces of equipment I could see in rooms off the corridors. When we found Aleko's room I hovered in the doorway, not wanting to intrude, but Aleko seemed to be in cheerful spirits and beckoned me in; warmed already by the bottle of brandy Kakha had brought, and insisting on immediate hospitality, he opened it.

'I feel better,' he told Kakha. 'There's a pretty nurse who gives me a bed bath every morning. They give me morphine. My mother is bringing me my favourite, liver and pomegranate every day. The doctor said I was lucky. Another millimetre and I wouldn't be able to walk. I can wriggle my toes now. Look!' Aleko wriggled his toes.

We congratulated him. He was going to be able to walk, but to me he seemed pale and voluble, his eyes were glazed with a reddish lacquer. It was the first time I had met him; he seemed strangely jolly for the occasion, as if he were trying to entertain us. He told us all about the nurses and which ones were pretty and which one he was trying to get to be his personal nurse when he went home.

'I'll need care,' he said seriously. 'I need someone to change the bandage and give me my injections.'

'Jesus Aleko you're a lucky bastard.' said Kakha. 'You're going to be able to walk. You nearly killed your mother with worrying about you.'

Aleko waved his hand dismissively. 'She always worries. I'll get her some chocolates,' and Kakha and I laughed with him.

Aleko's mother was known in Kakha's block for being somewhat of a hypochondriac. Once I had been staying over (too late, too long sitting with a bottle of vodka downstairs in Levan's Magic Room) and the whole block had been woken up by her calling an ambulance because her blood pressure was lower than usual. Kakha's mother, in her nightie, straining to see what was going on at the window, was not impressed with her theatrics, 'Her blood pressure is always so high that when it drops to normal she thinks it's an emergency!' Aleko's father was a colonel in the Interior Police and I had seen him once or twice, playing backgammon with Kakha's father in the yard in the evenings. He had a thick head of white hair and people said he was an honest man. After the ambulance had left he had come and knocked on the door to apologize for the noise and taken a cup of coffee with Kakha's father in the kitchen.

The operation to remove the bullet, which had lodged dangerously close to Aleko's spine, had cost $450. His father borrowed money from another neighbour who was, incidentally, the deputy excise officer in charge of impounding cigarettes, and quite rich.

The hospital room was bare dirty white paint. Aleko lit cigarette after cigarette with trembling hands and kept motioning us to drink another glass of brandy.

'Drink it, drink it! Otherwise I will drink it all and it will give me a fantastic headache from all the tablets I am taking. He's a stupid bastard,' said Aleko of his friend, pursing his lips so that a small amount of brandy could be poured over them. 'He nearly killed me. I told him not to bring a gun.'

Dato had the nickname Bandit Dato, but he was not really a bandit; he was only an average kind of idiot. Aleko had been his best friend. They were always together, since school, through their late teens when Tbilisi was full of Mekhedrioni and snipers. Aleko pretended to attend university for a couple of years, Dato hung about the streets. Together they earned a little money working for a Mekhedrioni lieutenant called Koshtaria, before Koshtaria got himself a bank and a proper suit. At the end of the bad times, in 1996, when the architects of bandit rule, Jaba Ioseliani, head of the Mekhedrioni and Kitovani, head of the National Guard, had been locked up and people began to be able to walk down the streets again, Aleko and Dato had fashioned themselves as *biznesmen*. They bought themselves a black BMW, bashed, seven years old with a cracked windscreen, and dossed on a couple of mattresses in Aleko's aunt's flat (she had left for Moscow at the beginning of the nastiness). They hung about, traded a bit of money, cash in pocket – nothing very serious, but there were still things that Koshtaria found them useful for.

One Saturday night they had been drunk – it had been someone's birthday somewhere – Aleko had been driving, cradling a bottle of tequila in one hand, racing down the river embankment road. They had decided to go to the casino. Dato was sitting in the passenger seat trying to connect the end of his cigarette to his lighter while the car was bouncing around. Beneath the Narikala Fortress in the shadow of the mountain, Aleko swerved to avoid a man crossing the street, forgot to brake, and hit a lamp-post.

Before the accident Dato looked like any one of the young Georgian men who stood about on street corners with bottles of beer and spat sunflower seeds into the gutters for want of anything better to do. His features were regular, handsome enough, nondescript, his black hair cut short, his clothes invariably a pair of black jeans and a black leather jacket. Sometimes he wore a black cap. He had a chunky gold watch that Koshtaria had given him once for services rendered and a gold cigarette lighter. He lost the gold cigarette lighter the night of the crash and always blamed the ambulance driver for stealing it.

Aleko, as Dato often said, was always the lucky one. Aleko had avoided getting arrested that time in Batumi; Aleko hadn't had his car jacked on the Mtskheta road; Aleko walked away with concussion. Dato suffered and was unlucky – and Aleko got fed up with hearing Dato whining about his suffering and his bad luck. That night the force of the crash slammed Dato's body, unsupported by a seat-belt, against the dashboard as the cracked windscreen imploded in his face. He broke two ribs and his left cheek was slashed open from his eye to his upper lip. The surgery had been less than meticulous and the resulting scar pulled at his lower eyelid and ran down his face like a Frankenstein seam. After the accident, he simply looked like a bandit. Everyone started to call him Bandit Dato; Lela always referred to him as Bandit Dato. But nobody ever called him that to his face; there was still pride in his eyes. It was said that his wife had taken away all the mirrors in the apartment.

After the accident Bandit Dato slipped into desultory *depressia* – a common enough complaint brought on by light deprivation, unheated apartments, unemployment, a death in the family or sudden poverty; in other words, by the usual symptoms of post-Soviet 'transition'. His physiognomy changed and his mood soured to match his perpetually vicious expression. He went to the Victoria Casino three or four times a week and lost all the money he borrowed.

I saw him there once. I didn't know it was him at the time, but afterwards I remembered the desperation and the scar. The desperation; casual, sneering and surly was the usual atmosphere of those places. There were never any women in them, just men with too much complimentary brandy in their stomachs, sour and losing, sitting alone at the tables and throwing their money away with a fake studied nonchalance. Bandit Dato, the man with the scar, was sitting by the roulette wheel piling chips on to the baize at every turn, littering the table with hope that was initially rewarded by the black 13 and the red 27 and then punished when the wheel decided to produce three 0's in a row while he was betting on black.

I looked up at the Casino uniform with a red clip-on bow tie. I had not covered the 0 either. He spread his hands wide in apology,

'The wheel of life,' he said with philosophical disdain; an inappropriate quality, I thought, in a croupier.

'Life is not life,' said Bandit Dato stiffly, throwing his four remaining stacks of chips on 11, losing them, and walking away.

An ordinary story. Dato's father was dead, his mother and his wife moved around him like satellites, avoiding his gravity. His little daughter shone her big brown eyes and did not know what to say to him. His food was prepared, his tea made, his socks washed. Lela said his wife complained that he spent all his time sitting in the cemetery by the grave of his school friend who had been killed in Abkhazia. Lela's kitchen window looked out over the Saburtalo cemetery – perhaps she saw him there, an unrecognizable figure in the distance, tracing the outline of the etched photographic portrait on its marble slab with his finger.

And then, finally, after months of nothing but existence, there was the knowledge of insult to add to injury. Aleko was sleeping with his wife. Caught in the tone of the tail of a telephone conversation; Dato knew instinctively it was something very intimate and serious. Aleko had managed to get a job as a driver for an NGO, Aleko had some money in his pocket and no wife to drag him down. Aleko was always the lucky one.

On 6 January, Orthodox Christmas, a week before Kakha and I sat in Merab's discussing the proceedings, Bandit Dato drove to Turtle Lake with Davit Badurashvili. Badurashvili was former Mekhedrioni, a cousin of Koshtaria's, an elder, a mediator, not exactly *vory v zakone* (he owned a petrol station on the Rustavi road), but certainly a man who held his own authority. He had red hair that was so unusual it created superstition. Badurashvili told Bandit Dato to come unarmed; Aleko had told him this too, it was just to be a conversation. But Bandit Dato had put his pistol in his pocket.

Aleko arrived with three supporters. They stood in a group, picked at the dry leaves on the ground with their feet and avoided looking over at Bandit Dato whom they knew; Bandit Dato was Aleko's friend, Aleko's friends had been Bandit Dato's friends. This tacit betrayal gave Bandit Dato a bitter smile; he tried to stand straight and look bored, to show that he didn't care. The cars were parked a little way off down the track, around them were the forest slopes above the city. There was a slight shading of snow on the ground.

After several minutes of conversation Badurashvili walked over to Aleko.

'You and Dato should go and talk this over,' he told him. 'This is between you both and some solution must be agreed between the two of you.'

Aleko nodded, threw his cigarette to the ground and began to walk over a small rise into a hollow that was out of sight. Bandit Dato walked in the same direction by a parallel route. He came over the rise and saw Aleko standing a little way off with his hands in his pockets. He went up to him.

'You have lost her, Dato,' Aleko told him. 'Let her go. It'll be easier for everyone.'

Bandit Dato was furious at such off-hand composure. He punched his friend in the face.

Aleko took a steadying step backwards but did not fall over. He felt blood in his nose and pressed against one nostril with his hand to snot it out. He wiped his nose with his open palm and then took a step forward and hit his friend back. For a few moments they punched at each other, blunt forearms masking sharp elbows, flailing in a violent grapple. Then Aleko delivered a powerful head smack and Bandit Dato fell over on his knees. There Aleko kicked him in the stomach and he coughed with a small whimper. Aleko started to walk away.

Bandit Dato sat himself up. Blood was in his mouth and his head; it pumped behind his eyes, carrying a strong current of adrenalin. He took the gun out of his pocket and fired it at Aleko. The bullet hit Aleko in the lower back. Aleko fell down.

'You fucking idiot!' Aleko began to scream at him, spitting frozen spit. 'You fuck – you fuck – I can't feel my legs –'

Bandit Dato dragged his winded rage upright. He limped over to Aleko's body, bent down and pressed the gun against Aleko's forehead. Aleko twisted around his torso and wrestled with the metal barrel the gun. Alerted, his friends came over the rise and saw the struggle. They shouted at them to stop and then one of them took out a revolver and, bringing it closer, walking with it outstretched, fired a single shot into Bandit Dato's leg to finish the thing.

Badurashvili had watched the scene from the crest of the rise. He did not go down and remonstrate. It was done. He walked back to his car with his hands in his pockets and drove away.

Aleko's supporters carried Aleko, his body-weight slung awkwardly between them, back to their car. After a moment's deliberation they went back for Bandit Dato. They found him mute, stiff, stifled, shot. He was breathing quickly from shock. They lifted him under his armpits and with enormous discomfort dragged him, limping, in the same direction. They put Aleko in the front seat and ratcheted the seat back to reclining. His eyes were glassy and afraid. He repeated that he could not feel his legs, but as they were bending them to get him in the car, he cried out in pain. They put Bandit Dato in the back seat squashed between two of them and took him home.

'I had to say yes, where else could he have gone?' Lela told me in a whisper on the telephone. Bandit Dato's wound hadn't been bad; the bullet had passed cleanly through the muscle. The wife knew, the wife had already gone, packed a suitcase and taken his daughter. But his mother was afraid for him, worried about who would look for him and find him and do something worse so she called Lela, her old friend's daughter, and asked if he could go there to recover, somewhere where no one would think to look and where there was an extra room.

'This is Tbilisi,' I told her. 'Everyone will know where he is within twelve hours. And then the police will come and arrest you for assisting an outlaw. And I'll have to bring you food every day in prison and pay an enormous bribe to the judge so that you get a suspended sentence.'

'The police won't come,' said Lela, explaining it to me. 'It would reflect very badly on Aleko if he called the police. No one ever calls the police when it is something like this.'

'So who is he hiding from?'

'I don't know. Aleko. Aleko's friends. Badurashvili. Badurashvili might want to scare him. He took a gun with him and he wasn't supposed to.'

'But Aleko's father is a police colonel.'

'I don't think anyone will come here. After all Bandit Dato had a good reason for shooting Aleko. Probably everyone thinks that what has happened is enough. There is a kind of justice already.'

Aleko's father had also been considering the ramifications. Kakha repeated to me a conversation between his own and Aleko's father that had taken place in his kitchen. Aleko's father, Kakha thought, was taking some respite from his wife upstairs who had wailed for days that her son would never walk again.

The conversation was this: there was no legal guidance to steer through this moral mishap, but luckily no one had died and there was no need for revenge. Each aggressor had wronged, each was guilty and each had been punished. This was clear and understood. There were other angles to think about, however. There was always the possibility of Badurashvili exacting some retribution for Dato's blatant trespass against code, but Badurashvili, Aleko's father felt certain – and he knew Badurashvili slightly from similar incidents in the past – would not want to worsen the situation. He would probably leave Dato alone. Dato now cut a pitiful figure in the story, Kakha's father reminded him. He would simply sink beneath the surface. Aleko would be all right, and the woman who had run home to her parents with the child – Aleko's father admitted he had not talked to Aleko about this – what would happen to her and a small girl? A child that might become his surrogate granddaughter! In any case, Kakha's father assured him, it was always the fault of a woman, her parents would have to support her now.

I went to visit Lela. I wanted to see Bandit Dato for myself. It was a Sunday afternoon, the graveyard across the opposite ravine was full of a funeral party sitting on the marble benches around the grave of their departed. The light was poor and grey. I felt for the torch in my pocket and walked up the twilight staircase.

'Oh! It's you, that's OK, come in. He's asleep at the moment,' she whispered.

We sat in the kitchen and Lela put a kettle on top of the kerosene heater.

'Are you hungry? Do you want *matsoni*, yoghurt? I have cheese also, and some *lobio*, bean stew?'

I nodded, plates and bowls appeared from the fridge. I was always hungry in the winter.

'It's because without electricity I can't see to cook,' I explained. Lela laughed.

Lela was blonde like me and everyone always thought we were sisters. We bent our heads together across the tiny kitchen table. The wallpaper was faded rose clusters, lacquered yellow near the stove. There was a bowl of tangerines on the table and black-and-white portraits of Lela's dead mother and father on the wall. All this was my familiar home. Whenever I was sad, whenever I was cold or hungry or bored, whenever there was no hot water at home and I needed to complain or to be fed tea and pancakes or to lie about talking about love and Thomas, I came to Lela who took care of me.

'I told her he'd broken his leg and he had to stay with us for a while because there are too many nephews and nieces in his parents' flat and he can't get any rest.' Lela lived with her grandmother, a tiny bird-like woman who slept in an alcove off the kitchen like Cinderella and washed up all our cups of tea for us.

'Where is Buba?'

'She's gone to pay the electricity bill,' said Lela with exasperation. 'She is eighty-four and she insists on going all the way into the back of Saburtalo by *marshrutka* to stand in line and wait and pay in full. It takes her about three hours and she does it every month.'

'That's ridiculous,' I said, incredulous. Nobody ever paid their electricity bill.

'I know. I can't stop her. She just says otherwise it's as if we were stealing the electricity.'

'What electricity?' I said, pointing at the kerosene lamp.

I told Lela I had seen Aleko in hospital.

'He's recovering. He looks all right, he looks in shock, confused, but OK. Kakha says he'll be out of the hospital in a couple of days.'

'I think Bandit Dato will take longer. I told him he needed to have a doctor look at his leg, but you know, he won't allow me to call one. His mother is worried about him, he is very weak, he cannot walk.'

'Does he know his wife has left?'

'Yes, he knows that. But honestly, sometimes I am afraid with him here. Not of the police, but him. Sometimes he cries in his sleep, he screams names out and wakes me up – Buba sleeps through anything; she's practically deaf. He just lies in bed and does nothing, he doesn't read. He's completely different from what he used to be – before the accident, before his face was smashed – he was so handsome. I think he has been bad for a long time. One of his friends came when he was first here and brought him drugs, heroin I think. He moans, but he doesn't speak to me much. I can see him smoking the heroin in his room and then he becomes calm. But he won't do anything, I can't get him to take a bath – I tell him he has to wash the wound with alcohol, I gave him the vodka, but I think he drank most of it.'

'This,' I said, suddenly realizing the reality of the situation, more than gossip, actual bodily, bloodily harm, 'is mad.'

Lela gave me a half-smile, 'I know. It's ridiculous. I am harbouring a fugitive drug addict with a bullet hole in his leg.' We caught each other's eye, we grasped the edge of the insanity of it and began to giggle. We held each other's hands, clinked our mugs together and laughed. It was mad. There was nothing to be done about it.

'What are you laughing about?' Bandit Dato, roused by our sudden hysteria, had limped into the kitchen on a wooden crutch.

He looked at me, confused. Bandit Dato was bent concave and looked emaciated. His face was a sickly yellow colour, realigned into dissonant cubism, his features did not fit the bone structure, his skin was pulled and scarred. I remembered the face from the casino; the one in front of me was a shadow of that diffident swagger.

'Hello,' he said with a thin, annoyed voice; I had intruded.

'Do you want some tea?' Lela asked him.

'Yes. Tea,' said Bandit Dato as he levered himself awkwardly on to a stool.

'It's all right. She knows the story,' Lela told him. 'She's a friend. You can trust her. She has news, she's seen Aleko and he's recovering.'

'I saw him four or five days ago,' I said, measuring my words for sure fact. 'He is in hospital. But I heard he will be going home soon.'

Bandit Dato did not respond, but looked straight at me. His eyes were blank.

'He's all right, he's normal, he can move his legs,' I repeated. His expression remained passive. The news that he had not paralysed his friend seemed not to penetrate.

He was floating in convalescence; he took no responsibility for time. He knew he had done something wrong and perhaps that knowledge hurt, but the pain from his leg distracted him from the emotional and it was postponed for later. He only wanted to lie in the protective shelter of Lela's dead parents' bed and hide beneath the pillows. His mother brought him food, Lela made him tea and he felt like a child again. He did not have to think about anything yet, there were no discussions in this limbo, there was no future, there were no consequences. If he closed his eyes and succumbed to the numb of the heroin, the throb in his leg lessened and his head ceased to ache. He did not have to talk or decide. He was only there, sitting in that kitchen at that moment, drinking a cup of tea and feeling the hot liquid soothe his throat. He had abrogated, cauterized self to the extent that neither his mother's bustling concern that his leg would be infected, nor the worry that the Mekhedrioni would exact a punishment for his behaviour, nor the news that Aleko would walk again made any impression on him.

When it was summer again and Tbilisi was so hot that it was impossible to imagine having ever been cold, Lela and I drove up the mountain into the cooler altitudes of Tskineti to swim in Lawyer Dato's pool.

'Let's stop by and see Bandit Dato,' suggested Lela. 'His mother is always asking me to stop and see them.'

'He's better now?'

'His leg is better,' Lela agreed.

'And what is he doing?'

'Nothing, I think.'

Bandit Dato's mother Sophiko was happy to see us and sat us on the balcony in green wicker chairs, went back into the house and reappeared some moments later with a tray carrying tea, a plate of lemon slices, red water melon, peaches, apricots, cherries, grapes and ice cubes.

'He's just coming,' she told us, smiling weakly at Lela. Lela and I felt compelled to avoid the obvious topic of conversation and set about providing animated chat about the weather which had been 40 degrees solid for a month, the dysentery epidemic, the oil scum on the Tbilisi Sea reservoir, the water shortage and other summer distractions.

Presently Bandit Dato emerged wearing a pair of denim shorts and a T-shirt. He looked terrible. The last six months had scratched at the surface of his skin so that it was reddened with spotted skin-burn like razor rash. His face was drawn tight over his skull, his eyes retracted beneath hoods, staring and wide. He was still using the heroin.

'Hello,' he said, managing a formal smile. He was awkward in front of us and I could see that he had shut himself away from visitors. The formalities were painful for him. 'I'm sorry about the state of my shorts –' he seemed embarrassed; they were spattered with green paint. 'I've been painting some garden furniture.' And he waved his hand over the balcony where we could see several stools, a bench and a crudely nailed-together table all painted the same livid green.

Lela managed the conversation; Bandit Dato said almost nothing and I looked over to the edge of the yard where the perimeter fence had also been painted green – recently and badly, paint had been dripped all over the surrounding grass. I surveyed further; the balcony itself had been spared so far, but the door into the house was green, thick-coated paint poured in oozing streams full of rubbery bubbles that looked half dried and sticky.

We drank our tea respectfully, making a succession of precarious small talk. Each comment – Lela's promotion, my recent visit to Yerevan – each piece of news seemed to make him wince. The rest of the world was moving past him and had left him behind. As soon as was politely possible we made our excuses and left.

'I've never seen anyone look so bad,' I said in the car to Lela. 'What is he doing painting everything green? The chair I was sitting on – layers of sloppy paint, the fence, the door – soon he'll paint the whole house green.'

'He has no future,' said Lela, lighting a cigarette. 'He'll be dead in a year.'

'And Aleko is living with his wife and child.'

'Aleko is living with his wife and child,' confirmed Lela, blowing smoke and the atmosphere of tragedy out of the window into the clean summer air. 'The child visits him occasionally I think.'

'So that's the end of the story.'

'Not really Pushkin is it?'

'No.'

Rustavi

THE CAR BROKE DOWN in Rustavi. I can't remember now where Kakha and I were driving. To see Kakha's neighbour's cousin about a diesel boiler perhaps, or maybe it was the time we tried to see the monastery at M—. Baba the car, as old as me, had had a difficult winter. Kakha kicked open the driver's door (it was always stuck; he meant no particular violence) and commenced, wrench in hand, to bang at the engine.

Rustavi is only twenty kilometres down the road from Tbilisi. The road is paved with a World Bank loan and lined with gaudy plastic imperial petrol stations. A large sign announces RUSTAVI in Cyrillic, Latin and Georgian script. Rustavi is an average Soviet industrial city, a stand of tower blocks thrown up suddenly out of a herdsmen's plain. The blocks, eight or ten storeys high, as regular as bricks, march one after another in an equidistant parade along the main road. They are dead grey – the colour of a leached cloudy winter sky – twenty or thirty years old, pock-marked with crumbling concrete, scabbed plaster, rough and peeling paint. Some great grey God put them there, squashed foundations against the dry land and lifted concrete boxes one on top of another. The same god who brought people down from the mountains and prised them from their villages to work in the factories towards the great Industrial Future.

The windows in the blocks are square, the balconies strips of narrow reinforced cement stacked like columns of vertical dominoes. Over the years, people have walled in these balconies with a rough collection of breeze-blocks, red-brick, tiles, corrugated iron, plastic sheeting and window frames, to make an extra room. The overall effect is patched and patchwork; small efforts of DIY individualism. Some balconies have been left open, a wood-burning stove set down in the corner, lines of washing strung up, baskets of apples and potatoes stored. Behind each one there is a family, a kitchen table, a collection of beds and relationships; second wives, grandmothers, teenage sons and babies.

At night in Rustavi piles of rubbish burn in the street, a few people sit around them drinking *chacha* or beer or warming their hands. The streets are dark; electricity minimal, a couple of hours at night, maybe – more often not – half an hour in the morning, maybe – not enough to heat a bathful of water to wash with. The blocks sit in the dark quietly, enfolded by night shadows; in some of the windows there is a faint yellow glow of candlelight, but not in many. Candles cost too much money to burn.

On the other side of town are the chemical plants and the concrete factory which is still working thanks to Turkish investment – there's always a demand for concrete somewhere – apparently the hope engendered by cheap construction springs eternal. Industry is spread out either side of a road, an ordinary Georgian road; dusty, potholed, covered with loose sand and grit, reclaimed by its verges. The land is a wide horizontal, flat, blown dry by winter and wind. Bushes were bundles of twigs; the colours only brown and olive green, grey, khaki,

yellowish. Beneath my feet was the close-up detritus of stones, dust
and dirt, small patches of grass and broken glass. Mud-water flowed
through a drainage ditch dun-coloured and solid. I watched my shoes
move, one in front of the other, traversing some small infinite piece of
earth, a nothing piece of anonymity. A small beetle with striking red-
and-black markings was moving about; his left legs followed his right
legs, shifting his bright little body in a staggering zigzag.

My mind was numb, bored by the broken-down car, blanked out
by the view, which was entirely unremarkable, conceding as it did only
the dead ordinary collapse of everything. I watched the beetle, but it
failed to metamorphose into anything; not Kafka nor even a bare
thought.

My gaze rose up (perhaps in the hope of finding the eternal muse
of the sky), took in the perpendicular chimney-stacks, cooling towers,
telegraph poles. The sky was blue (*the sky was blue* – true enough, but
hardly a discovery of inspirational dimensions); there were a few high
serried clouds; no cumulus puffs to make shapes out of; no pine-
apples, no dragons, no caricatures of Brezhnev.

We pushed the car across the road, down a short track and
stopped it in front of a gate set in a wall. Kakha decided to walk back
into town to find a mechanic – or a taxi, whichever appeared first.

An iron pipe propped on leaning supports ran a foot off the
ground around the wall and I followed it to a corner. Some way off
white steam was being pumped into the air from a tower supported
by scaffolding. At my feet lay the concrete foundations for some kind
of building that had never been completed, concrete supporting posts
stood in a row falling over. Bits of twisted iron, wire and rusted
reinforcing rods were lying about everywhere.

I sat on the pipe for a while, swinging my legs shallowly. Kakha was a little way off now, walking, clip clip along the road, waving at a very infrequently passing car for a lift.

After a while a shepherd came up the road moving a small flock of sheep in front of him with a stick and a dog. His face was brown and he wore a grimy tracksuit. The sheep fanned out across the grass by the wall and the shepherd, seeing me, gave a nod and came over to sit next to me.

'It's your car?'

'Broken down. My friend has gone to find a mechanic.'

'Ah. Broken down,' the shepherd repeated.

I offered him a cigarette but he declined, pulling out a paper packet of cheap Russian cigarettes and lighting one of his own. He was in his early thirties, he held a certain gentleness in a white smile.

'You live in Rustavi?' I asked him.

'In the village over there,' and he waved his staff in a general direction. We began to ask each other polite introductory questions, listening for a moment to the answer, nodding, smiling and then staring off companionably into the distance again. 'Where are you from originally?' 'Are you married?' 'Do you have children?' 'How old are you?'

He was an Azeri whose family had always lived on the plain. He had never worked in the factories, but his brother had and now it was difficult for him to live with no job. 'He doesn't know what to do with himself. It's *depressia*. He doesn't have anywhere to go during the day. All of them are like that.'

He often came to graze his small flock here, he said, because there was a patch of low-lying ground which flooded often and gave sweeter grass. His sheep were scrabbly and dirty, crowded each other in the usual moronic manner of sheep (and their stereotypes) and regarded us with an inborn irritated wariness manifested by an occasional bleat of futile protest. The shepherd picked up one of the lambs, ignored its crying, swung it upside down in his lap and inspected its feet, flicking out flecks of stone with his thick-ridged fingernails. 'This one is only three days old,' he said, smiling paternally, benevolently, patting it as it scrambled to the ground and skitted off towards its mother.

He scanned his familiar horizon. 'Now all of that,' he said, sweeping an arm in the direction of the railway, where a train loaded with cylindrical oil wagons had remained rusted stationary for the past decade, 'is closed down. My father remembers when there was nothing here in these borderlands, when we were the last village before the desert...'

So we sat there, the two of us, each contemplating the foreground and the background; the chunks of disused building / warehouse / factory / plant strung out like a necklace, or a chain, or an archipelago or the ruins of a crenellated fortress or a row of shipwrecks in a harbour (I was mentally twisting metaphors to pass the time) and the interminable history which hung about listlessly. Everything was very quiet; the air was still and warmed by the sun-warmed haze, hardly breathing. There was not even a hum from the semi-operational Turkish rescued concrete plant. The herd nibbled at the edge of the factory scrap. The grass grew over the factory scrap. The Industrial Future had stopped working and was disintegrating into the plain earth.

Large Abandoned Objects

IN EARLY OCTOBER 1999, Cormac and Kurtz and David and I, four journalists together, drove up to Abkhazia to see incumbent Ardzinba win the presidential election. There was no doubt that he was going to win the election because there were no other candidates.

We drove from Tbilisi along the M27, through Imereti, through Kutaisi, through Abasha and Mingrelia to Zugdidi, where palm trees began to grow in the gardens and horse-carts replaced cars on the roads. I stared out of the window and mentally collected LAOs, Large Abandoned Objects; they were my driving pastime. Rusting tractors, bits of pipeline, lines of coal cars shunted and left along a rail line, half-built bridges and apartment blocks standing concrete and empty; a skeletal, burnt-out crane hanging over them. Bits of the past left, ruined collective farm barracks and factories with all their windows smashed and their plant ripped out for scrap. Remnants of something else – a civilization of sorts? – scattered everywhere, lumps of concrete and bits of twisted metal, lying about to stub your toe on. Everywhere lay the debris of the Soviets, the husk of an empire. Mostly there were hundreds and hundreds of piles of reinforced concrete slabs, rotting, crumbling, rusting from the inside. In the villages ruined shops were abandoned, miles of counter and shelves left permanently empty;

instead people fashioned kiosks from scraps of metal fence and corrugated iron and bits of wood tied together with wire and sold Viceroy cigarettes from them. Weeds had overgrown monuments to the Great Patriotic War, weeping mildew spread over marble bas-reliefs of a happy worker paradise. The architecture had become that of Ozymandias.

We drove through Zugdidi and came to the bridge across the Enguri that marked the cease-fire line into Abkhazia. The bridge was dilapidated and there were a few women dressed in black walking across it pushing small handcarts. At either end there were Russian checkpoints, sandbagged, breeze-blocked pillboxes and giant concrete antitank jacks. We got out of the car at the far end to show the Abkhaz our passports.

'Igor!' Kurtz cried, advancing, catching sight of a Russian officer who was sitting with his feet up in the sun and drinking a cup of tea with the Abkhaz militia.

'Kurtz! Where in hell have you come from? There's nothing going on now you know. It's all quiet.'

'Igor. Still here? I thought you were going back to your nice wife in Tula.'

'Ah. Pah! They've sent me back to this backwater. Just for a few months.'

'We're just here for the election.'

'Oh, the election.'

'Will you share a morning shot?' And Kurtz produced a hip-flask from a pocket and held it out for Igor, 'just to wet your lips – the best Carolina moonshine!'

'The local stuff isn't strong enough for you eh?'

Kurtz winked, 'This is just for special friends, you know, I've only got a half pint of it left.'

After that there were no problems with our credentials. The Abkhaz pretended to make a telephone call, but our passage was assured. Kurtz agreed to let an Abkhaz guard ride with us as far as Gali town. He was adolescent and spotty, with a new, raw uniform and got in the back seat between David and me and stuck his Kalashnikov out the window.

We slowed down for the Gali town checkpoint, but did not stop. The Russian soldiers had taken off their blue peacekeeping berets and their shirts and were sitting on an APC (armoured personnel carrier) smoking cigarettes. They waved us through desultorily; they were bored. A little further along, where the two bridges were blown out, we passed a Russian convoy headed by a tank, coming to relieve them. The column of Russian troop trucks was moving slowly. Underneath the khaki green canvas the soldiers stuck their heads out. Each face was different: blond, wide-spaced cheek-bones of the Mongol-Slav, long-eyelashed innocence, narrow eyes and narrow foreheads of the far eastern tribes, red-cheeked adolescence. But each one carried the same expression: distance, unlined youth, trepidation; alone and inconsequential. They were boys. The Georgian partisans were always taking pot-shots at them and laying mines in potholes for them to drive over. Two days earlier, perhaps these recruits had heard whispered through the barracks, two Russian privates asleep at a checkpoint had been hacked to death with axes. 'It was nasty,' Igor had told us, rubbing his hands together with satisfaction. 'When I went to inspect the incident there was still bits of brain stuck to the wall.'

Past the burnt houses and overgrown gardens, rose bushes blooming over concrete foundations, homes stripped of doors, window frames, razed. And what was Gali? Full of ruins. And what was Abkhazia? Probably the largest abandoned object of them all.

Kurtz was chewing on the stump of his cigar and unscrewing the cap of his large hip-flask that was full of Carolina moonshine.

'Macco?'

Cormac shook his head, 'It's too early for me.'

I was thinking out loud, 'There should be another word for an election when there's only one candidate. It can't, can it, be called an election by definition? Election implies choice, after all, *choosing by casting votes*. You can't choose if there's only one guy with a box by his name.'

'You could call it a *complicity*. As in "Tomorrow we're holding a complicity; we'll pretend to have an election and you'll pretend to vote freely and fairly,"' David suggested.

Kurtz thought that calling it a *farce* would be more to the point, 'As in "The results are now in for the parliamentary farce held over the weekend."' We debated *affirmation, assignation, astigmatism* past the Ochamchire minefields until we came to the outskirts of Sukhumi.

'Jesus this place is a shithole,' commented Kurtz. 'I forgot. Last time I saw it there were bombs exploding everywhere and I had to sit on the filthy slippery deck of a fucking Ukrainian cargo boat for fourteen hours to get out to Batumi. I swore I'd never come back.'

In Sukhumi the only place to stay was the Aitar, a strange sort of outpost, a UN compound camped in a sixties-built Soviet sanatorium full of peacocks and camouflaged unarmed UN observers; it was hard to know which was the more decoratively useless. I had stayed here on my previous visit. The garden was planted with lush high palm trees, there were fish in an ornamental pond, birds sang sweetly. The electricity was mostly on, thanks to large UN generators, and the water was usually hot in the evening and in the morning. The rooms cost $5 a night. It felt almost colonial, Somerset Maugham. A writer sat in the corner of the civilian commissary, watching the BBC World News, taking notes down in a worn notebook with the stub of a pencil while the Polish UN political officer was hunched opposite, trying to prise the spy out of him. A pair of Bangladeshis watched for the cricket score and drank Coke.

At night the population of the Aitar, about a hundred international officers and an equal number of support staff – administrators and drivers and interpreters and women who worked in the human rights office and the NGO lot, Spaniards and Dutch and French, Acción Contra el Hambre, Red Cross, Médecins Sans Frontières – sat about and drank beer and talked about things like the Pakistani general's leaving party, whether or not the truck driving up from Trabzon that brought fresh supplies of Coke and Snickers bars would be on time and if the Russians were letting people through the border to Sochi that week.

There's a German, an Indonesian, a Jordanian, an Estonian, a Swiss, and a Portuguese and they're sitting on the Black Sea coast – I met an officious bureaucratic Indian with lines drawn down from his mouth: 'No. We know who you are but we cannot issue you with an ID until a memo has been sent.' There was a jolly, hard-edged German called Peter; blond, fresh-faced, rosy-cheeked, crew cut: 'I am a professional soldier, and the job of the professional soldier is to be brave, yes? Here, we are not allowed to be brave, it is frustrating.' There was an impecunious Albanian who had hitched all the way from Tirana to the UN transport plane in Istanbul, arriving in towns along the way and looking up Albanian families to stay with in the phone book. At night a slurry Irishman held up the bar with a glass of whisky in one hand, 'I'll tell you one thing I know –' cocking his head at the assembled. A trio of Englishmen sat about being polite to each other; the confident, competent colonel up from Zugdidi for the weekend, easy authority in his voice and a no-nonsense approach, rolling his eyes at the bureaucratic UN, and at the mess surrounding him; Sandhurst Ralph, shy and formal, almost diffidently stiff-upper-lipped, but very decent, with a stash of Bovril and Sainsbury's sage and onion stuffing in his fridge; and John, pink-and-ginger-coloured, with freckled hands and thinning hair, who might have been an accountant except for the uniform when he agreed with my effusive description of Sukhumi paradise by saying, 'Yes, well there are some nice parts.'

'Nothing's changed, Wendell,' said the Polish political officer, 'since the last time you were here. Only the nasty stories change, week to week. And after a while even those seem to be all the same incident.'

Nothing was working. Nothing had worked since Moscow stopped sending directives and especially nothing had worked since the bombs had wrecked the place. There was a semblance of life in Sukhumi, but mostly its head was down and its listless subsistence gaze directed at the pavement. Abkhazia was in limbo but the limbo had gone on for almost a decade and time had been stretched so far between two worlds, that of the Soviet Union, which was gone, and whatever else was supposed to come after it, that the limbo had become everyday life and you couldn't see over the edge of it to a future.

'Nothing's changed,' said Shalva when I found him at the bar of the Russian compound on the beach. 'You see, Wendell, the stones are just the same.' He had lost some of his KGB formality. I noticed a cluster of early grey hairs among the black. His head was between his hands as if he were trying to squeeze some meaning out of his thoughts.

'Yeah, well,' I said, 'have a cigarette.'

'It's impossible to get out of this place – I had an invitation to London, now I have another to a conference in America but I have no passport. Just an old Soviet passport.'

'The Russians cancelled them this year didn't they?'

'Yes they cancelled them. You can't even travel to Moscow with an old Soviet passport any more.'

On the day of the election Kurtz and I went to watch people voting in the main polling station that had once been a library but was now a mass of burnt books. Cormac and David stayed back at the Aitar with hangovers trying to fiddle the sat. phone dish into the right position in order to file their stories. We asked people who they were voting for. Since there was only one possible answer, Kurtz and I found this very funny. The first man we asked was an Armenian who said,

'Of course I voted for Ardzinba. He won the war! He is our natural leader!'

The second man was a Greek who declared 'Ardzinba is our God!' and the third was an Abkhaz who replied, 'Well I can't really see any alternative,' with a wry smile on his lips.

Later, independent international observers from Kabardino-Balkaria and Nagorno-Karabakh were happy to confirm the official result: Ardzinba had won with 99.6 per cent of the vote.

'Allah be praised!' said Kurtz, steadying his embroidered Turkish skullcap on his head. 'Now let's go to the Russian compound and get drunk again.'

*

All summer long the Russian compound was an extended Soviet party. The sunset over the sea was perfect, like the postcards from a decade before that could still be found on sale in the shops, dusty, propped up behind a load of greenish soap cut into slabs, the ubiquitous Iranian washing powder called Barf and stacks of Monica Lewinsky chocolate bars. In the Russian compound, it was always the decade before. The cafés along the promenade were full of young Abkhaz and Russian soldiers on furlough with their families. The gardens were well kept; fireflies danced blinking green neon among the hibiscus, palm fronds and banks of jasmine; each tree was neatly labelled in botanical Latin and Russian. There were red mosaics of Lenin at the end of the avenues that ran through the foliage between the different sanitoria. Russian girls with frosted blonde hair and dressed in high white stilettos with their thighs on show and chests squeezed into elastic pink nylon gauze or shiny silver leatherette or red lace halter tops trotted arm in arm with a man with a smile on his face and some money in his pocket. The music blared tinny amplified Russki pop; drum machines and impossibly catchy two-note choruses. It was life before the Great Collapse; it was holiday.

We were all drunk. The white plastic café table was littered with the remains of shashlik and tomato salad and vodka bottles, beer bottles, carafes of thick sticky local wine, packets of cigarettes, ashtrays, lighters. The men were drunk and I was drunk and the music flowed over the vodka that we drank to Ardzinba ('on the day of his historically insignificant victory') and to peace in the Caucasus ('because it's important to drink to at least one myth during an evening...') and to Shalva ('because the KGB is a noble fucking institution with a grand fucking tradition,' said Kurtz, smoothing his moustache laconically between his fingers; Shalva glared at him but could not bring himself to reply, because to reply would have been to admit it) and to Cormac ('and all the girls he's loved before') and to David ('our correspondent in Azerbaijan, up to see how the other end of the Caucasus works –') and to Kurtz ('… to Kurtz; master of the checkpoint!'). I tried to drink a toast to the Georgians who missed Abkhazia because they were missing all the summer fun but everyone went quiet for a second and I shut up. Cormac had his arms around some girl who was different from the girl at the UN compound he had kissed the night before. Shalva had settled into his private atmosphere of benevolent moroseness. They started to play Abkhaz national music and several Abkhaz young men patriotically got up to dance, stamping their feet in intricate drunken heel-to-toe patterns, in circles, kicking out their legs and holding their arms outstretched. Kurtz stuck his cigar between his teeth and ascended the dance floor to demonstrate his skill of Turkish chair-dancing. 'It's taken me years of practice with the great masters to perfect it,' he explained with a gleam in his eye. We made noise and were incoherent and we thumped our fists on the table and laughed louder and louder.

The lights from the Russian compound were the only lights around the harbour and they shone on the surface of the sea.

'It's my birthday the day after tomorrow,' I told Shalva, picking up a bottle of beer and peering down it to see if anyone had put their cigarette out in it.

'Happy birthday. How old will you be?'

'I will be two years older than you.'

'You will always be two years older than me,' Shalva said sensibly.

'I want to go to Gorbachev's dacha.' I said, wilful. 'Can you arrange it?'

'Gorbachev's dacha?'

'Up near Pitsunda.'

'Oh. I don't know. It's a Presidential Palace now. It's guarded. It's not open.'

'Please, Shalva, please. It's my birthday.'

'I'll ask,' said Shalva.

Shalva wouldn't come with us to Gorbachev's dacha. He said he was busy and I didn't ask why. But he came up trumps and arranged everything with the President's office and the KGB and the Foreign Ministry and the National Guard and the militia. Kurtz, Cormac, David and I drove up with Philip, the writer from the Aitar, who decided he needed a rest from his botanical studies. We took provisions: five quail, half a side of smoked beef, tomatoes, potatoes, chillies, three litre jars of red wine, one three-litre jar of *chacha* and several boxes of matches.

Gorbachev's dacha had been finished in 1990. And then the Soviet Union broke apart and everything was moot; there were suddenly borders everywhere and cars driving around with Kalashnikovs sticking out of the windows. After all the worrying about balcony proportions and views of the sea and numbers of bedrooms and size of swimming pool and décor, Mikhail Sergeyevich and Raisa Maximovna never even got to go there.

We arrived in the afternoon and stood in front of the massive yellow stone structure. Kurtz was momentarily lost for words.

'Fuck, it's huge,' he said and walked around it.

'Last gasp of Soviet luxe,' commented Cormac.

'Look at the stained-glass windows all around the staircase –'

It took us an hour to explore it, from the study and the dining room through all the bedrooms and their adjoining bathrooms (Raisa had apparently insisted that all rooms should have ensuite facilities), and downstairs to the cinema and the swimming pool and the sauna and the guards' quarters and the bomb shelter under the hill... The parquet was virgin and unscratched, the swathes of beige-foam-embossed wallpaper unmarked. The bathrooms were vast and lined with speckled tiling. Beds were placed in ballrooms. The furniture was the Soviet grand style of cheap veneer rip-offs trying to be pre-Revolutionary curlicued rococo, the carpets factory-weave brown scrolls, the dining-room chairs heavy carved wood and upholstered in green flock velvet, the light fixtures came from a sixties hotel foyer, all starburst steel and knobs, and the mirrors and table lamps were strangely encrusted in elaborate Meissen-esque ceramic flowers and birds.

'Oh my God,' said Philip.

'Oh my God,' said David.

'I know, I know.'

We were peering into the corners and trying things out. The taps in the bathroom spewed water all over the floor, the kitchen was lined in cheap chipboard and Formica cupboards, the curtains were nylon lace.

'Is this the best the Sovs could do?'

'What a load of crap.'

'Ugly crap.'

'But monumental crap.'

'It's just what you'd expect,' said Philip, articulating for us, 'it's the Soviet Union: a giant metaphor, impressive only for its sheer size but actually full of empty space and tat.'

'Well, who's in for a tickler?' Kurtz asked, unscrewing the lid of the *chacha* jar.

*

We sat at a picnic table under the stars and made a barbecue and ate the quail and tried to eat the smoked beef but it was too stringy. We gave cigarettes to the guards who were all good local friendly boys wearing their best fashionably square-toed leather shoes with their camouflage uniforms. They told us about their families and their children and said that it wasn't a bad job and mostly they got paid and they were lucky because there were hardly any jobs at all in Abkhazia and they were grateful that they had managed to get this one through a cousin or a cousin of a cousin.

Kurtz was in a happy growly mood and was prevailed upon to tell his famous story about the time when he had forgotten to take off his Chechen Vechen T-shirt trying to get through a Russian checkpoint near Gudermes.

'There was this goddamn colonel. I told him I couldn't speak Russian. But I told him I couldn't speak Russian in Russian. So he just thought I was a Chechen. And the Chechens had taken my passport. Or I'd lost it – I can't remember. I didn't have anything except my Memphis library card. And they couldn't read it because it wasn't in Cyrillic and then they found my copy of the Koran in Arabic...

We drank all the wine and then drove the car on to the beach and went swimming and then couldn't get the car back onto the road because there was a big concrete step in the way.

It was my birthday and everyone agreed that I should get Misha and Raisa's room. I lay in the enormous bed, itchy from the salt seawater and imagined a 2 a.m. knock on the door and an aide excusing his intrusion, but would I like to come and give the order for the army to open fire on demonstrators somewhere or other. I imagined standing at the top of the entrance steps, ready to welcome a foreign secretary of state, extending my hand and leading him personally to his room to show what a good fellow I was. I imagined the feeling of insulated authority and the fear that must have existed around the edges of the comfort zone. All those kilometres of parquet corridors and people whispering in them.

As it was, everything fell apart and we, like the rest of the inhabitants of the post-Soviet Union, were camping in what was a shell of its former self. That night we had toasted me and the sentences that I was yet to write and then Philip, with many sentences already published, raised his glass and offered a new one: 'To Misha, the poor bastard, to his late wife, and to the whole racket which went to hell in a handbasket.'

Khevsureti

THE FIRST TIME I drove the single-track shale road into Khevsureti it was spring. The car shook us over the rocks; in Lower Khevsureti, on the south slope of the Caucasus range, we passed by the villages with their blue-painted beehives, summer meadows flush with short green grass and yellow meadow flowers, copses of beech and elderwood. Suddenly a white Niva loomed towards us, scattering dust in its wheels, careening as it swerved and disappeared around a bend. Before we had time to think, a Khevsur on a white horse came galloping after it. Saddleless, he gripped the bridle with one hand, the other arm thrust into the air like a victorious Alexander; his mouth was opened in a battle cry of exaltation. He was dressed in the usual mountain uniform: a worn and dirty pair of tracksuit trousers, riddled with cigarette burns, muddied, torn at the crotch, and a grimy singlet. A Kalashnikov was lashed across his back. His shoulders were burnished bronze, his eyes were blue.

Apfi and his family lived in a three-roomed dwelling below the abandoned city of Mutso backed up against the high flank of the Chechen border. The walls of the hut were weather-beaten grey, fashioned from slate, bricks, plaster, basket-weave birch branches and corrugated plastic sheeting. The windows were uneven holes and without glass. The floors were dry tramped earth. In two rooms there were a number of beds; iron bedsteads, straw mattresses, a few rolled blankets, two or three icons on the wall, some faded magazine pictures and a small red-framed mirror, a hairbrush, a bucket of water and a small enamel jug, and two kerosene lamps. They had no kerosene for these lamps.

Hung bloody over a bit of broken chicken-wire-and-wood fence and covered in flies was a fresh goatskin. 'We have just killed it,' Mariemi, the eldest of the seven children, their sub-mother, told me. She was eleven or twelve years old with robust, dark, heavy shining eyes and red apple cheeks. She took a step closer and hugged the fence post, smiling shyly.

'What do you want your children to learn in the winter school in Shatili?' I asked Apfi who squatted in front of me, drunk, red-and-bronze-faced with a head of matted overgrown hair. We sat on the grass slope with a neighbour of his, passing a plastic Coke bottle half full of *chacha* back and forth. ('This is the poorest family in the valley,' Zaliko had told me, as we drove up in his heavy rattling bumping Soviet Army jeep. 'Apfi had a fight with his father – I don't know what about. Now he drinks too much – but oh, what a storyteller he is; when he's drunk he makes poems about everything, his wife – their cows. Funny and very good – but he is a lazy bastard, the woman does all the work and at the end of the summer I try to bring them a sack of sugar. They don't even have enough to feed themselves.') The ragged brood was dispersed – in order of height and age, Mariemi, Lela, Tolkha, Mindia, Ushisha, Dedika and Gaga – dressed in worn-through cast-me-downs with torn bits of rubber village shoes on their feet and dirt smudged around their mouths. Mindia was an albino. Dedika was digging carrots in the ploughed plot that ran down the hill from the hut. Tolkha and his younger brother Ushisha, carrying rods as long as themselves, were fishing in the stream that tumbled down the ravine behind the hut.

Apfi passed his hand over his mouth and spat, considering my question. Sano, his wife, put her hands on her hips and smiled at us. Her hair, pushed back behind her ears in a solid mass, was streaked with grey, her hands engraved with dirt. On her face were black marks, somewhere between bruises and scars, and when she talked to us, heaving the baby to her waist – 'I will get some tea. Mariemi, fetch the leaves that are drying. Will you have milk? In the evening there will be milk' – she tried to cover the marks with one hand.

The neighbour who was sitting with us, blond like the ancient Khevsurs, began to finger the muzzle of his rifle as if it were a woman's nipple, around and around, caressing it with his hands, stroking the inside of the barrel. There was something wrong about his face, I noticed. It was too pale, too open. There was a scar across his cheek-bone, but this was not it. His eyes were washed pale blue, like an early-morning sky, innocent and idiotic, but this was not it either. It was his mouth, I thought. The teeth slanted inwards and the lips parted wide, exposing too much upper gum. He smiled like a stupid impassive shark and gripped his Kalashnikov proprietorally.

Apfi considered my question thoughtfully. His eyes were bloodshot and glazed. 'I want them to know how to know the time. To use a watch, for example,' he said, looking over at Zaliko. 'If they go to the town, they will need to know this.' The neighbour stubbed out a cigarette in the grass, balanced the gun on his knees and fired a couple of bullets absently at a rock on the opposite hillside. The shots sparked a loud echo in the valley and Gaga the baby began to cry. Sano quietened him, rocking him against her breast and holding out an apple to distract him.

'And they should know how to count money,' continued Apfi, taking a swig of the *chacha*, 'how many kopeks make a lari and how many lari he should get for a cow.' I nodded. Zaliko took up his balalaika and began to pick at the strings. The notes were brief and discordant, whining and broody. He began to sing gently, laughing, putting his thoughts into rhyme.

'Time and money,' sang Zaliko, 'time and money.' He made up two fine verses about time and money and everyone laughed along with him. Then he put down the instrument and added, 'Time and money: I don't like these things.'

On the Chechen Border

RUSLAN ('HALF THE FUCKING population of Chechnya is called Ruslan,' Kurtz commented) brought me a video that had come out from Grozny through Shatili. It was October 1999. We had returned from Abkhazia to the news that the Russians had invaded towards their old cordon on the Terek River and were shelling Grozny. The video was Chechen propaganda, war porn. Ruslan put it in my video player and sat back with a cup of tea with me to watch it; he wouldn't accept vodka.

In one sequence of the film the camera panned over the body of a young woman splayed dead on the cold floor of her house. A female relative held the woman's son by the hand and forced him to look at his mother: naked abattoir flesh, grey-yellow and smooth; her foot had been blown off and lay close by. A huge rent in her belly, through her pubic hair, slashed open black, unimaginable, tangled gore – it was impossible to see what it was except horror. The small son was screaming with distress; still the woman held him firm and pointed at the corpse. 'This is what they've done to your mother,' she shouted at him, cruelly, bitterly, 'don't ever forget it. This is what the Russians have done to your mother!'

There were scenes from Samashki rubble, a crowd of women.

'We just want to live in peace,' they said to the camera. One small boy came forward and looked straight into the lens, 'I don't want anyone else to die,' and he listed those who were already dead, 'not my friends or my relatives, my parents or my grandparents.' The women crowded, bustling, imploring, begging. In the background the men shuffled with their heads cowed and ashamed, the elders wearing dirty black wool trousers with a mismatched suit jacket and a trilby on their heads, the younger ones in black leather jackets and black jeans. They were all sullen and unshaven.

There were various hospital interiors on the videotape, where corpses lay pre-death on cots amid grimy blankets. Cadavers with sunken cheeks and hollow hopeless eyes that had not the strength or wit or hope to ask for anything. One emitted a death-rattle like a heaving automaton, breath scratching at life and tearing it away. There was a toddler without an arm and dozens of quiet children with bloody bandages taped to their faces. A wounded twenty-year-old woman in shock asked about the baby she was carrying but no one would meet her eyes and tell her. In the operating theatre the surgeons operated without gloves, sewing up the mortal flaps and rents, pushing viscera back within the confines of skin with their fingers. The pictures were hideous, hand-held video, green light, smashed people: iron against flesh, not human at all, only animal and butchery.

I drank my vodka because I needed to. Ruslan's face was soft, but his expression was resigned and severe and when the video was finished he talked about going back to Chechnya to fight. But he didn't have the beard of a *boyevik*, a fighter, and he didn't have the contacts to get him back across the border through which he had fled a couple of weeks before. His Soviet passport would not travel and he had become a refugee. The Russians had closed the borders between the southern Caucasus and the northern Caucasus; later, around Christmas time, they were to send paratroopers into the Argun valley and seal the Shatili route into Georgia completely.

I was sitting in Tbilisi (or rather lying in my usual repose, in bed with the notebook computer hauled up on my knees), watching CNN reports. Cormac was going crazy with phone calls from journalists and photographers: 'How can I get into Chechnya? Are they letting people through the Georgian border? I'm from the Oslo paper X and I need to find a translator who can take me to Grozny.' Kurtz was living on a mattress on my balcony. He said he slept better in the open air.

John Kurtz, old Caucasian hand, nicotine stained. Kurtz was forty, an American with a vigorous strength strapped to thick bones. His head was covered in waves of grey and black hair, his eyebrows were coarse, wiry and overgrown and he had a bushy moustache that rivalled that of 'the Great Moustache'. His face had a veneer of brutality: large-pored, often shiny with sweat, red from vodka, grinning or grimacing. He was not a particularly violent person, but his heft and his drunkenness and his mood swings, arm swings, belligerence – his pride – led you to believe that it looked like he was going to hit you at any moment. In a word he was exactly Caucasian. He liked to wear an Azeri carpet cap on his head, he spoke several Caucasian languages badly, with a rasping American accent. He looked like wherever he was. In Azerbaijan they took him for an Azeri, in Abkhazia for an Abkhaz, in Chechnya for a Chechen. This was partly why he was called the master of the checkpoint, but the moniker had as much to do with his customary hip-flask and his swagger as anything.

He'd been in the Caucasus longer than anyone could remember; longer than Georgia had been a recognized sovereign state. Before the

Caucasus he'd been in Turkey hanging out with the PPK for a couple of years. He said, in one of his less guarded moments, that he'd stood on the flanks of Ararat with a PKK commander who was carrying a rocket launcher on his shoulder and stared down, out of eastern Turkey, to the plains below them.

'What's that?' he had asked, pointing at the concrete factory outside Yerevan that was pumping dust into the clear blue sky.

'Those are the Armenians. Another lot the bastard Turks tried to annihilate,' the Kurd had replied.

'And that,' said Kurtz, looking around at his rapt audience, 'was the first time I thought of hopping over to have a look at the pre-former Soviet Union, or whatever it was at that time: it was certainly not in control of itself; chaos.'

That was only one of his stories; he had a hundred. The Caucasus in the early nineties were full of stories. Maybe even some of Kurtz's stories were true. Maybe even some of them had actually happened to him. Probably they were composite fantasy, like all the best stories. After a while he'd told so many people so many stories that they got repeated second hand, third hand and became myths. And beyond the myths there were always the rumours. There was a tale of an estranged Karabakhi wife, but no one had ever seen her. There was also a version that she was in fact a Kurd, that he had married her in an abandoned Armenian church in Baku so that she could get a green card to the US. In any case, this was all personal, lost in the midst of legend and we were too scared to ask him about it.

Kurtz had friends, but he also had enemies. It would be simplistic, but not inaccurate to say that his friends were the Caucasians and his enemies were the Americans. The American government (he hated to pay taxes and he never paid taxes), American 'operatives' who kicked about the place ('you tell them all your funny stories and then they don't tell you any of theirs') and especially editors of American newspapers who wouldn't print his stories because America wasn't interested in Armenians throwing Kurds out of their homes in Kelbajar or Azeris burning Armenian shops in Sumgait or Georgians lynching Ossetians or Russians bombing Chechen hospitals or Abkhaz playing football with the heads of Mingrelian children. Or whatever was happening that week. 'Where the hell are you again, Kurtz?' they'd say down the phone, the crackling impossible phone line, 'who are those people? They've fled? I dunno, Kurtz, we've got this big thing about Srebrenica on the front page already.'

But the Caucasians he loved and he was loved in return. His old friends, people met along the way, local commanders in Karabakh and the old woman whose kitchen table he had cowered under during the siege of Sukhumi call him simply 'Kurt!'

'Ku-urt!' they'd cry, catching sight of him after an intervening year or a battle-scared week that felt like a long-lost year. 'Ku-urt!' they'd cry, rushing up to him with outstretched arms, to embrace him, clap him on the back, throw their heads back with the surprised joy of reunion. 'Oh Ku-urt! Do you remember that time! You crawled under the little table in the kitchen when the artillery was very strong one night! The windows rattled and you were curled under the table! Oh Ku-urt! You were as frightened as a child! (We were all frightened – what a terrible night it was –).' Or the local militia chief wearing camouflage and infantry boots sitting in a fly-blown empty office with cracked windows and a mobile phone tossed on the desk, 'Ku-urt! You old bastard! We all thought you were dead!'

With Westerners in the Caucasus, Kurtz was ambivalent. He

fought too much. He turned friends into hurt grievances. He railed, he tore, he abused. In the barrel chest, the raised glass of *chacha*, the thumping fist on table, the late-night roaring, 'Let's rock this shit-hole', there lurked an undertow – the obvious kind of undertow, at least for a war correspondent. An undertow like a stench, the powerful sour smell of spirit that seeped through his pores. Laconic alcoholism. Common enough, even endearing, but impenetrable as a suit of armour. Nothing could get past the bluster. 'It's my black dog,' he'd say of his own depression. And then drown the wretch in *chacha*.

The undertow, if you could see through its swirl of discord and twisted verbosity, was in fact underbelly, soft underbelly; the white place, sensitized and exposed. His capacity for injury and slight was enormous. His capacity for generosity and tenderness towards his friends was infinite. Too often, it was impossible to tell which reaction you were likely to provoke.

Kurtz had been brooding for days, waxing and waning through a series of bottles of vodka, interrupted by swigs of my single malt whisky. The cigarettes piled their stubs in the ashtray; smoke curled from his nostrils like a dragon's. He forgot to eat and slept interruptedly between four and nine in the morning. I could hear him banging around in the bathroom; I could hear him connecting to his email. He sat in the kitchen grouching with his thick two-tea-bag tea, smoking, drinking shots of brandy and bottles of beer and anything else that was lying around. 'Shall I go back through the Azeri border and Dagestan?' 'How can I get a Russian visa?' 'I'm pretty sure I could walk through Khevsureti into Chechnya.' He clogged his moustache with his fingers and scratched at the underside of his unshaven chin and at the greasy sides of his temples. And then he pronounced, in a great booming voice, his opinion:

'The Chechens are fucked. Fucked by the Russians sure, but worse, fucked from behind. Your Ruslan: good-looking, fine young man. But talking a lot of nonsense. In between worlds and realities. Pushed around by the Sharia courts for traffic accidents, their sisters wrapped in headscarves and pushed around anyway. Hassled and harried by kingpins and shysters. Half Russian half of them. Russified down to their core. But refusing a glass of vodka, or saying that Chechnya should be an independent Islamic state – it's all a load of shit – but good people. But left with nothing to believe or trust in, to go back to or forward to.

'Ah Samashki,' Kurtz settled his frame, rested his elbows on the table, pulled out his perennial pack of red Marlboros, and smiled his jaded war correspondent smile. 'I was fucking there –' stabbing the air with his index finger for emphasis, 'I was there before the war. I saw the children of my friends get massacred, I was there during the war and after the war. Macco and I were the first people in after the massacre and do you know what they said to me? There was this old woman, used to cook for me, macaroni, about all there was left in the place. And she comes running up to me, Ku-urt! she says, we have been so worried! She told me her son-in-law – he was some fighter, I'd met him a couple of times – had gone back through the Russian lines to see if they'd beaten me up. They'd heard that I'd got sent to a filtration camp or something. So in the middle of this massacre in which her daughter had been killed, probably raped and God knows what else, in the middle of this she had been worried about me? I wanted to say: why the hell aren't you worried about you!'

Cormac and Kurtz and I sat in the Manhattan Bar in Tbilisi. David was there; Thomas was there. Thomas bit his nicotine-stained fingernails, chain-smoked and looked sexy. I sat next to him, feeling heat. All Caucasus hacks, all talking, all war stories.

'You're either a cowboy, or overly inspired by the story, or have some personal attachment to the Chechens,' said David sensibly. Well, I thought, all of these are around the table and they're still not going.

'It's not the same any more,' Cormac was leaning back in his chair. 'We were treated like diamonds in the first war, you could leave your sat. phone on the street and no one would ever take it. Now the editor won't even let me go. They'll fire me if I go.'

'I want to go, I can meet these Chechens who can take me tomorrow, but I don't know; it's shit. I am nervous. I hate being nervous like this,' said Thomas.

'And what is this anyway?' answered Kurtz. 'What's the point? Isn't it just voyeuristic?' We could not answer him because we did not know. A French journalist who had disappeared in Grozny the week before had turned up on a videotape in Moscow, chained to a radiator, battered, pleading for rescue. 'Well it's one way to beat the black dog; beat him back with fear,' Kurtz concluded, bravura in the bottom of his glass of whisky, sucking back on the stump of his fake Cuban cigar bought for a buck on the Turkish border.

Kurtz was seething, swearing. The nasty Caucasian decade weighed on him. He was still chasing the tail of the war dog; perhaps he felt a kind of responsibility to haul his exhausted self back into the thick of it. Perhaps it was only habit. What the hell else was there for him to do? But his eyes were rimmed red and stared blank; you could see he was tired of it, bored and tired of being scared.

A compromise was fashioned: Kurtz would accompany me up to the Georgian–Chechen border to look at the refugees coming across. I would call Shamil, a Khevsur friend of Zaliko's, and see if he could take us. On the way Kurtz would think about what to do next. 'Let's blow this shithole,' his voice rang with finality and decision, and he slammed his glass down on the table, as if he meant it; whatever it was.

In Khevsureti time is expansive. It wheels around with the sun and sleeps at night, slips between the seasons of alternating snow and clean wind. There is only one road into Khevsureti, a rocky track cut in the seventies. The Niva banged over every pothole, rock, stone, puddle, gushing stream, boulder, flint.

The road ran higher and higher until my ears popped. Leisurely winding up the southern meadows of the Caucasus, then over the pass descending along the Argun River on to the northern face of the mountains. On the road there was only a very occasional car packed with refugees and baggage and a few Khevsurs walking from village to village with backpacks and fishing rods. The scenery was enormous, filling everything and stopping words.

This was the place where rivers come from. Traced up to the monumental spine of the Caucasus; to its valleys and ridges, its peaks with teardrop drifts of snow packed into rocky crevices, swathes of steep baize-green meadow-grass, tumbling fissures of scree, grooved mountain streams hurtling almost vertical from the patches of forest and ancient fortresses built on high outcrops. Great mountains above, rising straight up from the river, no strip of horizontal, no easy plateau; a single step was a three-foot climb. The sky changed every minute: first it was raining lightly and mist lolled around the peaks and then the clouds cleared and patches of hot sunlight shot through the cold high air casting bilious travelling shadows on opposite slopes.

It was further than another time. Shamil was driving and had taken off his watch. I sat in the front seat with my knees up on the dashboard, Kurtz sat in the back with a leaking petrol can for company. He smoked almost continuously.

There had always been Chechens in these mountains, in twos and threes, on foot, on horseback, smuggling cigarettes and guns. Sometimes they had friendly relations with the Khevsurs, sometimes they fought them over cows, horses, women and pasture. Feuds ran long and deep. They fought in the footsteps of their ancestors; for honour, not hatred. They knew each other well; wedged between them was ambivalence, suspicion, language and religion, but there was also respect. A century before, when the Khevsurs killed a Chechen they cut the right hand off the corpse and hung it next to the door to their home.

The mountains on either side were steep and monolithic, the sun had sunk over their rims and the light was grey and cold in the late afternoon. Banks of scree tumbled like static waterfalls on either side. Rivers of slate, stopped. Streams ran across the road indenting it with mud craters. The banks of sloping loose shingle were falling down.

'Landslides,' said Kurtz. The road was packed grit. Around a corner a rusty yellow digger was parked. It seemed that any breath of wind or fall of rain would send a mass of slag and jagged flint down on us.

How does it stay up? I wondered, there's so much of the mountain that's sliding off itself. How, after all this time, does the mountain remain?

Kurtz was thinking out loud about the first war. He was spouting war stories, driving through Chechen checkpoint after Russian checkpoint, drinking tea with the Chechens, vodka with the Russians, swapping his black *pappakha* for his grey military *shapka*. Tracking

Basayev through Shatoi for an interview the week after the raid on the Budyonovsk hospital. He remembered that Cormac had said that the story was worth dying for. Cormac had once famously shouted into the phone (the last bloody phone line in Gudermes), furious at his editors in Moscow who wanted him to pull out, 'There aren't enough fucking Hemingways any more,' and flung the receiver down. Later, driving back to Samashki, Kurtz had leaned over to him, haggard with fear and exhaustion, admitting defeat.

'We're going to die because I'm too tired to remember which fucking hat I'm supposed to wear. And nothing we ever write about this shithole, no matter how much we love this place, will make a blind bit of difference.'

Beneath the right edge of our car was a sheer drop on to steep rolling grassland that stretched far towards the next set of sharp rock peaks that glared with dull menacing snow. The road wound down. Fishtailing across the Argun River, stone cold and rushing white. Past a couple of abandoned concrete barracks. (Large abandoned objects, even in Khevsureti.)

'How many people are there in Khevsureti now?' Kurtz asked.

'About four hundred in Upper Khevsureti – but most of them come down in the winter and sell their cows and return in the spring,' Shamil answered. Shamil looked like a friendly wolf, he had yellow eyes and a sharp nose and a good strong smile with strong white teeth. He looked like a mountaineer; he had a full bushy beard, white and grey in places and the compact, skinny, muscled body of someone who could walk for several hours uphill carrying an old man on his back. He was happy, like all true mountain people, to be back in the mountains, but he shook his head at the refugee cars we passed, overloaded, full of quiet suffering people, grinding up the road.

Shatili, the main village in Upper Khevsureti, came into view, a scant row of boxes hanging on a hillside. Rebuilt as a gift from First Secretary Shevardnadze in the seventies. A few poor houses, a few poor chickens, some rose bushes which were thin and thorny in the cold altitude. On a flattened piece of slope there was a helicopter pad and a radio antenna.

Around a promontory were the bereft towers of old Shatili – abandoned in the fifties, its slate walls leaned into the rock and weathered against the mountain so that it had become part of the hard scenery. Piles of flaky slate tumbled down its old narrow lanes, walls had buckled and hung open, the basket-weave balconies were leached grey, worn by the wind. Where once Khevsurs had kept cattle and tradition, shook pints of cream into molten butter, stitched small crosses on to the embroidered hems of their tunics along with small silver coins and covered their heads in chainmail. An English ethnographer watching them do this in the early twentieth century had deduced that the Khevsurs were descended from a remnant of a Crusader army that fought with the Georgians against the Turks.

'But the Khevsurs were never anything to do with the Crusaders,' explained Shamil, decrying the old, foreign legend. 'They fought with them, perhaps they copied their armour. There was never any written history – it's difficult to know. The Khevsurs were always considered the crack troops of the Kartli kings; it used to be a great honour to send a son to the royal bodyguard.'

Shamil was born in the last village in Khevsureti, in Hone, where the valley rounded into a bowl against the mountains and from whence a tributary to the Argun sprang. For the first five years of his schooling, before his family was moved out of the mountains to a suburb near Tbilisi's airport, he went to the village school along with ten other children. In the winter the families of Hone moved to their upper village, high and safe above the threat of avalanches. In the summer, hay grew on the upper slopes and the kitchen gardens yielded potatoes, cabbages, tomatoes, beans and maize.

His parents had named him Shamil after the great Chechen warrior of the nineteenth century; the original *boyevik* that Lermontov and Tolstoy fought against and that Tolstoy's hero Hadji Murat betrayed. With this name he went hunting across the border during the summer with ready Chechens. A very noble name: often he had been drunk to, often he had drunk in return, to its original holder. Local mountain vodka that smelled like cow shit but was surprisingly smooth in the throat. With the ancient rhythm of a swooping glass raised, vodka spilling over on to the table, glass clanked against glass, then swooped back towards the mouth and upended with an elbow loop and a turn of the wrist. Then Shamil would play the balalaika and stamp his feet with the old songs and the women would come in from the kitchen and dance while the men clapped them.

Once he had been a guest in a Chechen village, he told us. A small feast had been prepared and everyone was sitting at a rough narrow table laid with flat bread and fried potatoes and a dish of stewed goat. He had caught the eye of a small dark daughter who was watching shyly from the doorway. She blushed and in trepidation, lest his glance be noted, he had buried his gaze on an innocent blank wall where no one would find it.

'Your grandfather was a bastard,' the host was thundering, beating his palm on the table, 'a face like a mangled cow's arse, a temper like a rabid dog – he stole my grandfather's horse; a horse that was as high as a house and as mad at the world as he was. (A part of my grand-mother's dowry – some say given in revenge by her father.) The great horse kicked half the corral down during the theft (loyalty to his true family, no doubt), but your bastard grandfather paid no attention, whacked him on the nose with a chunk of wood and climbed straight up on to his back and rode away.'

Shamil had kept his eyes staring at the wall; the wall was neutral. He withdrew his hands to his sides.

'Stolen! Well –' his host, who was a hardy rough fellow, smiled, pleased with the tense expression on the face of his guest, 'that's all past – decades have rolled over these mountains since the old bastard fell over his own feet in the dark and cracked his head open. Now we can all drink together and forget all that shit. Ha!' And he stuck his glass in the air and Shamil banged it with his and looked over to the corner of the room where the rifles were stacked.

Shamil told us this story and thumped the steering wheel with a great grin, remembering. 'I was worried, I was a guest, but my grand-father had stolen a horse. It's not an easy situation to find yourself in. That girl was beautiful, though. I never saw her again.'

Below Shatili, in the cold mountain shadow, on a small stretch of land next to a bend in the river, we could see several groups of refugees squatting by a fire. Shamil stopped the car and we got out to talk to them. Their stories were the usual refugee stories:

'They're bombing the road.'

'There's nothing, no one is left in Grozny. Everyone has left.'

'We've got nothing here. Not even bread for the children.'

'The thieving Russians are coming back.'

'There were bodies by the side of the road.'

'We had to walk for hours in the night.'

The men were dressed in jeans or tracksuit trousers, cheap

coloured factory-knit sweaters and suit jackets. One or two wore a mink *shapka* on their heads. The women had rubber village shoes on their feet. They had a few blankets between them in which they wrapped the smallest children.

Kurtz stood in the middle of a circle, swapping phrases in Chechen. One man, inevitably called Ruslan, smiled his gold teeth under a thick black beard.

'The Russian planes are coming again and I am trying to take my family out. Then they bomb us on the road.'

'It's bad in Grozny?'

'Bad? Pah. It's quiet in Grozny. Everyone has left Grozny!'

'And why do you think the Russians have invaded again?' One man shrugged, one nodded as if it were always a foregone conclusion. Ruslan pushed his cap further off his forehead.

'It was a bad thing that Basayev did,' he said truthfully, casting his eyes at the ground. 'No one in Chechnya supported him when he invaded Dagestan. He is just a fighter who likes to fight.'

'We are very peaceable people.' A woman had pushed into the circle to have her say. She wore a flowered headscarf and several layers of clothing. She was perhaps forty, unremarkable except for her manner; she had shoved herself forward with an ample bosom and spoke belligerently, rapidly. 'We are peaceable people. And they come with their bombs. I had a son and they killed him. And now I have another son, my only son,' Kurtz saw that she was dragging a very small boy along by the wrist, 'and they will kill him too. Nobody cares! Nobody does anything. They build their fat dachas and drive around in their fat Mercedes and we poor people endure because poor people always endure –'

Kurtz took off his Turkish cap and silenced her with his hand.

Slowly he took out his hip-flask from the interior of his jacket and began to unscrew the top.

'Do you drink?' he asked the woman. These were a Muslim people, it must be respected. But they were also a Soviet people, so most of them drank.

'No I do not drink.' She stood her ground. The small boy beside her looked up at her.

'Well then *I* will drink for your dead son,' said Kurtz, unscrewing the cap of the flask and inverting it so that it became a shot container. 'And I will drink for all the dead sons of Chechnya.' And he waved his hands wide with expanse so that everyone understood and fell silent in respect. He drank the thimble with his elbow jutted out and his forearm parallel to the ground in ceremony. When he was finished he passed the tumbler around the men, most of whom drank from it solemnly and hid their thirst for the spirit, proposing noble toasts. The woman, defeated, shaking her head, left the men and went back to sit against the heat of the fire.

I found her there and took her details down in my notebook, scribbling to keep up with the invective. Her name was Marina Kaftarashvili, it was a Chechen name with a Georgian suffix. She was thirty-six years old. Her husband had stayed behind in Chechnya. She had no job – God above, no one had any job! She had been travelling for two days with a party of eight other refugees, mostly neighbours. They had walked overnight along the narrow track to reach the border post. One of the children she was travelling with had developed a cough and there was no medicine for it.

'May I see your passport?' I asked and she brought it out and showed it to me.

'You are a Georgian?' Her passport was Georgian.

'I am Chechen,' replied the woman proudly, standing defiant with her legs astride. 'Kistenka.'

The Kisti were Chechens who had settled in Georgia in the early nineteenth century – refugees and outlaws of the early Russian campaigns. They lived meanly in villages in the Pankisi valley that backed up against the high Caucasus. There were several thousand of them and some had gone back to Grozny and to relatives in Chechnya after the Russians had been driven out in 1996.

'Just when you think you've heard of all the tribes,' said Kurtz coming up behind me and offering me vodka from his hip-flask. 'Shall we go and check out the border?'

'It's two kilometres further,' said Shamil who had been passing out vodka and bread, pressing them into the hands of the women, who were less particular about accepting charity than the men.

'Yeah, let's blow this,' said Kurtz, stretching his shoulders against the weight of the sky. 'Let's do it before we don't.'

The afternoon was darkening and chill and the Shatili Khevsurs were herding their cattle home along the road. The cows hefted one foot in front of the other and moved gracelessly, interminably forward as if obstinacy was crossbred into their Spartan mountain suffering. A contingent of Georgian security forces had come up to augment the usual company of border guards. They had built a small camp on a flat bit of ground by the river consisting of a couple of tents, a rusted cabin and a generator. A slim pine log had been stripped, lowered across the road and weighted with stones as a barrier.

Two soldiers wearing bear shearling coats and crisp new uniforms with bowl-shaped helmets stood about.

'*Gamma Jobat.* Hello.' Kurtz walked up with a stiff swagger, belly swelled with breath, master of the checkpoint. Rocking like a gangster, feet planted solidly apart as he faced the guards, arms flung open in an exaggerated welcome and to show that he was not carrying any weapons, smiling broadly, he walked forward with his packet of cigarettes outstretched. 'Take some cigarettes,' he told the soldier boys. The guards each took several, lighting them with cupped hands protecting flecks of glowing red against the wind and secreting the extra ones in their pockets.

'You been up here long?' Kurtz asked them.

'Not so long,' said one.

'Couple of weeks; since this business started,' said the other, nodding towards a small metal folding table where a third guard was laboriously recording the particulars of a family at the end of a long list of names.

The refugees stood around pointing out spelling to him. Their baggage was heaped in the middle of the clearing. The soldier stamped their refugee cards, issued by the Red Cross in Grozny several years before at the time of the last war. Stamp, stamp, without looking up. When he was finished he waved them through with the back of his hand and they ducked under the barrier (none of the soldiers bothered to raise it for them) and walked slowly onwards.

'The border is now closed,' said the third guard, getting up from his seat and walking towards Kurtz. His face was blank dismissive camouflage authority.

'It's not permitted to come any further,' he said flatly. Kurtz waved his press accreditation at him. The soldier took the laminated document and inspected both sides of it with a scowl. Kurtz spread his hands wide, 'We're not doing anything. We just want to talk to your commander.'

Kurtz looked at me and whispered under his breath, 'There's

always a Tweedledum and Tweedledee and then there's always a fucking moron.'

'No,' said the soldier and turned away.

There was a silence. The two soldiers paced uneasily, trying not to look at Kurtz while fingering his generous cigarettes in their pockets.

'Can you fetch your commander?' Kurtz addressed the one who was standing nearest to him.

The soldier glanced over at his recalcitrant comrade who was walking away down the incline to the encampment.

'Wait here,' he told Kurtz with resignation and gravity.

After several minutes (Shamil and I sat in the car with the doors open, smoking and eating bits of bread we tore off a loaf), Kurtz was rewarded with the sight of a colonel walking up the escarpment with his hands in the pocket of a brand-new stiffly ironed camouflage uniform. He smiled at us graciously and introduced himself with a formal handshake.

'Well you can see there's not much happening here,' he said, neutral, benign.

'Refugees,' I replied

'Some refugees are coming across, yes. But they are mainly Georgians.' The colonel was impassive and protective.

'Georgians?'

'Georgians. Chechens with Georgian passports. They come from Pankisi. And now they are going back to Pankisi.'

'How many of them have crossed?' asked Kurtz, poised pencil over notebook.

'About a thousand in the last two weeks. There has been no trouble.'

'And they have to walk across the border?'

'There's no road over the border.' The colonel smiled tightly, 'There is a road on the other side, but it stops about three kilometres away. So they walk the last few steps.'

'Along the cow track?'

'Yes, as you can see,' the colonel waved his arm in the direction of another herd treading uncertainly down towards the river, 'mostly it's just used by the locals. They take their cows up to graze over the ridge.'

'And refugees with Russian Federation passports?'

'They are refugees. We cannot turn them away. And so we register them and they come through.'

'No problems?'

'No, there has been nothing unusual.'

'How many guards are there here now?' I asked.

The colonel smiled broadly, 'Oh, I cannot tell you that.'

The colonel was smug and relaxed and Kurtz disliked the way he swallowed his smiles with an inward private humour. He was supercilious. Kurtz felt the old checkpoint feeling, a mixture of performance nerves and uniform foreboding. The guards paced nonchalantly with their guns. Towards the end of the interview Kurtz actually yawned. The colonel had refused to answer a question about traffic moving the other way.

'This is not a border,' said the colonel.

'But you are wearing the uniform of a border guard,' said Kurtz, deadpan.

'It's a temporary border; during this – *situation*.'

'One-way traffic.'

'Refugees tend to flee in only one direction, yes.' The colonel turned sarcastic, and then he turned on his heel and walked back down the hill.

Kurtz chewed. Then he began to try to engage the recalcitrant guard in conversation, drawing him into chat with his hip-flask. The guard shook his head.

'I don't drink.'

'Ah,' said Kurtz, understanding, taking in his dark brown skin and black hair. 'You are an Azeri.'

'Yes. I am an Azeri. From Rustavi.'

Kurtz slipped into Azeri. 'May God watch over you here.'

'If it is his will.'

The Azeri's name was Arif. After a few minutes he began to smile at Kurtz and even went so far as to accept a cigarette from him.

'You know there is an American here,' Arif told him, now thoroughly charmed by Kurtz's collection of Armenian jokes.

'An American? Another journalist?'

'No, a refugee. He came over yesterday morning, but he has no visa so we cannot let him pass. Someone from the American Embassy is coming to pick him up.'

'A refugee. He has an American passport?'

'Yes. He is with his wife and small daughter. She is about this big –' Arif put his hand level with his mid-thigh. 'We put them in a tent down there. He is complaining that we didn't give him any food. But we gave him rice.'

'Can I talk to him?'

'I can get him.'

I sat in the front seat of the Niva, which was parked up next to the barrier. Shamil was wandering about, staring up at his mountains and looking over anxiously at Kurtz; it was getting dark. I took out my notebook and wrote things in it. It seemed important to record every detail very precisely – this little microcosm of petty border politics. I looked up and saw a puff of noiseless white smoke drifting a few kilometres away. The Russians were bombing. Kurtz saw it too and started to say something about it but then a man came walking quickly up the hill from the encampment with anticipation. He was wearing a good thick alpine jacket, jeans and a pair of stout hiking boots on his feet. His face was red brown, with a Semitic nose, black glossy eyebrows that almost met and a thick beard that he kept extremely neat.

'Hello,' he smiled at Kurtz, breathing from his climb and his adrenalin. His face radiated relieved happiness. It was clear he thought that Kurtz had come from the Embassy.

'John Kurtz. I'm a journalist.'

'Oh. You are journalist.' The man was disappointed, but remained polite.

'You're an American?' Kurtz asked him doubtfully. His carefully trimmed beard was Wahhabi; not a stray whisker had been allowed to reach below the line of his upper lip.

'Yes. I was naturalized. My name is Omar al-Kurdi. Originally my family came from Jordan.' Omar al-Kurdi spoke calmly and gently. His face was young under his beard and unlined.

'From the Chechen diaspora in Jordan?' queried Kurtz.

'No. No. I am not Chechen at all.'

'And where in the States are you from?'

'Oh, from Tennessee.'

'From Tennessee!' Kurtz roared back. Indeed Omar al-Kurdi had a faint Southern accent. Perhaps that's why it had seemed gentle at first.

Kurtz took his camera out of his pocket to record such a strange and anomalous being.

'Please,' said Omar al-Kurdi, taking a step backwards to decline, 'I cannot have my picture taken. It's my religion. But I am happy to give you any information.' There was grace in his voice, there was worry in his eyes, but an artless sense of something pure in his gestures. He did not want to give offence; Kurtz assured him that he had not done so.

'You are with your family?' Kurtz was scrawling pencil across the page.

'Yes I am with my wife and my daughter. My wife has a Bosnian passport. She is Bosnian, we met in Sarajevo when I was working for a Saudi relief organization. And my daughter. She has an American passport. My wife is pregnant –'

Kurtz took a moment to digest this confusion and transfer it to the page with illustrative arrows.

'And you have been living in Grozny? You must be the only American in Chechnya!'

'Yes, well I was.'

'And what were you doing in Grozny?'

'I had a honey business,' replied Omar al-Kurdi without guile. There was nothing for Kurtz to do but nod.

'Why did you try to come south into Georgia?'

'We tried to get out through Ingushetia,' Omar al-Kurdi explained, carefully. 'But my Russian visa expired four days ago. Just four days ago! They wouldn't let me into Ingushetia without a Russian visa. I tried to get a new visa in Grozny but every time I went they said they had no forms and that Moscow had not sent them any forms. So I tried to ask them: how can I renew my visa? It was a vicious circle. They would not let us pass into Ingushetia. For two days we were trying. Then the Mafia took my car. My wife is pregnant, I am very worried about her –' Omar al-Kurdi lost a little of his poise, and his words became more ragged. Before he had been replying to ordinary questions, the kind of questions he might be expected to answer on a form; now he was trying to retell what had happened to him and his family; a story rather than facts. 'We had to retrace ourselves,' he continued. 'We found a bus and tried to get south, but they are bombing the road.'

'During the day?'

'And during the night. You cannot drive with your headlamps on, otherwise the Russians will use this as a target. In every town there was some damage and people lying dead from bombing. Then we got lost walking. We had to walk all night and then find a different route. It's not easy in these mountains. My wife is pregnant. She is not well. She nearly had a miscarriage. And now they won't let us into Georgia because my visa expired four days ago. Russian citizens can pass. But they won't let us through – we've been sitting in that tent for two days. I am very worried about my wife –'

Kurtz saw the taut expression on his face; the unsubsided fear of the past few days was mingled with the apprehension of the uncertain days that were to come. He put his hands on Omar al-Kurdi's shoulders, square and reassuring, and twitched the corners of his big moustache into a smile.

'Everything will be fine,' he told him. 'They've radioed to the American Embassy and they are sending someone up to get you.'

Omar al-Kurdi smiled back; he wanted to believe him.

'What will you do?' asked Kurtz, 'Where will you go? Back to the States?'

'Or to Jordan, I have family there.'

*

Dusk fell. The soldiers raised the barrier for another herd of cows that meandered, milling around the car, bumping it with their flanks. Shamil was talking to the herdsman whom he seemed to recognize. They stood off to one side, heads bent together; Kurtz was still occupied with Omar al-Kurdi.

'Your brothers are all through these mountains,' the herdsman told Shamil, lowering his voice, 'and these idiots don't do anything – pah, just walking about on the spot.'

'My brothers, you say. My brothers!' Shamil laughed at his friend. 'They're all a bunch of criminal narcomen,' he added easily.

'They're all through these mountains,' the herdsman repeated, ignoring the dog that was standing next to him and looking up, imploring him to raise his stick to the more reluctant cows, 'there will be trouble for it!'

I was distracted from eavesdropping by another car arriving, in fact two white pick-up trucks, brand-new Chevys with winching gear attached to their front bumpers. Two men got out of the front truck, three from the truck behind it. One man stayed in the second truck, passively staring out of the window, seemingly uninterested in the scene in front of him.

The men were Chechens, dressed in black jeans and sweaters; a couple of them had mobile phones attached to their belts, one had a bandage wrapped around his knuckles, another had a gun in his pocket. One was grinning as he bounced out of the car in a pair of Nike Airs and came over and offered me a bottle of Coke.

'Thanks,' I said and smiled back at him; they were full of coiled energy and seemed jolly.

Kurtz had his hip-flask out and was passing it around. He had already thrown back his head laughing and was clasping each of them in the half-bear-hug and back-slap of the Chechen greeting. ('Always feels like they're checking you for weapons,' he told me later.)

Kurtz and the Chechens milled around the barrier; the guards eyed the group suspiciously but did not try to wave them away. The conversation was piecemeal; fragments of enquiry, unfinished sentences, non-committal. There was an amorphous quality to the scene, no one was quite sure what the other was doing there and it was not really politic to ask.

'You're waiting to go over?' probed Kurtz but the Chechen he was talking to only shrugged.

'The refugees below Shatili look like they're going to have a cold night of it.' Kurtz tried again after a few moments.

'Cars come and take them out of the mountains,' came the reply.

'So there's a relay service?'

'Something like that.'

One of the Chechens was allowed through the barrier and walked down the slope to talk to the colonel in the encampment. The others stretched their legs and stared the soldiers down, passed words between themselves, smoked, put their hands in their pockets, paced about. They were young and fit and arrogant.

I looked into the second truck where the lone man was still sitting unconcernedly. He had sandy hair and didn't look Chechen at all.

'Hello,' he said with an English accent. 'You're journalists?'

'Yes. Looking at refugees.' He nodded at me. 'What are you doing up here?' I asked.

'Mine clearance,' he said, getting out of the truck and leaning against it, 'I'm going back in – well, hope I'm going in – tonight – if these fellows can fix it – to restart the operation.'

'You're going back into Chechnya in the middle of a war to dig up mines?' I was incredulous.

'My name's Rob,' he said and extended his hand politely; he did not seem to think it was funny. Perhaps it wasn't. He was slight and compact; he wore a pair of jeans, a checked shirt and a cotton zip-up jacket. He looked like nothing in particular. Except there was a clean line across his forehead, an almost imperceptible determination.

'So you know these people?'

'Never met them before – it was set up in Tbilisi –'

'Have you got a Russian visa?'

'Nah. They don't like anyone helping the Chechens. I'm persona non grata. I'm not here and there's no bloody border either.' Now he smiled; *that* was funny.

'You've been before?'

'Spent two years in Chechnya, running the operation. Had to pull out in May – kidnap attempt.'

'What happened?'

'Usual thing. They'd been trying to snatch me for months. Never travelled anywhere without a convoy. Ambush. Four of my bodyguards were wounded. Basically I legged it.'

I took him for ex-army, minimum number of words, maximum amount of fact. His mood was calm and bored; he was waiting.

'Do you trust these Chechens?' I asked him.

Rob shrugged. 'They're all right. Been drinking since we left Tbilisi. They got into a fight on the way with some bloke whose dog we ran over. That's why he's bandaged his hand.'

There was movement around the barrier; the colonel had returned with the leader of the Chechens to allow one of the trucks through the barrier.

Rob remained, kicking at the stones on the road with his boots, occasionally exchanging a few words with the two other Chechens (including the one who had offered me the Coke) who had stayed behind with him.

'Getting dark now.'

'Bit colder.'

'Have you got another cigarette?'

Kurtz had engaged the colonel in another series of fruitless questioning.

'Where is the truck going?'

'Just a kilometre further,' said the colonel.

'Why?'

'They said they're picking something up.'

'What for?'

'You'll have to ask them that.'

I ducked under the barrier. The colonel watched me but he did not stop me. We were not actually on the border; it wasn't a border.

The road continued straight towards Chechnya for a couple of hundred yards, but then turned sharply right along a perpendicular valley through which ran a tributary of the Argun, up towards Hone. Two mean, broken-down slate hovels, plague huts, stood on a spit of grassy cliff, where the two rivers met. A very steep, narrow, dirt path led down to them. They looked like no more than caches of stone. I looked through the bars of a tiny window into one of them. By now it was dark and I couldn't see anything until I shone my torch on the interior. There were two stone shelves inside piled with human bones.

I walked back to the car with my hands in my pockets. A single electric light bulb was strung up over the folding table at which the refugees were processed. Everyone was milling about in the darkness, avoiding its bright glare. Kurtz and Shamil were standing by the car. Shamil was trying to persuade Kurtz to call it a day. Kurtz was reluctant; he wanted to see what would happen.

It didn't look as if anything was going to happen, there was an atmosphere of complicit boredom. Two of the Chechens went up to the barrier and hissed at the guards to get their attention.

'Comrade! Get us some bread will you?' one of them ordered. His tone was arrogant; the soldiers ignored him. 'Get us some bread. We're hungry. Bread!' He slapped his hand on the flimsy barrier which wobbled. One of the guards went to pace further off, the other mumbled something back at him. The Chechen demanded, the soldier shuffled, demurred. 'I haven't got any,' he said. The Chechen railed at this and stamped his feet, petulant, aggressive, losing interest.

After a couple of minutes he came over to me. 'We need your car,' he said. 'Lend us your car for a couple of minutes.'

'What do you need it for?'

'We have to pick something up.'

'It's not my car,' I lied, 'you have to ask Shamil.'

Shamil was sitting in the driver's seat with his arms folded across his chest. He shook his head at the Chechen and turned his palms upwards; what could he do? The Chechen walked off down the track to take a piss; he did not bother to walk out of view. Rob stood about saying nothing.

'Where have they gone in the other truck?' I asked him. He shrugged. The machinations were nothing to do with him.

Kurtz tried to engage the Chechen with the gun in his pocket in conversation, but the cordiality of half an hour before had gone. He said nothing; they were all waiting for us to leave.

'I don't like these people.' Shamil explained, still holding his arms protectively around himself. 'During the day it's fine; but at night – they'll take your car and there's nothing you can do about it.'

After another twenty minutes or so of standing about Kurtz gave up.

'Let's blow this,' he said, swinging his legs into the car. 'They're not going to do anything with us watching them.'

Shamil took us to one of the houses in Shatili for the night. We drove past the clumps of refugees still waiting for a taxi or a bus or a relative to take them out of Khevsureti. ('They charge what they like; fifty dollars a person; or you have to wait three days for one of the buses they send from Akhmeta,' we were told when we asked.) Shamil parked next to the last house in the single row of houses in the village. Two small boys were playing in the street with a stick; they ran off when they saw us.

A young man, untalkative and uncongenial, showed us into a room in the house in which there were four beds. He was tall and thin with a long narrow face and a knife-edge nose. I asked him if there was anything to eat; he said he had milk and would try to find some potatoes.

Kurtz and I sat in the kitchen with bowls of hot milk, writing up notes and drinking vodka. I had checked the bathroom: rusted old enamel bath and a filthy enamel sink; cracked tiling, patched ceiling; certainly there was no running water.

But the kitchen was snug with a huge cast-iron stove in the corner and a boiling kettle on top of it. The room had worn, painted wooden floorboards, damp walls, papered in places long ago, a mould-ridden ceiling, faded red plastic tablecloth. There was never any hot water.

There was always vodka. Kurtz stared at the bottle of vodka on the table which was already half drunk between us and blurred his vision at it.

'I am beginning to realize,' he said, 'that if I had to choose, I'd take vodka over hot water most of the time.'

'They've obviously got some system,' said Kurtz after a while. 'They've got the stiff-necked colonel paid off; they've got their network waiting on the other side; the Ministry man even hinted to me in Tbilisi that there are guns and rocket launchers going over the mountains all the time.' He had stopped writing and leaned back heavily in his chair. 'Until it snows in about three weeks. And then the passes will be blocked.'

The colonel was guarding his authority; holding it tightly to his chest; it didn't look as though Kurtz was going to get a chance to slip through his border. He wasn't equipped to walk over the mountains and there was no one to take him. He looked down at his notebook. He had a few refugee interviews: a bizarre American Wahhabi with a Bosnian wife and an Englishman bent on demining in a war zone. Where was the angle? Just random, absurd – almost ridiculous – a line on a map, a stripped-pine barrier and twenty-four soldiers (according to Shamil's local intelligence), guarding the entrance to a war.

Our host returned with a bowl of potatoes and began peeling them over a bucket in the corner of the kitchen. He nodded at us, but said nothing.

'I hate these goddamn borders, checkpoints, bullshit,' Kurtz looked up at me with bloodshot eyes. 'All that peculiar tension, who can pass, stop, questions, forms, documents. I am tired of these ethnic wars; who the hell cares if they keep killing each other. If I were younger I'd walk into Chechnya and take my chances. But now I've grown accustomed to my skin – perhaps I just can't be bothered. Perhaps I want to stick around a bit longer with this fucking black dog tethered to my ankle. I don't know.' At this, the sum of the whole long day, the sum of forty years and a decade of Caucasus wars, he closed his notebook, tossed it across the table and reached for his glass of vodka.

Aslan of Adjara

GEORGIA HAD FORGOTTEN ITS two hundred years of Russian and Soviet Imperial order as quickly as a bottle of vodka is drunk. In a short decade it had reverted to its comfortable medieval self: peasants farmed their plots and suffered in the winter, and the ruling class of whatever they were – bandit politicians, the odd warlord, shallow academics – ruled in their own manner, in the manner of their ancestors; locally, badly, with deep pockets, petty rivalries and occasional violence. The idea that Georgia was a sovereign state with a flag, a democratically elected government, a seat at the UN etc. was entirely notional. The last time Georgia had been an independent, administratively coherent nation was under David the Builder in the twelfth century and the experiment had been brief.

Aslan was a king with a fiefdom called Adjara, a dictator with a secret service, a president with bodyguards. He had his own television station, his own 'tariffs' excised on the border with Turkey; he had his own police and they had their own black Gore-Tex uniforms and sub-machine-guns. He had independent relations with the Turks and with the Russians (which means he took money from them). He had a bomb-proof black Mercedes, just like Shevardnadze's. He had power and absolute control. It was his own; Aslan Abashidze owned Adjara.

The capital of Adjara is Batumi and in the autumn sun it was lovely. Like a brochure, the skies were blue, the sea was like glass, the sun shone warmly on the grassy esplanades and avenues that ran along the beachfront. The summer crowds had gone. The bamboo groves rippled over shadow, the cafés were quiet; baklava and coffee. Graceful turn-of-the-century holiday villas were brilliant with new white paint. The little streets and lanes that fed into the back of the port were full of boutiques and bars and small hotels and galleries; above them a single minaret pierced the sky.

Aslan watched all of this. He looked down from the walls of offices and foyers and halls upon his minions and subjects. His face was on posters plastered twenty deep or more on every vertical surface in Batumi. It was the week before a parliamentary election and Aslan was head of the opposition Revival Bloc.

'I know! What can I do?' Aslan smiled at me, disingenuous; his blue eyes twinkled with a hard edge. 'Some stupid guy put up all these posters! It's like an anti-advertisement. I'm trying to think how to take them down.'

I smiled back and raised an eyebrow. 'But why is yours the only face on view?' I asked. 'There don't seem to be posters for any other candidate! Anywhere in Batumi.'

'Oh, that is their affair!' he said, dismissing the subject and rambling off about mandarin oranges.

Aslan was short, as is traditional for despots, but relaxed and handsome, with wings of pure white hair and eyes of an intense sea blue. He stared at me to see if I would meet his gaze. He made his little jokes, he spun an easy patter. Lackeys who came in and out of the room ferrying messages were deferential as courtiers, leaning into a shallow hovering bow to relay their information in a rushed whisper.

143

I admit I almost liked Aslan. Of course the guy was bananas, but the whole country was bananas. He was at least a banana with a smirk and real authority; Holly Golightly's favourite kind of banana: the Top Banana.

The room in which we met was grand. It was furnished with a suite of white leather rococo furniture and an enormous polished walnut circular coffee table. Above us hung a huge crystal chandelier. Citrus tea and cakes were brought. The interview lasted almost three hours. In that time Aslan did not answer any question directly. This was the commonplace apparatchik practice. Aslan was used to his polemic; it was a polished certainty, and things like questions, facts, statistics or other people's stupid opinions simply slid off its shiny surface. Sometimes I found it difficult not to smile at his serious congeniality; he said such silly things with a straight face. From time to time he doodled on a piece of paper to illustrate a point; he drew boxes and then crossed them out for emphasis.

At first there was a very young, very nervous interpreter, who did OK, relaying our conversation in a stuttering strangled falsetto. But Aslan was clearly displeased with his efforts and so after half an hour he summoned his son who had studied English, Aslan explained, in England. As the interpreter was dismissed he looked over at me, utterly miserable, as if he might begin to cry. I tried to defend him, saying that there was really no need to change interpreters, that he was doing a fine job; it was to no avail.

The day before, Aslan had opened a 'Centre for Democracy and Regionalism' in Batumi, an event attended by a formless group of Brussels types, NGO worthies and the resident Turkish Consul in Batumi. Aslan seemed to be trying to establish independent diplomatic relationships with these people; perhaps in the future he thought he could get development aid directly without it going through Tbilisi.

Needless to say Aslan was in favour of regions. 'Regions should have their own economic spaces. Their own budgets,' he pronounced. He said that a region was 'just like the family. Each family leader should look after the members of the family.' Perhaps a little paternalistic for most democrats, but still a nice sentiment.

Father, godfather; Aslan had money and he took care of his people. He had money from the trade with Turkey that he controlled. Batumi had a relatively decent electricity supply, pensions and government wages were paid. He had built a factory that made speedboats. Most importantly he had kept Adjara out of the civil war of 1992–3. He had headed off a column of Kitovani's National Guard tanks, sealed the Adjarian border with Russian soldiers from a nearby base and disarmed the local police. And while the rest of Georgia was caught in the Mekhedrioni mêlée, the Abkhaz war, the Ossetian troubles, Adjara sat on the Black Sea and was safe.

And he took care of his family. Giorgi, his son, arrived for the interview dressed in black cashmere with long black eyelashes that blinked over a pair of red-rimmed hungover eyes. Giorgi, I knew, had his own black Mercedes and owned the largest nightclub in Batumi, called Dianaland after Aslan's daughter.

In Adjara, Aslan was king. But his kingdom was small and no one had ever heard of it. I had a feeling this bothered him. And it probably bothered him that his arch-enemy, Shevardnadze, seemed to spend his days whisking between Washington and Moscow and Berlin, handshaking heads of state and finding himself at swank receptions where he was toasted as the great reformer with crystal glasses and fed fillet of beef. Aslan was adamant that Shevy had been Gorbachev's puppet, a cipher, who had done whatever he was told and should not take any credit for ending the Cold War whatsoever. Aslan hated Shevy.

'Shevardnadze has planned to liquidate me,' Aslan told me very seriously. 'I will not go to Tbilisi because they plan terrorist acts.' Aslan had not been to Tbilisi in many years and he had forbidden his family to go there. 'We found one terrorist hiding in a government building in Batumi – I don't know what could have happened.' They had found other would-be assassins, specially picked orphans, he said, hiding in the bushes with antitank missiles along the road from Batumi to Kobuleti where he had a house. 'They would destroy me everywhere. Tbilisi was helping these people, they gave them guns and boats. Our house is close to the sea and they wanted to fire on the house from the sea.'

If Shevy had his assassination attempts, then he, Aslan, must have them too. Aslan was petulant on the subject; his easy-going sly-fox political chit-chat went out the window; he became slightly deranged.

'Shevardnadze sets up his own assassinations as shows!' he told me, barely controlling his outrage at such heinous deception. 'And always before an election, you'll notice! How is it possible they missed with an antitank missile at three metres?'

There followed a catalogue of slights: Shevy had destroyed Batumi's bid to host the European Chess Championships, despite the nice new building Aslan had built for the purpose; Shevy had soured a hazelnut deal with Hillary Clinton's brothers worth $114 million ('$114 million for nuts?' I repeated incredulously. 'That's nuts!') with a phone call to the White House.

'Shevardnadze is for no one. Not north, west or east. Shevardnadze is like a windsock.'

The main point of contention between the two was money. Tbilisi wanted Aslan to release more of the Adjarian cash flow into the central budget than he was at present doing. With the exception of Tbilisi, Adjara was by far the richest region in Georgia. There was the Turkish border money, hazelnuts and mandarins which were good, exportable cash crops and a local economy injected with lari every summer when the fancy Tbilisi élite headed to the Adjarian coastline for their holidays because they could no longer go to Abkhazia. Batumi had new banks built out of marble and gold mirrored glass; new hotels went up all the time and the bars along the beachfront had good sound systems and large collections of multicoloured cocktails. There was an air of bustling prosperity.

Shevardnadze accused Aslan of withholding 25.5 million lari from the central budget over the previous two years.

'It's crazy. It's only blackmail,' said Aslan, waving his hand derisively, crossing out more boxes on the pad in front of him with sharp pressurized downward pen-strokes. 'They want to say that they cannot pay salaries and pensions because Abashidze will not pay.'

Aslan was particularly upset about Tbilisi's efforts to send a British company, ITS, to supervise customs on the border.

'ITS cannot come here. They are trying to block the flow of goods into Georgia.' Aslan was quite categorical, he resented the intrusion. 'They are not investing anything,' he complained. (Investing in what? Local friendship?) 'I told them if they invested some money they could stand on the border no problem.'

ITS never did get a foothold in Adjara. From time to time teams of international tax advisers were sent from Tbilisi, but officials in Batumi simply shrugged and refused to hand over figures. It was hard to blame them. At least in Batumi you knew where the money was going; in Tbilisi it just disappeared. In Georgia, politics was personality and in the end it just depended on who you were related to.

At the end of the interview, Aslan presented me with a gift pack which included: one video documentary of the assassination attempts, a personally signed copy of a pamphlet entitled 'The Adjarian Autonomous Republic in Figures', one bottle of Yves Saint Laurent perfume and a Mont Blanc malachite ballpoint pen – not fake. I watched the video; it was an odd mix. Half of it was taken up with testimonies from people admitting that they had tried to kill Aslan on Shevardnadze's orders and the other half was footage of Aslan and his would-be murderer together: Shevy and Aslan speeding around Batumi harbour in an Adjarian-built speedboat, Shevy and Aslan planting a ceremonial tree, Aslan greeting the presidential plane on the tarmac, side by side, Aslan and Shevy, their bodyguards in tow, discussing matters of state. I had the feeling that however much Aslan protested hate for Shevy, secretly he wanted to be Shevy.

'I hate all this political stuff, I really hate it,' Giorgi told me while Aslan was taking a telephone call and I was waiting to shake his hand and wrap things up (I was exhausted). We exchanged a chagrined look, 'But you know when my father asks me to do something –' he shrugged; it wasn't easy to refuse.

'I'm sorry for taking so long,' I said, sympathetically.

'Oh, it's no problem,' Giorgi smiled, anointed Prince of Adjara, with grace and charm.

I left, clutching my bag of goodies, and walked down the wide expansive staircase accompanied by a press officer. The front doors opened ahead of us and a woman swanned into the lobby. It was Mrs Abashidze. She was middle-aged, large and voluptuous. Her hair was coiffed into a dark chestnut cloud above her head. Although it was only the middle of the afternoon, she wore an evening dress that clung to her curves and sparkled glitter over a large bosom. She did not glance around her but swept forward imperiously. The press officer and I, without thinking about it, flattened ourselves respectfully against the wall as she passed.

I went to sit in a café in the shadow of the monument Aslan had erected to his father in the park that ran along the beach. I drank three cups of coffee and smoked four cigarettes and felt better. In fact I felt wonderful; the coffee was strong and Turkish, the sun was warm. I began to think seriously that a benevolent despot was better than a bad democracy. But then perhaps I too had become a victim of the Aslan spell. The sun, the wine, the gracious hospitality, the presents –

A black Mercedes drew up, followed by a silver saloon car. Giorgi had found me through a mutual friend with a mobile telephone.

'Please allow me to take you to the station to meet your train,' he said, infinitely more relaxed out of his father's presence. 'It's so nice to be able to talk real English with someone. I miss England. I was in Cambridge. How is it now? Batumi – you know in the summer there are a lot of people here, a lot of friends and everything is open, there's a lot of fun here in the summer. But in the winter – it can be boring. Nothing happens and my father will not let me go to Tbilisi.'

I was taken to the station in convoy. Giorgi helped me find my berth and hovered on the platform attentively, moaning adorably about how boring he found all the politics. I was thoroughly charmed. (Indeed his eyelashes were very long.) I got on the train and contemplated my meagre picnic of sausage, beer and bread. Hmm, I thought, Adjara – can't wait to go back.

Istanbul, Cairo

AS THE CENTURY TICKED over to nought I stood on a boat in the middle of the Bosphorus. Cars trapped in jams along the banks of Istanbul honked, crowds of revellers waved at us and danced and threw their glasses into the water, fireworks somewhere up ahead burst into sprays of fiery sparks. I was crying soft tears. Thomas was talking on his mobile phone to his other girlfriend. My heart was broken. The party on the boat hugged and kissed each other. Kurtz barrelled around filling glasses with champagne, rollicking the guests, Cormac canoodled. Thomas could not kiss me because he was talking on his mobile phone to his other girlfriend and because his jaw was septic. He'd had a tooth pulled by a Wahhabi dentist in Nazran the week before.

It started to rain, it was cold. The boat finally drew into a quay and we found taxis – Istanbul seemed to be working; after all it was not Mohammed's birthday. I kept with the group but apart from it. I could not look at Thomas. Thomas could not look at me. There was another party that we went to. I suppose I talked to people. Later it was still raining and cold and we all piled back to the hotel. Thomas, running a fever, flushed, sweat in his hair, exhausted, filled up with the emotional wrench between two women and blood-infused mouth pain finally collapsed on the bed, coma-like, with his boots on. I took his boots off and pulled the blankets over him and lay down, squashed myself against the wall in the space that he had not sprawled across and lay there for a long time, wakeful, with tears running silent grooves from my eyes to my ears.

Thomas was very ill for three days. He slept and woke for a few minutes and could not remember where he was. I brought him medicines from the pharmacy that were not strong enough. I had the kitchen in the hotel send up soup. There was nothing else to do. Kurtz had disappeared into the city where he had once lived for several years; he had old friends to see. Cormac was holed up with canoodle. I left the hotel and walked. For three days I walked through frigid Istanbul.

The Bosphorus was cold iron grey hard; the Blue Mosque was grey too and the sky spat sleet. There were many things to see and that I could be distracted by: single singed black hairs from the beard of the Prophet Mohammed encased in gold and rubies in the Topkapi Palace, crowds in the spice market, straggles of Christmas–Ramadan tinsel, acres of authentically antique bashed tin water jugs, the vast graceful circles of Hagia Sophia, freezing fresh orange juice, bags of rose-coloured Turkish delight, milky coloured raki, persistent shoeshine boys, idiots who kept trying to chat me up in German, streets that wound up and down underneath my feet for miles and went past different neighbourhoods, shanty and smart, mosques covered in people – most of them selling pistachios, headscarves, cheap shoes, prayer beads, newspapers, blue glass evil eye charms, gold bracelets – as well as dealers who could probably produce for 'a special price just for you', out of a grubby pocket, another selection of hairs from the beard of the Prophet Mohammed.

I found the Armenian church in Galatasaray and lit three candles there. One for Thomas, one for Iceberg, his other girlfriend, and one for me. 'God help us in this mess of Thomas,' I prayed, probably out loud.

On the third day, Mike, the owner of our hotel, spied me, red-rimmed and pitiful, slumped in the corner of the sitting room. 'Apple tea!' he exclaimed, summoning a lackey to fetch it. I smiled weakly at him. 'Ah you need the *hammam*,' he told me sympathetically, 'there is a good one, quite close, three hundred years old.'

So dispatched, in convalescence, I walked up the street to the baths, paid my $10 and lay down on the marble. The *hammam* was a hexagonal domed room with sunlight beaming through star-shaped holes cut in the roof. Supported by an interior ring of pillars, each capped with Arabic calligraphy carving, the expanses of marble plinths and ledges and floor were smooth and welcoming. I washed myself in a stone basin using a copper bowl and lay on the warm marble. I opened my book; it was Giuseppe Tomasi di Lampedusa's *The Leopard*, set in nineteenth-century Sicily – recommended by a friend of mine who said that he had been amazed at its relevance to modern-day Georgia.

I was warm and embalmed in steam. My body relaxed from its hunched suffering, I faked a little hedonism. Di Lampedusa happily took over my brain in earnest concentration. Until I discovered that the young Concetta, who loses her love to a rival at the beginning of the story, finishes the book an old virgin collecting reliquaries for her private chapel. Hmm, maybe I should have bought a couple of the hairs from the beard of the Prophet Mohammed while I had the chance, I thought.

There are always moments of damned epiphany: but the *hammam* that day did not produce any. I left as I had entered, with such an awful pain in my chest that it crossed my mind that I should give up smoking.

Thomas recovered enough to be able to sit up in bed and tell me that he was sorry. I nodded dumbly; what else is there to do when you have lost? He took the next plane to Paris. I booked a ticket back to Tbilisi. The flight took off in the middle of the night; everyone fell asleep and when we landed several hours later I looked out of the window. 'This doesn't look like Tbilisi,' I told the person sitting next to me, peering suspiciously at the blazing terminal, 'there's too much light.' It wasn't Tbilisi. It was Istanbul again. We had flown almost all the way to Tbilisi but had been unable to land because a surge in the power lines in Kakheti had burned out the cable to parts of Tbilisi, including the airport. We spent fourteen hours in Istanbul airport and when I finally got home to my apartment on Vashlovani it was dark anyway because Telasi had come round and cut my illegal second line. Neither of the two units of Gadarbani that usually functioned was working. The power station was completely out of action. The city was down to six hours a day of electricity and in the weeks that followed this went down to four and then to three.

For a week I lay in bed in front of the gas heater reading by candle-light. I ate bread and jam and drank whisky. The pain twisted inside of me; I tried not to think but it was impossible not to think. I thought variously of loneliness, long distance and running.

After a week Kakha called. 'What, you think it's clever not to call your friends? Where the hell have you been?'

'There's no electricity. I can't charge the mobile,' I told him pathetically.

'Come to my office. There's electricity here. I've got a heater. I'll make you a cup of tea.'

'OK.'

There was a pause. Kakha said, 'Jeez, that Thomas is a bastard. I'll kill him for this.'

Everyone said that the winter was worse than any they remembered. It was colder than usual and there was less electricity than usual because Telasi had begun cutting second lines. There was nothing to do but wait. Wait for the electricity to come on to try to coax heat into the 'hot' water tank, wait for the electricity to come on to charge the computer, wait for the electricity to come on to see what you were cooking, wait for the electricity to come on to plug in the space heater in the bathroom, wait for the electricity to come on to watch the Russians pound Grozny on the news...

Kakha greeted me sympathetically.

'You're cold eh? Take this blanket and put it around your knees.'

'OK.'

'Jeez, Wendell, I'm sorry, Tbilisi in winter is a bad place for a broken heart.'

I spent the next couple of weeks in that room. Kakha had an office in an old Soviet office building. The corridor outside smelled of eternal communism; bread and piss. There was a bakery on the ground floor and a really bad toilet opposite.

'It's like something primeval, that stench,' I told Kakha, balancing pretension and my computer on my lap, 'the very basic essence of everything.'

Kakha was translating news reports from Chechnya from Russian into English. I tried to write, staring off into space grasping my palms around some elusive sentence, the word for –

'How can I say it?' Kakha would ask, peering around his terminal at me. 'The Chechens are withdrawing their forces?'

'Retreating,' I would reply.

'How can I say it? The village was suffered by a poison cloud?'

'The village was suffocated by poisonous gas.'

'How can I say it? There were twenty-eight casualties. Or should I say twenty eight dead?'

'Were they Chechens or Russians?'

'Chechen.'

'Then twenty-eight dead.'

'All the figures are stupid anyway.'

'Exactly. It's only a small effort at evening out the propaganda.'

The hills outside flushed aquamarine at dusk. There was snow higher up, thin and blue. The shadows were deep indigo and soon they would be gone and there would be only blackness.

'I am miserable,' I told Kakha one day. 'It's miserable enough to be miserable, but it's unendurable to be miserable and cold and dark all at the same time.'

'I know. But you will learn things. And eventually it will go away.'

'I think I will go away,' I said, suddenly thinking of something that hadn't occurred to me before, 'I think I will go to Cairo.'

'The thick Nile mud, sun-dried into bricks, made an excellent and very cheap building material,' explained Joyce Tyldesley in her book about Nefertiti that I had picked up in an English bookshop. I looked around me. The most incredible thing was that the air was warm and there was

sunlight which shone through, actually hot in patches. I took off my jacket and realized that I had not been warm for a long time. My toes began to uncurl themselves, I left my hands outside my pockets, swinging alongside my hips, I breathed. Cairo's buildings, ten storeys high and wide, built as boxes with balconies, were L shapes, squares and rectangles. In between were piles of rubbish. They were all brown, the same shade of earth and sand, the colour of the banks of the Nile, clay dust mixed with muddy water. But Zemalak, where I stayed, had an air of quiet prosperity. There were embassies mixed in with the apartment blocks, there were trees; there were many doctors who advertised their speciality, gastroenterologist, hepatologist, orthodontist, Samih Sadeh, a urologist. In the morning from my hotel room I could hear the sound of birdsong mixed with children squawking, playing in the school playground.

Walking in a new city is always fine in the side-streets until you hit the big roads. Several lanes of traffic, across a bridge, access roads and ramps, scant pedestrian comfort, the odd traffic island amid cars, staccato toot-toot. There were a lot of cars in Cairo, they were all noisy and bashed in and aimed right at me. There weren't any crossing points at all, everyone, the crowd in beige and brown and bits of pale blue, the women covered in headscarves and chadors, and me edged our way haltingly through the cars that were stop-go in the traffic. Like this, against the odds, I found the museum. I realized that I had not thought about Thomas for at least an hour. Cairo, I decided, might just be random enough to work.

Everything was new and unknown and no one knew where I was. I could unwind and just look. I could just think. I could have a hot bath whenever I felt like it! Tutankhamun was turquoise, gold, lapis lazuli, carnelian, blue faience, amethyst, alabaster, gesso gilded wood.

He had a leopardskin mantle covered in gold stars, a gold pomegranate cup, golden flies on a golden chain awarded as an honorific, cobra bracelets, stools in the shape of duck necks, scarab rings, a necklace of gold interlinked seashells, hawk's-head-clasp beaded collars, ebony and ivory inlaid boxes. The whole thing was completely alien. The colours, the sunshine, the hot water, the electricity. Here was civilization.

I sat in my hotel room and worked. I went for long walks and drank fresh orange juice or hibiscus tea and smoked *shisha*. I went to the bazaar and bought souvenirs. I lay in the bath and read second-hand copies of *Hello!* magazine. I went to the Pyramids and walked around them, alone, one foot in front of the other, just like in Istanbul. One foot in front of the other, I thought, and maybe some day I'll get somewhere. The next day I found the Armenian church and lit three candles. I felt self-contained and a bit better, but I still cried most days.

The father of my best friend from school was Tim Webb and he ran a tour company in Egypt. He took me for a drink in the Ambassador Club Bar.

'You look terrible,' he said. 'I think I should send you down the Nile for a week or so.'

I went down the Nile and learned all about the Eighteenth Dynasty and visited the Valley of the Kings and dressed up in a local *gallabaya* with a cheap belt made of coins like a handmaiden and played silly games with fruit with a group of elderly Americans. It was fun.

One night I confessed to a nice woman from Baltimore that I was in Egypt to escape a broken heart. I think she reminded me of my mother. She listened sympathetically.

'And where is he now, dear?'

'He's in hell. Where I told him to go. He's in Grozny.'

*

One night I sat with a Nubian in a domed mud house on an island in the middle of the Nile talking about love. His feet were bare and cracked and covered with the fine dry silt that covered everything. He wore a *gallabaya* and a turban wound around his head. We smoked hashish. He was wise enough and his smile was perfect white against skin that was the same dark brown as the dry Nile silt, but still it hurt and would not stop.

One night I sat with Tim Webb and a large gin and tonic in the Ambassador Club Bar. He told me that it would get better but I did not particularly believe him. I drank five gin and tonics in order to numb this feeling. We talked late and when the bar was closing I got into a taxi to go back to my hotel. The car window rushed by in a blur of different-coloured lights. Perhaps there were important sentences, I thought, perhaps somewhere there were things that could be said that were true. Perhaps even, 'time heals' would turn out to be one of them. It was good to be drunk, I thought, when the night has extended itself and 'one more drink' becomes three. And when the conversation turns serious and intimate, when secrets are exchanged. There is a depth in alcohol, I thought, slurrily, when it's already five in the morning and far too late and there are empty bottles all over the table. The taxi glided along the river; palm trees and lit-up restaurant ships. Once, I remembered, in Tbilisi Thomas and I had waited until five in the morning and everyone else had gone home; we weren't ready to go home. Instead we went to the casino where I tried to play black-jack on the poker table and after we had lost fifty bucks or a hundred, we still didn't want to go home and we found a taxi drivers' place that was open and had *khashi*, tripe soup, for breakfast. And afterwards we still didn't want to go to sleep and we sat in my kitchen drinking whisky and talking about important things. It was nine in the morning, ten in the morning, the city was awake again and walking to work. At eleven he kissed me. It had taken us twelve hours to fall in love.

I was in Cairo for two months and at the end of it I felt functional. Not well, but well enough to leave the sanatorium. I had written five stories. Two of them I even liked; that wasn't so bad, I told myself. I flew to Azerbaijan, to Baku.

Ali and Nino

I STAYED IN BAKU with David who wrote for the *Financial Times*. Tom was staying with David too, collecting interviews for a book on the Nagorno-Karabakh war. Tom was very intelligent and had co-written a book on Chechnya and lived in Moscow for four years. He was the perfect diligent journalist, thoughtful and unbiased and English and charming (he made us tea in the morning in a teapot with tea-leaves). Tom went out in the morning wandering through the old Armenian quarter and talking to refugee Azeri families who now lived there; chasing up has-been Azeri generals from the war. David got up at noon in a flap and went into the office for ten minutes before coming out again to have lunch with someone. They were nice to me and said they liked my stories and they didn't say anything when I sat on in the enveloping darkness of the Opera one rainy Sunday evening and let the tears drip. In the daytime I wandered about the city and stopped in little Georgian restaurants and read and wrote notes in other people's margins.

There was one book about the Caucasus that I held in high esteem above all the others. All the time I was trying to steal stories for my collection, anecdotes and incidents and roundabout tales of Caucasus extremes and write them down, this book, an ordinary paperback with a dull, ugly green cover (the edition I had was published by Robin Clark Ltd, a tiny little imprint, since defunct, that specialized in 'foreign literature' of the obscure rather than classical variety) sat beside my bed, lay in my bed, underlined and thumbed and ragged with reference, reproving me with perfection. *Ali and Nino*.

Tom had come from Armenia the month before. David had come back from surveying Turkmenistan (Turkmenbashi's face, apparently, was emblazoned on everything: the money, packets of tea, posters and a large revolving statue of the man in the centre of Ashgabad). Ghukassian, the President of Karabakh, had just survived an assassination attempt by the war-hero warlord Samvel Babayan with bullet-riddled legs; a bomb had gone off in Makhachkala; we were thinking about driving north to Kuba to look at the Mountain Jews ('commune with my people,' said David with his tongue in his cheek), or taking a ferry across the Caspian to Iran, now that Iran was opening up. We talked through the omnipresent Baku–Ceyhan oil pipeline conversation and Shevardnadze's upcoming election and by how much he would fix the vote and whether President Kocharian was managing to consolidate power by splitting the Veterans' Parties in Armenia after the October Parliament shooting, and why he fired Sarkissian's brother as Prime Minister and who he would replace him with.

And we talked about books. We talked about Caucasus books: Dumas' *Adventures in Caucasia*, Mandlestam's *Journey to Armenia*, Pushkin's *Journey to Erzerum*. We laughed about Lesley Blanche's purple prose in her book about Shamil, *The Sabres of Paradise* ('... *it had secretly been every woman's dream to be seized, flung over the saddle of a purebred Kabarda steed and then forced to submit to the advances of some darkling mountaineer'*) and rehashed our opinions of Thomas Goltz's *Azerbaijan*

Diary and wondered why Goltz was planning to ride from Baku to Ceyhan with a barrel of oil on a motorbike.

But the book that we talked about above all others and which one of us always carried about with us in case we needed to make reference to it, was *Ali and Nino*. *Ali and Nino* was a novel, a Baku love story between an Azeri boy and a Georgian girl, set during the turmoil of the revolutionary years in the early twentieth century.

We had our favourite bits:

And it's not a good thing that all these foreigners come and tell us how stupid we are... 'Poor Georgia,' sighed the beard. 'We are between the two claws of a pair of red-hot tongs.'... It just showed: there really were decent Armenians. This was quite a disturbing thought... Of course the execution of a blood feud can sometimes be a bit awkward, shots missed or more people killed than necessary...

... and then there was the geography lesson where the Russian master tries to convince his Azeri charges that it is better to belong to progressive Europe than to backward Asia... the part where Nino is kidnapped by the treacherous Armenian and Ali rides to rescue her on a pure red Kabardino steed... the way in which the eunuch in Persia tries to educate Nino in the traditions of the harem... the description of Ali and Nino's simple life in an *aoul*, a mountain village, in Dagestan... Armenians in Karabakh boasting of how old their churches are... the descriptions of Baku, its inner town and outer town... the old illiterate oil barons... the Bolsheviks at the gates...

On every page, through the mouths of a hundred characters, a thousand observations, came the old, pre-Revolution Caucasus that was uncannily echoed by the one we could see around us. How could it be that eighty years later it was all exactly true?

Ali and Nino was our guide and our touchstone, beautifully written; gem-like, compact, full of perfect sentences, rich but never verbose. The story is epic; but it is the details that clutter up the background – the wizened wise Azeri cleric, Nino's outrageously hospitable Georgian cousins, the soft-fat Armenian – the deft precision of observation that made it so funny. I could pick it up at random and read any paragraph and it would make me smile.

Kurban Said was a pen-name. The author of *Ali and Nino* was born Lev Nussimbaum, probably in Baku, probably very early in the twentieth century, probably to a German-Jewish businessman father and a mother whose origins remain obscure. He and his father left Baku, probably around the time of the revolutionary upheavals, spent some time in Istanbul where an adolescent Lev seems to have converted to Islam and taken the name Essad Bey. Father and son then ended up in Berlin in the twenties and Essad Bey, by all accounts, set himself up as an exotic Asiatic, parading lurid tales of Caucasian romanticism, wearing a turban and hanging out in cafés while writing biographies of Stalin, Nicholas II and the Shah of Persia. *Ali and Nino* was written in German, published in Vienna in 1937 under the name Kurban Said and copyrighted by a certain Austrian baroness called Elfriede Ehrenfels. Kurban Said–Essad Bey–Lev Nussimbaum died in 1941 in Italy of a blood-poisoning disease. He was alone and penniless and fleeing the Nazis.

The times had been in tumult, biographies and names changeable and unclear. Recently the old Baroness Ehrenfels had made a claim to have written the book herself. She had been a good friend of Essad Bey's; he had told her tales from his Baku childhood and she had incorporated them in a love story. And there were others who thought that the man who called himself Kurban Said was not the author.

'The details in the book are very good,' said Rustam Ibrahimbekov, the famous Azeri screenwriter who had written *Burnt by the Sun*, musing, in his office in Baku. 'How could Kurban Said have remembered all those details from his childhood? He was only a boy when he left.' Ibrahimbekov told us that he had written a preliminary draft of the screenplay of *Ali and Nino*; the Hoomani brothers, owners of Baku's only cinema, rich Azeris with American passports, were going to put up the money for a film version. Tom and David and I went very quiet. A film? We were sceptical. 'I think we will have to change some things,' Ibrahimbekov continued. 'The Armenian for example – I think we have to make him more sympathetic.'

Ibrahimbekov told us that there was some discussion in Baku (some parts of *Ali and Nino* had been translated into Russian and published in a local literary review in the early nineties) that an Azeri writer had written *Ali and Nino* and that Kurban Said had plagiarized him. 'There are many parallels, many similar incidents,' said Ibrahimbekov, 'the man has since perished in the camps, but I can give you the phone number of his son.'

Tom went to see the son, Fikret Vezirov, who he described as being 'a serious, rather ponderous man, seventy years old, big jowls, thick glasses, who works in the cabinet office'. His father had been a famous Azeri writer, Yusif Vezirov, who used the pen-name Yusif Vezirov-Chemenzemenli and had been born in 1887 into a famous Shusha family. Chemenzemenli studied law in Kiev. In 1918 he was the Ambassador to Turkey of the first Azerbaijani Republic. In 1921 he moved on to Paris, where his younger brother was studying. In 1926 he went back to Baku, wrote and taught in the Oil Institute. In 1940 he was arrested, in 1943 he was shot in a prison camp, in 1956 he was rehabilitated.

Vezirov the younger called Lev Nussimbaum a fraudster, a 'charlatan', not a Bakuvian, who wrote twelve books 'of an adventurist nature' but had nothing to do with *Ali and Nino*. '*Ali and Nino*,' he declared, 'is a pure Azerbaijani novel.' His father, he said, had written *Ali and Nino* and managed to get it published in Vienna through a cousin who lived there. There were too many details that matched: Kurban Said must have been an Azeri. 'He even knew all about a special kind of Shusha cheese, which only a man from Shusha would know about,' Vezirov argued.

I was rereading *Ali and Nino* and a curious thing was happening. I felt that I had not only read it before, but that I had *heard* parts of it before, that its stories were somehow familiar.

Ali Khan Shirvanshir narrates the story. He is an Azeri; he has a graceful, sensitive, hard, clean, desert soul. '*I loved the flat sea,*' says Ali, '*the flat desert and the old town between them. The noisy crowd who come looking for oil, find it, get rich and leave again are not the real people of Baku. They don't love the desert.*' His opinions are Eastern: '*An open face, a naked back, a bosom half uncovered, transparent stockings on slender legs – all these are promises which a woman must keep. A man who sees as much as that wants to see more. To save the man from such desires, that is why women wear the veil.*' And Ibrahimbekov is right, in that the details are all right – it's just that the stories, the characters, the incidents – they seem at second glance to be copied down from local legend. Almost as if *Ali and Nino* were a guidebook in disguise. Everything is at its most obvious, almost Caucasian clichés.

For example, Ali's name is Shirvanshir. Before Azerbaijan was invented, Baku was the centre of the Khanate of Shirvan. Nino's name is, similarly, the most famous, the most traditional Georgian girl's name – after St Nino. Nino is carried off by a treacherous Armenian.

(Everyone in the Caucasus hates the Armenians; in the same way that Mittel-Europeans used to hate the Jews – sometimes violently, sometimes just with superior little jokes.) In Tiflis, Ali is overwhelmed by Georgian hospitality and is taken to the sulphur baths to recover. Georgian hospitality is famously extreme; the sulphur baths full every Sunday. And in Karabakh and in Dagestan, the local legends recounted to Ali are the same ones that appear in every nineteenth-century travelogue: Karabakh poetry competitions which resulted in the death of the losing poet or the Imam Shamil ordering his own mother to be whipped for disobedience and then taking the punishment himself...

And there are a couple of mistakes: Nino, a Georgian, describes her religion as Greek Orthodox. Hmm. And Ali talks about speaking his native language of Tartar. Tartar is spoken by Tartars, not Azeris.

I was sure Kurban Said had written the book. Somehow, it was almost too perfect to have been written by a local...

Tom, David and I mulled over all this at length and then decided that we should go on the first, inaugural *Ali and Nino* tour of Baku and rang Fuad Akhundov, Baku's enthusiastic and encyclopaedic tour guide.

Here was Baku before us. As Ali/Kurban Said explained:

There were really two towns, one inside the other, like a kernel inside a nut. Outside the old wall was the Outer Town, with side streets, high houses, its people, noisy and greedy for money. This Outer Town was built because of the oil that comes from our desert and brings riches. There were theatres, schools, hospitals, libraries, policemen and beautiful women with naked shoulders. If there was shooting in the Outer Town, it is always about money. Europe's geographical border began in the Outer Town and that is where Nino lived. Inside the Old Wall the

houses were narrow and curved like oriental daggers. Minarets pierced
the mild moon, so different from the oil derricks the House of Nobel
had erected. The Maiden's Tower rose on the Eastern Wall of the Old
Town...

Ali and Nino, the Baku guidebook... and we pondered that it was no
small irony that eighty years later Ali's Inner Town house was likely
to have been refurbished by one of the oil giants, BP, Amoco, Pennzoil,
that have bought concessions in the Caspian.

At the turn of the century, Baku was a boom town. For centuries
the sweet oil from the Apsheron Peninsula was used for lubrication
and anointing saddle-sores on raw camel skin. The Russians sold the
first oil concession in Azerbaijan in 1872. The factories in Moscow
needed fuel. Suddenly, there was a generation of oil barons, the
overnight mega-rich. Local boys, illiterate peasants, field drillers who
were sent into the deep wells to dig in the lee of seeping methane,
cobblers' sons, barrow boys. There was money and the foreigners
came too, German engineers, the Nussimbaums, the Nobel brothers.
In 1872 there were 14,500 people in Baku; by 1914 this had grown to
214,000.

Fuad knew everything about Baku, every building, every builder
and every ghost.

We saw Ali's school, now the Azerbaijan State Economic Institute,
opposite Nino's school. We saw the Ziziananshvili Gate where Ali
defended his city with a machine-gun that looked like 'a Russian nose,
snub and broad'. We saw the peculiar Venetian gothic architectural lines
of the Muslim Philanthropic Society built by Nagiev, a famous miser.

But my favourite story was that of Hagi Zeynalabdin Taghiev
(1823–1924), an illiterate stonemason who struck oil and money and

who founded the first secular Muslim school for girls because 'an uneducated woman is an uneducated mother; what can she give her children?', built a theatre and a department store and spent lavishly on philanthropy. His first wife died and in 1896 he married Sona, the daughter of an Azeri general in the Russian army (a rare career high for a Caucasian). She was only fifteen and he had met her when his eldest son, Ismail, married her elder sister. They had five children and he built her a palace in the European quarter of Baku with her monogram carved into the lintels above the door.

Ali and Nino danced at a reception in this palace... *'the ball was at Seinal Aga's house, in the big hall with the ceiling made of rock crystal'*... Afterwards the Soviets turned it into a dry history museum, but Taghiev's nouveau taste was still visible; one ceiling was entirely gold and another was covered with elaborately oriental mirrors. Taghiev was known for his magnanimity. One day he happened to be at the market and the peasants crowded round him, complaining, entreating; the price of fish had gone up and they could no longer afford it. 'I will bring the price of fish down!' he declared with the booming authority of a despot. Taghiev went immediately to the place where the Caspian fishermen landed their catches. Making a great show, with his valet and chauffeur in tow, he took a ring off his finger. It was a large gold ring studded with diamonds. 'Bring me a live *kumtum* – a small one!' he commanded and at once the fish was brought to him. Holding the ring up in the sunlight so that everyone could see how the gems gleamed, he took hold of the poor thrashing fish and wrenched the ring on to its tail. He carried the fish to the edge of the wharf and threw it in the sea, where it lay on the surface for a few moments, dazed, and then swam off with its jewelled tail flashing, into the depths.

The next day the fishermen scoured every inch of the Caspian and landed an enormous catch. The market was flooded with fish and the price fell.

'It sounds like a fairy tale but a man like that could easily sacrifice a diamond ring to his popularity,' said Fuad.

There were many times I felt the echo of Ali and Nino in different places. Baku always seemed to me to be their city and I would sit in the little parks next to the walls of the Old Town and imagine a nook where they might have stolen a kiss on the way home from school. In Tbilisi Tom spent a morning once climbing up to the shrine of Griboyedov and Nino Chavchavadze (one of Nino's ancestors), to see where Nino had finally said goodbye to her Georgian childhood before she married Ali. And when I was writing in Karabakh I used to climb up the Shusha Gorge to clear my head, the place where Nino's family had picnicked before the First World War broke out.

Shusha was a special place. It was a Karabakh town, half Armenian and half Azeri; perched on a giant plug of rock on one side of the Shusha Gorge. A thousand feet below was the river and in the distance, where the mountains began to level into rolling plain, was the village that would become Stepanakert. At the turn of the century Shusha was full of newspapers and cafés; I saw postcards of it; there were mosques and churches almost side by side and a large covered market. It was a place for idle intellectual chit-chat; some said it was the second town in the Caucasus after Tiflis. In the summer the fancy families from Baku, Armenian and Azeri and Georgian alike, came to Shusha to escape the heat and relax.

In the gorge below there was the remains of a small village, tumbledown stone walls and roofs covered in grass where we spread our own picnics. In the autumn it was an indescribably beautiful place, red and yellow, rosehips and berries, the sheer cliffs of the gorge above, blue sky above their rims and the river running through it, smoothing curves in the limestone. We used to walk through the ruins overrun with blackberry brambles, down by the old stone bridge. Further along, into the deep cut of the gorge, wet foot across the river, there was a huge umbrella of mossy outcrop, dripping with a curtain of spring water which made a cave full of rainbows when the sun shone.

Shusha was sacked twice in the twentieth century, once by the Turks in 1920 and then again in 1992, when the Armenians took the town with tanks and the Azeris who had rained down artillery on Stepanakert below for months, retreated. It's mostly burnt now, blackened blocks, walls, masonry; the Armenians have rebuilt their churches and left the mosques to rot. But you can still climb the minarets of one and look out over the magnificent view and imagine what was. There are only three thousand people living in the shell of Shusha now; it's sad and empty. In one of the kiosks we found Viagra bubblegum for sale (with a free pornographic sticker); Turkish, circumventing the blockade, traded on the Georgia border. Ali and Nino's world was gone, and yet history in the Caucasus persists in repeating itself.

By now it was April; in Georgia, Shevy was having his presidential election. There was bound to be electricity for the week before the polls and David had to cover the proceedings. And so, finally, after three months, I went home.

Azerbaijan is flat desert to drive across, the road is long and boring. Ali's desert is interrupted with salt flats, until the region near the Georgian border (Aliev and Shevardnadze handshake of friendship on a billboard) where there is greenery and a few prosperous villages that grow tomatoes and cucumbers and have built themselves beautiful new filigree tin roofs with the proceeds.

At the border David and I found a taxi that would take us the last forty kilometres to Tbilisi. The driver was garrulous and friendly and Georgian; he wanted to take us to his village for a meal before we completed our journey. The landscape was pretty: green hills with flocks of white sheep and lambs gambolling and trees that swept blossom all over the road like snow. I began to think about my friends in Tbilisi, about Kakha and Lela and Alex and Zaliko and all the Datos. I thought about seeing them again and sitting with them, fireplace, red wine, walnuts. The weeks that I had spent in Kakha's office I had also spent staying with Lela. She gave me half her bed and brought me tea in the morning. We talked and talked about Thomas and she was adamant on my behalf. 'He will cry!' she told me fiercely. 'He will cry! You do not believe me but you will see it.' Kakha had been staying in my flat while I had been away and I imagined him reading my books all through the winter. He was always much better read than I was. Most of all I imagined being with them all again and laughing about silly things like Zviadist breakouts from jail, Shevy's plane nearly crashing on the way back from a Summit, Lika's new boyfriend; the usual things. I was going home to people who loved me and when I thought about it like this and realized how much I had missed them, I began to cry. I snuffled and wiped my nose with the back of my hand.

'It's not Thomas,' I told David who was looking at me strangely, 'I am just happy to be back in Georgia; I don't know why I'm crying.'

Election

THE NEWS WAS ALWAYS BAD:

Tbilisi airport will stop functioning as of 10th July because of a debt incurred by the air travel of government delegations. An Iprinda correspondent has learned from a reliable source that the Georgian state airline company, commercial airline companies and Georgian air traffic control have decided to go on strike. The source said that it was important that the state and above companies came to a mutual understanding, because the companies are trapped in a difficult situation, unable to make payments because the state is in debt to them.

Iprinda news agency, 10.7.98

Employees of the Zugdidi [West Georgia] bread factory today went on strike demanding payment of wage arrears dating back to May. As a result, the bread factory has stopped working. According to the source, if the bread factory does not resume work in the next few days, refugees in Zugdidi will face hunger because their source of food is bread.

Iprinda news agency, 15.12.98

The Minister of Georgian Defence, Lieutenant-General Davit

172

Tevzadze, denied the claims by the mass media that soldiers of one of the military units of the Armed Forces of Georgia, stationed in Akhaltsikhe, are allegedly on strike due to absence of foodstuffs supply. Speaking at the sitting of the government of Georgia on July 14, Davit Tevzadze informed that in the above-mentioned military unit there is currently a 15-day reserve supply of foodstuffs

Black Sea Press, 14.7.99

The ITERA international group of companies has reduced supplies of natural gas to Georgia by 30 per cent because of non-payments for the current supplies... Under an agreement signed at the beginning of October 1999 the government of Georgia undertook to timely pay for current gas supplies, but in October-November the outstanding amount for them reached 3.8 million dollars. That is why the supply of gas to Georgia was cut after the repeated mentions on the part of ITERA.

RIA news agency, 17.12.99

AES-Telasi [Tbilisi electricity grid operator] has halted power supplies to the Defence Ministry over the Ministry's 300,000-lari debt for electricity. Aleko Mchedlishvili, aide to the Georgian defence minister, told Kavkasia-Press that this could paralyse the entire defence system.

Kavkasia-Press news agency, 23.12.99

Members of the Georgian Justice Council and Chairman of the Tbilisi District Court Davit Sulakvelidze have said that they will resign if the authorities fail to pay salaries to the judiciary regularly.

Kavkasia-Press news agency 10.1.00

*

Shevardnadze was going to be re-elected on 9 April 2000. He was not popular, but his election was nevertheless going to be a shoe-in. Shevy was always like this: contradictory. A conundrum of irony; contortionist, supreme politician: he kept turning out to be the opposite of what everyone had thought he was.

Shevy was a career communist who became a Western media darling, the warm and fuzzy democrat who dismantled the Iron Curtain as Soviet Foreign Minister. He was a communist who became a democrat who became President of Georgia at the behest of a warlord cabal who had ousted the legally elected Gamsakhurdia in a violent coup. He was a calming anti-use-of-force member of the Politburo who resigned, warning of crackdowns in the Baltic states. Two years later he was wearing camouflage fatigues covered in concrete dust from artillery bombardment in a basement in Sukhumi, ordering the last-ditch Georgian offensives against the Abkhaz. He was a reformer who had, in the mid-eighties, instigated the famous 'Abasha' experiment in Mingrelia, where farmers were allowed to grow their own produce and sell it at a market; it had been the first private enterprise in the Soviet Union since Lenin. But one of Shevy's close advisers admitted to me once (in mid-2000, I think, when the economic crisis had got worse; it was always getting worse) that there wasn't a single person in Georgia who had a fundamental understanding of macroeconomics, least of all the President. Shevy was a crusading anti-corruption leader during his years as head of the Georgian Socialist Republic; there was hardly a family in Vera who didn't have someone in prison for raking cash out of the system. But as President of the Republic of Georgia he never prosecuted a single government official for corruption despite obvious and appalling levels of abuse.

I could never figure him out. I think the Georgians understood him, but it was a deep Georgian thing and impossible to explain. He was caught in the Georgian–Soviet mix, as everyone was, stuck somewhere between the clans and the bureaucrats. The Georgians may have understood him in some way, but they didn't particularly like him. The country had been without much electricity, heat or employment since the early nineties. His government had managed to replace transition with regression and had failed to deliver a bathful of hot water for most of the previous winter. But he had put the Mekhedrioni and the warlords in jail; there was no more shooting on the streets; he had his international profile, he had IMF loans and World Bank money on his side. His re-election was assured; there wasn't much of an alternative.

Shevy's main rival was Jumber Patiashvili, the old communist leader who had replaced him as head of Georgia when he had gone to Moscow in 1985 to be Soviet Foreign Minister. Patiashvili was supported by the Revival Bloc, Aslan Abashidze's fractious and fairly useless opposition. But this was a bit odd, because Aslan was running for President too.

I went to one of Patiashvili's rallies in Tbilisi. The place was full of the older constituency, the nostalgia people who hoped the clock could be turned back in some way; refugees from Abkhazia who thought he could get them home, men in their fifties who thought he could give them their old jobs and respect back. Patiashvili postured with a grave voice and knitted brows, a slew of phrases came out of his mouth, but none of them worth quoting. During his speech there were occasional bursts of applause as the babushki beat their hands together fervently.

'The Soviet Union will return; you'll see,' said one.

'No it won't,' said her neighbour sensibly, 'history doesn't repeat itself.'

'Well I got my pension this month,' replied a sprightly lady with soft white hair, her smile betraying a trace of cynicism. 'I wonder why.'

'What's the difference?' said the first one. 'Twenty lari. It's not enough even for bread.'

Generally there wasn't much enthusiasm for this latest round of sham democracy in the Caucasus. Shevardnadze's Citizens' Union Party, the CUG, had put up lots of posters everywhere; the German Chancellor, ever grateful for Shevy's role in reuniting Germany, flew in to lend a bit of credibility; the state TV channel reported with a Shevy bias, but as far as everyone else was concerned, nothing was going to change nothing.

'We receive nothing. The government gives us nothing,' they said, repeating themselves over and over, in the market in Bolnisi, in shops in Tbilisi, in the streets in Rustavi. At the watchwords of Western political campaign, Future and Change, they simply shrugged their shoulders and rolled their eyes in mock cynicism at the ceiling. A taxi driver in Bolnisi was as tired of it and indignant as the next man. 'So, we're in the European Union [*sic*: he meant the Council of Europe] and we're talking to NATO: what difference does that all make for the working man?' He told me he did not have enough money to fix his cracked windscreen. No one did in Georgia; half the cars on the streets had cracked windscreens.

There were some who bothered to vent their frustration with Mr Just-give-me-five-more-years-and-I-will-bring-you-electricity-and-jobs-just-like-I-promised-you-five-years-ago Shevardnadze. Eggs were thrown; there were outbursts of heckling. One pensioner yelled so much in front of the presidential procession that an aide angrily asked him what he wanted. 'Just give me twenty lari,' said the pensioner, thinking quickly, and the aide fished a note out of his pocket and gave it to him. 'Wish *I'd* asked for something,' the pensioner's friend told me afterwards.

It was all fairly desultory. Shevy smiled and waved and kissed babies, but he seemed worried; there were cracks in the veneer. He wanted to win properly, with a great big mandate. And so the word went out to the CUG faithful, the officers in charge of polling stations, regional organizers. Shevy would undoubtedly win, but according to the constitution 50 per cent of the electorate had to vote in order to validate the election. No one I knew in Tbilisi was going to vote; there was in fact an unofficial passive boycott. Vote for what? What was the point?

Polls were difficult to come by, but numbers gleaned from the international community of observers and diplomats and journalists, overheard from CUG sources and bandied about in bars at the end of the day, gave Shevardnadze about 55 per cent, Patiashvili about 35 per cent, and Aslan the Adjarian 8–10 per cent. The numbers for the other hopeless hopefuls – one candidate who claimed to be the Second Coming and an ex-Mayor of Batumi running from a jail cell (one of several people serving time having been convicted of trying to kill Aslan) – were negligible. I bumped into an old friend, the smarmy CUG 'volunteer', now with a new Mercedes and a seat in parliament.

'So what are you going to be doing on election day?' I teased him.

He smiled sharkily, 'Oh, you know, what I always do.' (Ballot stuffing.)

Everyone knew the Shevy landslide was coming. In the week before the polls opened the question was not so much who would win by what margin, but whether the result would be mildly fixed or superglued.

Then a curious thing happened. On the day before the election Shevy flew to Batumi.

'Shevy wants to persuade Aslan to pull out,' said Lela.

But Shevy was guaranteed victory – why was he bothering to negotiate with Aslan? On the eve of an election! Aslan was trailing pathetically in the polls and had not even bothered to leave Adjara to campaign; he was no threat at all. There were old and intractable questions between them, things that could hardly be negotiated in half an afternoon: Adjarian status (which had never been constitutionally defined) and Adjarian contributions to the national budget. Why would Shevy allow Aslan to play the kingmaker and politick about the place like a peacock – why hand him political capital? And why would Aslan receive the man who he had so often publicly accused of trying to have him killed?

Lela and I sat on her bed and watched the news. Aslan and Shevy emerged from their meeting in the Batumi sunlight. Aslan smiled for the cameras in a pleased and smug manner. He shook Shevardnadze's hand. Something had been settled. David called; he had been writing a deadline piece about how the election was being held on the same date as the troops massacred demonstrators on the streets of Tbilisi in 1989.

'What's going on?' he wanted to know.

'No idea. It's a complete mystery.'

Shevardnadze flew home and less than twenty-four hours before the polls were due to open Aslan announced that he was pulling out of the race.

*

On election Sunday we went round a few polling stations in Tbilisi. They were largely empty apart from a few observers. Those in charge, however, were happy to assure David and I that a goodly percentage of their electoral lists had shown up and voted, even if they did not seem to be doing so at the moment we had arrived to see them do it. We drove up to a couple of villages on the Mtatsminda plateau; it was rainy. There the polling stations were even emptier.

'The observers never showed up,' explained the man overseeing the vote in the small village of Chughureti – it was hard to tell if his tongue was in his cheek or just depressing the truth.

Later on Sunday afternoon we heard that some voters in Batumi were still voting for Aslan; either they hadn't heard that he had pulled out of the race at the last minute or his name was not crossed out on the ballot paper as it should have been. David and I excitedly concocted a theory that perhaps Shevardnadze's visit to Batumi was not so inexplicable after all. Consequences: Aslan pulls out of the race, endorsing neither Patiashvili, his colleague in the Revival Bloc, nor Shevardnadze. But a portion of Adjara still votes for him – pointlessly. What happens? The ballots are spoiled but they're still counted in the turnout figure. Thus Shevardnadze boosts the overall turnout (which he was desperate to do), without having to lose votes to Patiashvili. We were very impressed with our conjecture and it fitted the theme of the day: Shevy, the great political politician, practising the art of politics.

But then on Monday morning there was a final twist: the result. Shevardnadze had won with 80 per cent, Patiashvili had taken a mere 17 per cent. Turnout was generously put at 66 per cent.

Eighty per cent! David got on the phone to his editors right away. Who would have thought that the CUG would have the gall to manipulate the figures so high? Sixty per cent, 65 per cent – possible, plausible, perhaps even likely – but 80 per cent was ridiculous. The party faithful had gone too far. The OSCE, the European organisation overseeing the proceedings, later agreed in a press release that *'observers reported a series of identical signatures on the voter lists, group voting and the presence of unauthorised persons, including police and local officials, at the polling stations... it became apparent during the counting that ballot box stuffing had taken place.'*

Gorbi, an independent polling company, interviewed twelve thousand people in Tbilisi, Rustavi and Kutaisi: their exit polls had Shevy at a more modest 51 per cent and Patiashvili on 24 per cent. And then I thought about the visit to Aslan, again, and couldn't understand, again, why, if they were going to fudge the vote so completely all along, any deal had been necessary. It was all suddenly nonsensical. (As if it had ever made sense.) And anyway, what did it matter? Shevardnadze was always going to win. Shevardnadze won. I looked around my kitchen. As if on cue, the lights went out, came back on after five minutes and went out again.

There was a beguiling feeling in the Caucasus in the year 2000 that things were stable. The convulsions of the early nineties had subsided; life went on every day in the normal manner. Shevy was in power in Georgia, Heydar Aliev was a bit sick, but his grip on Azerbaijan was hardly diminished. In Tbilisi there were more cars on the streets, new businesses opened, businesses closed. In the morning there were people walking to work, there was even a kind of rush hour at 10 a.m.

But there was also a feeling that anything could happen. There was never any clear surface in the Caucasus. There were only mountains and valleys, crumpled distance, potholed roads. You could never see where you were going.

For example, a random event: the previous October gunmen opened fire in the Armenian Parliament killing the Prime Minister, Vazgen Sarkissian, the Speaker of Parliament, Karen Demirchian, and six others and took fifty deputies hostage for the night.

I remember standing on the street outside with David and Cormac, watching lines of soldiers form up and police Ladas drive up and down. Cormac was trying to call the head gunman, Nairi Unanian, holed up inside, on his mobile.

'We only entered Parliament to create a fright,' he said when Cormac eventually got through.

After a few moments of talk, Cormac put the phone back in his pocket. 'He said it wasn't about Karabakh,' he told us, puzzled.

Unanian and his band surrendered early that morning and were taken away to prison where nobody had any access to them and they were never heard of again.

The bodies of seven of the eight dead politicians were laid out in open caskets on the stage in the Yerevan Opera House, built, like everything else in Yerevan, out of pink tufa. Demirchyan's face was covered with a white cloth because he had been shot in the head. Over the course of the day 100,000 people filed past in a bundled grey mass. The light was gloom, an orchestra played violins and a choir sang behind a black gauze-draped curtain; an honour guard brandished their bayonets ceremonially behind the coffins. The dead men were dead and looked like wax, slightly yellowy, unreal and gone.

Everything in Armenia changed after the Parliament shooting. Factions realigned, the President wobbled and then regained some strength. Flurries of false hope about a peace settlement with Azerbaijan over the disputed region of Nagorno-Karabakh flew about, now that the politicians who had opposed compromise had been assassinated. But then the question was: how long would Aliev last? And who was in power in Washington or in control in Moscow... And then for a long time nothing much happened again. Unanian was a haphazard fanatic. He'd been shouting about creating a bloodbath for months, but nobody paid any attention. And when it was done, nobody could figure out why he'd done it.

The Caucasus was stuck on a geopolitical fault line: nothing was secure. When Shevy was getting elected there was a rumour that the Russians would invade the southern Caucasus. They'd beat the Chechens and then push south to Azerbaijan and Georgia. You heard it from government people and from foreign diplomats.

'Georgia's integrity is not secure,' Alex told me gravely.

'The Russians don't care – they want to take back what was theirs,' said a Pole with a Muslim name, a 'lawyer' for a Chechen Mafia gunrunner in Baku.

And then there were the rumours about Azeri oil; more discovered, not enough found, pipelines posited, the twisted chicanery between Russian interests and American money. Who the hell was going to pay the $4 billion they thought they needed to build a pipeline from Baku to the other side of Turkey to get the oil out? And if there was peace in Nagorno-Karabakh, wouldn't it be easier to route the whole thing through Armenia instead of through Georgia? And then Iran was softening and opening and there were millions of Azeris living in northern Iran. And how long – how long would Russia be weak? How long would the Russians put up with so much American machination in their back yard?

Where the rumours came from was impossible to know: local paranoia or the coded padding of feet in Kremlin corridors. Perhaps it was only melodrama, but still it seeped into the foreign news pages of the Western newspapers. The Transcaucasus: fucked up – but *strategic*.

In any case, this was the grist that fed our conversations that spring. Shevy had been re-elected. He'd fixed the election. We went out to dinner. David and Cormac and I, a few others; I don't remember. We went to Miraj, next to the *banyas* in the old town and sat surrounded by brick walls covered in carpets and ate shashlik cooked in the fireplace. At about eleven o'clock we heard an artillery barrage.

Conversation ceased and we dropped our forks and looked at each other.

'It sounded very much like –'

'It shook the table –'

We all tiptoed outside gingerly, stood beneath the shadow of the Narikala Fortress and cocked our ears in the dark stillness. Other people had come out of their homes and were doing the same. What was that? we asked with our hands, palms upturned to the sky. We couldn't see any smoke. Cormac called someone in the press office.

'Oh, it's OK,' he said, 'it's nothing. Apparently they were just practising the gun salute for Shevy's inauguration ceremony.'

Shevy's inauguration ceremony was held out on the steps of the Parliament. (Rebuilt after being shelled during the civil war, the hammer and sickle neatly chiselled off the façade.) We assembled: the press, the foreigners, the parliamentarians, the army, and distinguished guests, the *hoi polloi* intelligentsia, a stout babushka wearing her old green uniform covered in communist medals, several veterans of Abkhazia in wheelchairs and some florid generals with impossibly large generalissimo hats. Up on the high pediment ledge of the Parliament building stood a row of dancers, male and female, dressed in traditional Georgian costume; *cherkeskas*, long coats with vertical pockets for cartridges, *kinzhals* and floaty medieval dresses. Shevardnadze was inaugurated by the Patriarch Ilya II in front of a microphone. The rest of us gossiped, kissed acquaintances hello and talked into our mobile phones. Organ music blared from the tannoy. Shevy promised that we would soon see the new face of Shevardnadze: no more of that irritating corruption thing, and lots of economic revival. The soldiers, lined up opposite along Rustaveli Avenue picked their noses, shifted their weight from leg to leg, nudged their neighbours and yawned.

After a bout of final slow clapping, the order was given for the military parade. It was disappointing. The Georgian army marched past wearing creased camouflage combat uniforms and forage caps. There were no tanks or armoured cars or hurtling jets overhead. The vaunted artillery barrage was drowned out by a banging brass band.

Reaffirmed President Eduard Giorgi Shevardnadze went to Mtskheta to get blessed in the cathedral. I was whisked into a black Hyundai with AAA plates by a couple of parliamentarians who should probably remain nameless and we also went to Mtskheta to eat a big *supra*, toast our optimism and make cynical remarks about the coming Lordkipanidze–Zhvania political tussle. Thus fortified, we made our way up to the Shevy family compound for the official reception.

There were several hundred people at the party. It was held outside, under a dirty bit of tarpaulin which collapsed at the first gust of wind. Most of those present were men in suits glad-handing each other and politicking. There were the foreign ambassadors, 'Georgia! Ha! It's going down the tubes,' one told me; a couple of Shevy's pretty granddaughters; Misha (smoothie) Saakishvili, an up-and-coming parliamentarian who was soon to be given the poison chalice of a ministry post; a lost Scottish MP from the Scottish National Party who wanted to talk to the Georgians about devolution ('Devolution is pretty advanced in the Caucasus,' I told him); Irakle Managadze, president of the National Bank, who was chortling proudly, 'The lari is the only stable thing in the country!'; an agriculture committee member who was looking forward to his minister getting fired next week; a shark called Boris Berezovsky... Nanuli, Shevy's wife, was like a whale, hefted into an armchair and holding court with a superior smile.

Shevy played his favourite role of amiable elder statesman, grinning, shaking hands, bluff and personable. A male choir sang polyphonically.

The canapés were fine, Shevy's speech no more platitudinous than any other politician's, the champagne and lurid green tarragon fizzy pop flowed, but somehow the whole thing felt lame. Perhaps it was the cynicism and despondency of the conversation. A lack of forward dynamic, dulled optimism; the atmosphere of bandied quips and investitured smugness that made everything seem swampy, bogged down with vested interest. I shook Shevy's hand and to be honest it was a bit limp.

Giorgi

GIORGI WAS TWELVE. He had large serious adult eyes and the spry tensile body of a mountain goat; wiry, lean, young muscles stretched along long arm-bones. We were climbing up mountains in Khevsureti. It was July, three months after Shevardnadze's election. We had reached the saddle of the ridge above the village of Roshka after a two-hour climb and had collapsed panting. We stared dumbly at the view which stretched to the top of the world and was as peaceful as mountains always are, eternally so, as if it were impossible that Russians and Chechens could be fighting in them 'just over that peak', said Zaliko, scratching his beard and pointing. We were resting before traversing the narrow track of tramped shale that was the pass that would lead into another long green valley, lying exhausted, flat out, when Giorgi came bounding up the final slope, smashing the dandelions that grew short against the altitude wind with his rubber boots. We greeted him, waving weakly, and he stopped long enough to throw down a plastic bag in which he had a spare T-shirt and a sweater, and dance around us, grinning. He was pleased; he had run all the last part of the way, up from the lip of the curved meadow valley and along the rutted cow tracks, to catch us up.

'That boy is insane,' said my brother, who had arrived from New

York on a plane a scant twenty-four hours before and was in utter culture shock.

After the pass it was all downhill, but it was downhill for a very long way. At first we were as a high as a few strands of clouds and as high as the furthest snow which was lying piebald across the mountains and melting into rivulets which ran into streams which ran into rivers. There was watercress growing in the wet banks of rock and Giorgi gave me bunches to chew on. When we stopped we ate macerated lemon slices in a sugar sludge.

'It's good,' I said. It was the best thing I had ever tasted.

'Are you tired? Do you hate me for bringing you all this way?'

'Not yet. But we have not arrived yet.'

'Ah! It's not far now,' said Zaliko, lying, kindly.

A group from Roshka had left much later than us and went past, walking fast and nimbly, able Khevsurs in their rubber slippers and odd assorted tracksuit trousers and camouflage forage caps. We were all walking over the mountains to the village of Arkhoti for a horse-race. We had to walk over the mountains because there was no road. Among the group of Khevsurs there was a woman, Tamriko, with dark brown pretty face, red cheeks and strong black hair, and two brothers (Brother One had a small wound under one eye and a ring of bruise – he said from chopping wood; Brother Two was encumbered by a five-litre plastic jerrycan full of *chacha*) and our grand host, Giorgi's father, Zhura. The horse-race was to commemorate Zhura's father, Giorgi's grandfather, who had died a year before.

I was moving slower, but Giorgi kept by my side, running off for a few moments and then ambling on the spot, waiting for me. He carried my shoes across a frigid rushing brook when I wanted to keep them dry (his own feet were soaked), he lent me his stick on a snow bridge that was slick and icy and full of sun-melt slush patches, he made sure that when I slipped on the rocks and whacked my ankle I did not yelp too loudly and had not fallen over.

We all stopped for lunch in the middle of a meadow with a river running several hundred feet below us. We ate cheese and bread with chillies and drank Brother Two's *chacha*. The day was sunny and the air was clean and sharp and the view was amazing, the meadow around us lush and full of purple flowers, the river below strong rushing and white, but we tried to keep our ebullience in check, measuring our natural happiness against the weight of remembrance. The toasts were solemn.

'My father was dying in Tbilisi,' recounted Zhura with his glass of *chacha* resting on his knee in readiness, 'he lay in bed, my mother tended to him. He was ill and the illness became worse. He began to understand he was going to die. He was sixty-eight, he had lived, and he understood what was happening. "I want to die in Arkhoti," he told me, "I want to die in the place where I was born." I hired a helicopter. I found a doctor who would help us move him and a nurse who would come with us to Arkhoti for a few days. It was May and there was still snow on the passes; it would have been impossible to walk even without the snow. The helicopter was delayed two days because of the weather and my father grew weaker. At last we were able to bring him home. He was grateful and he died two days later. He was peaceful and there was new green grass in our valley.'

'For our guests.' Zhura nodded at my brother and I.

Michael (nicknamed Mishiko for the duration) sniffed his *chacha*, his first *chacha*, gingerly. 'Doesn't smell too bad actually,' he whispered.

'For our guests,' Zhura continued, 'my father asked me to remember him in this way, to organize a horse-race in the old way and to invite many people. But only good people. We are very glad Mishiko and Wendell are with us.' We were silent and respectful and raised our glasses, spilling a little *chacha* on to the ground to appease the mountain spirits and in respect for the ghosts of our ancestors, and drank.

Giorgi and I couldn't really understand each other, my Georgian limited to ordering more beer, his English to the word 'mountain' which was somewhat self-evident. But Michael sang old Dublin drinking songs along the way and we smiled at each other often and Giorgi never left my side, never left me alone when everyone else had overtaken me or when Zaliko was slowed down behind with a pack twice his weight and his customary cigarette hanging from his mouth.

At last, there was Arkhoti! Four roofs and an abandoned slate tower; cow shit and *chacha*.

'The river!' said Zaliko.

'The river?'

'Women must walk through the river. Ha!' Zaliko thought this was very funny. 'It's true. I did not tell you before; you would be too angry with me!'

I looked at him with malice. 'Now I hate you.'

'No I am being honest. You cannot walk past the village shrine.'

'What shrine?'

'This one, on the path.'

Three small heaps of stones were piled next to a tree on the slope above the river. There were strips of fabric tied to the tree.

'I hate you,' I said again, but lifelessly. I was weary. We had been walking for almost ten hours. The river was wide and fast and full of cold water.

Tamriko and I looked at each other. I looked down at her long skirt and her carpet slippers that had stepped so daintily around every patch of mud and stone and wet obstacle along the way. Giorgi, who remained unfatigued and impish, strode across the river which crested against his body up to his waist and showed us that it wasn't that difficult really. Tamriko and I followed, gritting our teeth at the world that would order us, tired and fractured, into the water just because we were women. We followed Giorgi and he darted ahead. Our footsteps were measured now, a tramp routine ground into them. But then they became squishy. Giorgi had led us into a bog. The mud oozed around our feet. The two of us together, Khevsur and stupid foreigner, in the same tone of exasperation and irritation and groan, said, out loud, 'Gior-gi!' Giorgi laughed and led us tripping, dripping up the slope above the bog which was steep and covered in thistles.

Thus tested, we strode into the village victorious, and drank from the sweet well that sprang from a bit of slate pipe into a slate bowl as if we were thirsty men after battle. The women clustered around me and took off my wet clothes and washed my feet in bowls of warm water.

Giorgi had a cousin called Giorgi who had come down from another village, Juta, where they used to trade with the caravans and all had the surname Arabuli. Zaliko thought they might be left-over Arabs who traded cowrie shells with the Khevsurs hundreds of years before. Cousin Giorgi was more mischievous-looking, less serious, a cow-kicking, stone-throwing, runaway child with such long eyelashes that you would forgive him anything. Giorgi and Giorgi shone their dark eyes at each other, linked arms and went off to hurl a football around.

We ate supper on a mud-and-slate veranda: *chacha* and soup, meat broth and *adjika*, chilli sauce, bread, cheese and hot milk. We toasted guests and toasted hospitality and toasted dead people and especially the special dead person we had gathered to honour and afterwards we slept like the dead on a large piece of blue UNHCR tarpaulin in a field.

We woke the next morning and went to have breakfast with Zhura's sister's family on their balcony. So many people had descended on Arkhoti during the night that they had to be fed in shifts: children and girls, and then the men; *lobio*, bean stew, tea, porridge, bread and cheese, *chacha*. Giorgi was nowhere to be seen and we were told that he had taken a horse back up to the pass to help more guests come down the serpentine path to the snow bridge.

'That boy is insane,' I told my brother.

Arkhoti was its timeless self; the slate tower watched the sun ascend the sky, more guests galloped in on horseback, stacked their guns by the wall, and went to wash the dust off their faces by the village tap. The cows were milked, morning and evening, pure white frothy milk into a silver pail set up at an angle on the mud-and-shit floor of a hoof-trodden pen. The milk was boiled to make cheese, the cheese was stacked in the damp cellar. The girls washed dishes and clothes by the tap, the men sat about and cadged cigarettes off one another. Zaliko walked up an adjoining valley to visit a poet who had a bandage around his hand. He had been shot by some Russians trying to infiltrate the border – 'Clear out of it, it's my land,' he had told them. The country of Arkhoti, we were reminded, *rodina*, motherland, in those toasts when Khevsur red-black sunburnt faces twitched near tears and held a red-black hairy hand above their hearts and drank.

Giorgi eventually returned from his ferrying, ran about with the other boys in the village, hurled rocks into the river and made them skip, begged for turns riding the horses, begged to be let up on to the back of a handsome grey Chechen mare with an intelligent and unfathomable character. Giorgi and Giorgi fetched and ran messages for their uncles. They plaited the horses' manes with coloured ribbons and picked up white quartz rocks and banged them together to make sparks, they whittled sticks into tiny stakes and helped to put up tarpaulin and tents for the visitors who kept coming. When he had a spare moment Giorgi would come and sit by me and I would ask him if he was well and he would reply, 'Good', and give a simple nod, quite satisfied with things.

On the day of the horse-race it was very hot. Four Englishmen (somewhat grimy, on a walking holiday and full of private jokes like a company of bravado) had walked down from Juta in the night. Zhura wanted me to make sure they were invited to the festivities. They scarcely knew what they had stumbled upon when we were led into a small murky hut. On the floor was a bucket full of dark murky beer, reserved from scant barley for special occasions. We each drank a mugful. Giorgi was not allowed any and when I offered him some of mine on the sly he was very well-behaved and shook his head to decline. The Englishmen said the beer tasted like off bitter. They laughed and raised their glasses and tipped the precious stuff away. The Khevsurs passed a single mug around, toasting, spitting, drinking, serious.

In the sunlight the sisters of the dead man wailed around a blanket covered with his possessions: his old moth-eaten fur cap, a thick grey worsted suit jacket, a pair of embroidered Khevsur breeches, a horse bridle from his great white stallion Sultan, his boots, his house shoes; his pair of binoculars and a leather knapsack. There were cowrie shells on the horses' bridles, coloured beads covered the ceremonial bottles of *chacha*. The riders swung themselves up on to their mounts, jerked at the bits with their rough hands, kicked the bare flanks with their heels, whacked the horses with a rope flail and streamed away down the valley for the start.

We sat on stones and waited for them to race back. They came from two miles away at a stretching gallop; dust flew from their hoofs. The grey Chechen mare of intelligent and doubtful temperament won (the prize was a cow) and the loser (a lad with a bony knife-edge face and bloodshot eyes who Zaliko told me had 'got some alcohol this morning') tried to fight him for it. There was a scuffle in the middle of a crowd of men. The loser was dragged away by his friends, red raged. Eventually negotiations prevailed and a hundred people sat down at a long long table filled with feast.

The Englishmen enthusiastically drained their *chacha* by the glassful, encouraged by the Khevsurs who thought it was a great sport to get the outsiders legless. I sat next to Zaliko who told me stories about the people around the table. The *tamada* was an old, vigorous man with a red wrinkled neck, white hair and an enormous mottled purple nose. He had ridden a donkey over the mountains from Kazbegi wearing a three-piece suit and a felt Svan hat. His voice was as strong as iron. A small man sat at the far end of the table and nobody would talk to him; he was the hired man who helped to milk the village cows; he was an outsider, he was being fed, but he was not included. Brothers One and Two appointed themselves refillers of the glasses and spent the afternoon pouring more *chacha* around. The winner and the loser scowled at each other at first, but there was enough food and *chacha* and after a while it didn't matter.

'That man – look,' Zaliko pointed, 'with the scar to his ear. He is a famous hunter. Once he gave me a great horn from a mountain goat. It can hold two litres. But you can only drink two litres of wine. *Chacha*, it's impossible –'

'It's not impossible! Only you must breathe carefully,' Zhura came down the table, listened to the conversations, quietened people for the toasts, made sure that the jugs of wine were full and that everything was in order. 'Mishiko! Drink!' he said, slapping my brother on the back. Mishiko, it must be said, by this time had fully assimilated the Khevsur drinking rhythm.

'I am drinking!' he told Zhura who clapped him on the back again and laughed.

The women did not sit at the table; they only served it. They brought large plates of boiled ox and small plates of tiny river trout and fried pancakes filled with liver and heart and plates of vegetables that had been cut up very finely into salads.

The Englishmen ('*goluboi*,' said Zhura disparagingly, 'poofs') became so drunk that within two hours they could not stand. They staggered off to their tents and fell over and went to sleep. A couple of hours later I looked in at them; they were unconscious, prone. Curiously, oblivious, one had his hand down another one's trousers. The feast table broke up into smaller groups as the other very drunk men went to sleep it off.

Michael sat on the steps to a house with a ring of children around him. He sang soft melancholic Irish songs and made popping noises with his cheek, which threw his audience into fits of giggles. Zaliko had got some vodka and helped the women milk the cows. I wandered about and looked at the enormous sky and the enormous mountains that almost filled it on every side. I sat on the slate ledge next to the village tap and smoked a cigarette and Giorgi came to sit by me. He was engaged in plaiting a bit of rope, enjoying the atmosphere which was familial and drunken and full of small groups of men patting each other on the back. The women were washing up in relays, the horses were grazing in the meadow.

'*Rogora khar?*' I asked him, 'How are you?' and he smiled with his serious eyes at the place he loved and at me, and replied as usual, 'Good.'

Minefields

I WAS IN ABKHAZIA walking in the minefields along the Gumista River in the north of Sukhumi. It was a year since I had last been there with Kurtz and Cormac and David. A lot of things had happened to me, a lot of things had happened in the Caucasus but Abkhazia was its unending stagnant pond. I was wearing a Kevlar apron and a sweaty breath-fogged visor that was too big for me and kept slipping down over my eyebrows. I was existentially, extremely, aware that the earth underneath my feet was not its usual eternal dumb self. I walked over it with small steps, stepping where I could see the footprints of where other people had already stepped. Cattle pasture, hazelnut plantations, overgrown ruins, rusted playground; river-bank, boulders, stones; bramble patches and weeds; soil, mud, silt and dirt. The ground and its underground were almost infinite.

The Halo Trust is the best NGO in the world. They dig up mines and blow up left-over ammunition and they do this all over the world in boring shithole war-zone places where no one else wants to work: Afghanistan, Angola, Mozambique, Somaliland, Eritrea, Cambodia, Nagorno-Karabakh and Abkhazia. For example, they were the only people in Chechnya between the wars, and apart from kidnapping, they were the largest private employer there.

I was quietly concentrating on my feet but Richard, Halo's Caucasus officer, was happy and unconcerned. The sun was shining and there was a black puff of smoke on the horizon from where a mine had just been blown up (on purpose). He had his hands on his hips and he was talking to Oleg, the Estonian supervisor, about the blast. Richard nodded and gesticulated the shape of the blast. Oleg had short-cropped blond hair, a fresh, serious face and was wearing a khaki boiler suit. When he wanted to indicate something he flung his arm out from his chest as if he was saluting the Führer.

'It was lying on its side,' said Oleg, earnest, arm outstretched, 'it is the floods in the spring that has achieved this position.'

'Still, another one gone,' said Richard, gritting his teeth with the dust that had blown over us. One of the fifteen thousand mines along the Gumista.

When the smoke had cleared the whistle blew and the deminers went back to work, burrowing like slow moles through their lanes; red-and-white sticks on either side marking the cleared land from uncleared land. The deminers worked methodically: they knelt down, first checking for trip-wires, and then cleared the vegetation with a pair of shears before passing a metal detector over a small area. If it signalled, they scraped away at the earth gently with a trowel. Usually they found just a bit of rusted metal or a spent cartridge and it was tossed in a bucket. The process was unimaginably laborious and pain-staking; cold in the winter, sweltering in the summer and always boring. The deminers were paid $180 a month. There were almost no jobs in Abkhazia and everyone wanted to work for Halo. When they found a mine it was blown up in situ. Behind the deminers was a trail of yellow sticks that marked where mines had been found and exploded. I walked through a swathe of about forty yellow sticks clustered close together.

'Is this where they found the skeleton?' I asked.

'Yeah, a skeleton with a pair of boots.'

'What did they do with it?'

'The man from the Abkhaz war graves commission came. He walked over, took a look, sniffed the air, declared, "Georgian!" And walked off. Clearly not interested. So we buried him over there...'

The Georgians had dug in along the river against the Abkhaz who were besieging the city for several months in 1992–3. The Georgians laid the mines to stop the Abkhaz, but they were not successful; up by the road bridge were monuments to Abkhaz who died taking the city. Their portraits were etched on black marble, always in uniform, with stripy Russian army T-shirts and Kalashnikovs gripped across their dead chests.

'It's the only new thing they've built in Abkhazia since the war,' said Richard.

'What?'

'Graves.'

Bob the bomb disposal man met us at the control point of one of the minefields. He was leaning against one of the monstrous armoured diggers covered in thickened steel with its tyres wrapped in massive chains. He nodded hello at Oleg. Oleg nodded curtly back and went to amend his map to include the newly exploded mine. Bob had been out by the airport looking at unexploded ordnance. He was about forty, short and wiry, sticking-out ears, cheeky, Scots.

'Blow anything up this morning then, Richard?'

'Couple of PMN2s; nothing interesting.'

'We found an aerial cluster bomb.'

'Did you?'

'Tail fin shorn off, the wee flange-things sticking out of the ground, nose down.' Bob had spent twenty years blowing things up for the British army. He had plenty of stories about things that had gone bang like Belfast milk floats filled with explosives and Second World War anti-landing-craft mines bobbing around southern English beaches and suspicious packages in the Sainsbury's car park that turned out to be a pile of porno mags. Bob was funny, both ha-ha and peculiar. For example, he had recently become a Muslim and got engaged again (Bob had several ex-wives). Bob had met his latest fiancée in an Omani hospital, where she worked as a nurse, when she had come to bandage him up after his circumcision. 'While I was embracing Islam,' as he put it.

But now he was precise, professional, and showed Richard the angle of the aerial cluster bomb with his hand: 'It was sticking like that out of the ground. Kids were throwing rocks at it. Bloody hell, I told them to stop throwing rocks at it.'

Halo boys, ex-British army, Sandhurst, competent, professional, disciplined, hard-working, straight-up. I should say that they were dedicated to their work, but that was not strictly true. I think that saving lives and making the world a safer place was not why they did it; rather they were dedicated to doing a good job efficiently; they liked being around explosives and they treated them with a mixture of soldierly pride and little-boy glee. They were not heedless to the effects of land-mines; they simply had to live with them every day. If anything, they admitted, as they got older they become more careful. I noticed Richard always wore his seat-belt in the car.

Walking back to the Land-Rover, Richard and Bob talked shop in strange sentences of jargon speak and acronyms: radiuses, diggers, distances, map co-ordinates. Radios crackled in the background. They talked about the six-year-old Abkhaz boy who had lost an arm, a leg and an eye a few months earlier playing with a mine. They talked about the Halo expat who was kidnapped with the UN up in the Khodori valley the month before; luckily only a Georgian kidnap, which meant three days of drinking *chacha*. For some reason there wasn't any fuel to buy in Sukhumi; there had been almost no petrol for two weeks and vehicle routes had had to be reassigned. There was equipment clearing Georgian customs, there were meetings with Ardzinba to discuss; there were questions about funding. But things were going well in general and Richard was pleased.

I listened. It was all extremely interesting. Halo worked close to the ground, they ran the whole programme in Abkhazia, employing three hundred people, with only two expat staff. Their local staff were very loyal. Halo knew the ins and outs and connecting patterns between the Abkhaz and the Georgians and the Russians and the UN and the partisans in Gali and the Abkhaz government-in-exile. When Halo had a truck stolen in Gali by a local bandit, it had been *returned*.

The next day we drove down to Gali. In Gali there were more minefields with red-and-white sticks and yellow sticks and blue sticks which marked the contaminated earth that had been moved into a pile. We sat in foetid, boxed-in armoured Land-Rovers, protected.

'Are you all right back there then?' asked Bob and I nodded mutely, wiping the sweat from my face.

'Don't worry,' he said kindly, 'it's not much further and then we'll stop and have a bit of lunch in Otarbaya.'

I was inured by three days of talking and joking about blown-off feet and whopping iron bombs, armed robberies and running through minefields to escape kidnap attempts in Chechnya. I watched the Gali villagers walking past through the thick greenish bullet-proof glass, I waved at the children who waved at us. This was unprotected every-day: cows whisking flies with their tails, pigs trotting along with a wooden triangle tied around their neck to stop them getting stuck in fences, two young girls hoeing a cabbage patch, a woman walking down the road in a pair of high-heeled wedge shoes going somewhere, a man sitting on a rock doing nothing at all. Some homes were inhab-ited, more were abandoned; rusting metal gates, overgrown yards, holes where there should have been wooden window frames and panes of glass. Everywhere, growing indiscriminately, was a dense jungle of fruit trees that smashed plums, apples, pears, lemons, mulberries, bitter red cornels and blackberries down against the pock-marked rubbly road.

The woman who cooked for the teams of deminers at the Halo House in Otarbaya, rotund, jolly, careworn, told me that she and her family sat up at night, listening for noises in the yard, waiting for dawn to go to sleep, because the bandits came at night and tied people up, threatened them with guns, took the money they had got for their hazelnut crop, took their television and left.

'Are they Mingrelians?' I asked her.

'Mingrelians. Abkhaz. What's the difference? They rob you just the same.'

After lunch Richard and I sat on the veranda with a view of the Russian checkpoint next door. Bob had gone off to investigate a box of RPGs (rocket-propelled grenades) that the cook's eldest daughter had found in a pigsty. We listened to a briefing on recent events in the

Gali sector: a Russian soldier had stepped on a mine and lost a leg at the knee, a peasant had blown his foot off trying to rebury a mine in his garden to protect his cow. Someone had blown up the large statue of a lion in the centre of Gali town and three gunmen shot up the empty UNHCR house because of a dispute between the watchman and the people he was selling gasoline to on the sly. There had been an attempted ambush of Abkhaz militia and small arms fire was exchanged. Locals kept reporting gunfire around Russian checkpoints at night and the Russians said that they had come under attack, but it seemed more probable that their soldiers were just drunk and firing in the air. A partisan-'businessman' running Viceroy cigarettes from Zugdidi claimed his car had been fired on by Abkhaz militia but the alternative story was that he was drunk and yelling obscenities at a Russian checkpoint and the Russians fired at him to make him go away. A busload of women coming over from the market in Zugdidi was held up by bandits and everyone was made to strip before being robbed. Gali was always full of nasty stories and these were pretty run of the mill.

In Gali there were a hundred tiny footpaths that wound between villages to other paths that led to fords and plank-bridges across the Enguri; lines of tramped mud and overgrown weeds that trailed down gullies and across sandbanks. The river was wide in Lower Gali, stretched in interconnecting channels across a generous flood plain, and people knew where they could cross it at different times of the year, to go to the market in Zugdidi, to graze cattle on flat islets of meadow or to run away from the Abkhaz. There was a railway bridge across the river which had been shelled. One of its middle arches had fallen into the river, but there was a series of steel planks laid across the gap and quite a lot of people used it. Underneath it was a great swathe of river-bank, pitted and scraped by the deminers. It had taken three years to clear.

Bob and Richard reminisced all the way back to Sukhumi along the M27, remembering Angola where they had to airlift vehicles into the Central Highlands because the roads were constantly cut by the fighting; living in a freezing tent in Kosovo during the first winter; the two Halo expats who were blown up by two linked mines, booby-trapped against demining, in a tank in Afghanistan. Bob and Richard were hard-boiled; I was beginning to feel hard-boiled too. Ethnic cleansing went by outside the windows of the car, but I was bored with looking at it. There was so much of it and all burnt houses look the same.

Later, laughing at myself and my new vocabulary (det. cord, primary explosive, firing cable), I sat on the beach with Shalva, with our customary beer. On this occasion I had brought him a cigar from Tbilisi (not a very good one; it was impossible to find anything very fresh) and a book of American short stories.

'And how are you? How is your news?'

'I have been to America,' said Shalva, grinning.

'They let you go!'

'You cannot imagine the papers I needed. And in Moscow they arrest you every few metres; they think you look dark, you are Caucasian, maybe you are a Chechen; they want to see your documents, to check everything. I had to go to the police station twice; for nothing! I was just walking down the street; it's impossible. And then when I arrived in New York the immigration guards; they asked me a hundred questions. I had only $60 in my pocket and they said, "How are you going to support yourself?" I felt ashamed, really.'

'You were in New York?'

'And Boston and Washington. I liked Boston.' There was a new confidence in Shalva; he was – I looked closer at a relaxed animation in his eyes and a curve of a smile at the corners of his mouth – enthusiastic. 'I liked America very much,' he said, having decided quite definitely about it, 'much better than London.'

'You went to London too?'

'I was in London on the way back for three days.'

'Yes, well,' I said, 'the English are not very friendly.'

'I did not have such a good feeling in London; but in Boston – they seem to know how to enjoy themselves in America. There were old women – and even they were enjoying themselves as if they were teenagers. I had the feeling of being at home in America. I had a good feeling. I can tell you honestly I feel as if I have left a piece of my heart there.'

'It's not all brilliant,' I told him harshly, somewhat annoyed at him for having fallen for the ease of it, the decency of the public institutions, the upright, forthright flag-waving democracy. 'It's competitive, America,' I said, 'you're judged by how much money you earn, and it's difficult for a lot of people. It's not an easy place. Everyone has to work very hard.'

'Here there is no work at all,' Shalva corrected me. 'Here there is nothing. I fell into *depressia* when I came back. You cannot know.'

'No,' I admitted, 'I can't.'

'And that stupid election –' Shalva shook his head as if he could hardly believe he had once told me, 'Ardzinba is our leader; we should support him united.

'Nothing changes here; it's not possible to organize anything, to *do* anything. They are privatizing, but everything is being sold to Ardzinba's wife.'

'What will you do?' I asked him.

'I have applied for a Russian passport. I was born in Russia so it's not so difficult. I think maybe in a month the documents will be ready.'

'So you'll be a Russian?'

'I'll be Abkhaz, I will always be Abkhaz.'

'Of course you will!'

'My cousin who lives in Moscow; he went to Moscow during the war; he is a Georgian –'

'It goes through the mother, I remember. I still think you're a Mingrelian.'

'You, Wendell,' said Shalva, teasing me, 'should not say such things. Not even to a good friend.'

'Mingrelian! You're all the same!'

'It's not the same. Be quiet about it! My cousin has said that he might be able to help me get some kind of job. Maybe translating.'

Shalva leaned back, flared a match and sucked the cigar until it lit. 'I look like Kurtz with this,' he said, rolling it from one side of his mouth to the other. 'How is Kurtz?'

'He's disappeared.' I said slowly. 'No one knows where he is. Maybe he's in America and not answering the phone. No one has had an email from him in six months.'

'That's bad.'

'I know. He was chasing the black dog. Perhaps the black dog bit him.'

We fell quiet. The sea was dark; the mountains behind us were finely etched blue silhouettes. Dogs were barking at each other, fiercely, up and down the road. Every neighbourhood dog was howling and snapping and yelling at its neighbour.

'Moscow!' I said at length, touching Shalva's shoulder.

Shalva smiled – there was always the future to think about – and replied,

'Moscow. Maybe. I hope, Moscow. I can't stay here any more.'

Shalva and I walked back to the house and found Bob and Richard sitting in the kitchen reading a year-old copy of *Loaded* magazine.

'She's all right, I like those Asian hens with a bit of meat on their bones there,' said Bob, drinking his Coke and fingering the page on Bangkok lovelies.

'Not my thing, really,' said Richard rather disapprovingly.

'Oh well. I found a flashette artillery projectile this morning,' Bob announced, pleased with his discovery.

'Really,' said Richard, brightening at the news.

'Yeah, Russian manufactured, contravening the Geneva Convention. Nice little bomb that explodes thousands of slivers of metal in all directions,' he added for my benefit. 'Found it in the car park of the maternity hospital, lying under a bench.'

11th August

HERE IS AN ACCOUNT of a certain day. This is what happened, for example, on 11 August 2000:

Richard and I got back to Tbilisi from Sukhumi late on the night of the 10th. I went home, threw off all my clothes and collapsed on to the bed and watched CNN. In the morning the television was still on and the news was the same. If I had listened properly I might have found myself well informed about Indonesian separatists or Malaysian separatists or Kosovo elections or whatever was happening and important – but that was all somewhere else and I had ceased to be interested by it; I had my little corner of complicated reality and it was enough.

I had a bath. I had a Russian lesson. I sat around thinking about doing something and had a cup of tea. There were green unripe grapes hanging on my balcony. I ate two peaches watching the street below bake in the rising heat. The tomato-widow, black crone with a bucket of tomatoes in front of her, had fallen asleep on the kerb and one of the street children, my favourite, Gika, who was tiny and nimble and ran fast everywhere, was stealing a tomato.

The phone rang; (aha! distraction) it was Richard in great consternation. News had broken in Moscow the day before: the Russian government had accused the Halo Trust of being undercover British agents who had used their compound in Stary Atchoi to train Chechens in terrorism. He read me the *Daily Telegraph* story that had come through his fax machine: '... *according to the FSB, the charity's topographical reconnaissance had the aim of including Chechen towns and villages in the "NATO co-ordinated system". It supplied guerrillas with communications devices and military equipment and recruited a network of local informants to provide military and political intelligence, the FSB claimed in a statement issued from the Lubyanka, its Moscow headquarters...*'

'Why haven't the Russians quoted my name in their press release?' Richard was indignant, but he was also trying to laugh about it; it was quite serious, but it was ridiculous. 'I've been in charge of the Caucasus for three years. Guy's just called from head office and told me they've arrested Alman in Grozny. We're persona non grata in Russia.' He was scanning the press cuttings coming through the fax, 'God knows if we'll ever see Alman again. He was coming down to Tbilisi this week to tell me how many of the metal detectors he had managed to hide under boxes of onions in someone's front yard near Gudermes – I suppose it'll be a bit difficult for him to make the meeting, poor bastard's in a Russian detention camp.'

'What happened to the rest of your kit up there?'

'The Russians blew up a couple of the armoured diggers with aerial bombs. The *boyeviki* took the vehicles. God knows. Ruslan was best friends with Basayev's cousin or something, some cousin or other – nothing to do with us; but it's a small place.'

'It doesn't look like you'll be restarting operations in Chechnya for a while.'

'No. Probably never; unless the Chechens win.'

'And the Chechens won't win this time.'

'Probably not, no.'

The Russians didn't want foreign organizations operating in Chechnya so they called them spies because they would see things that were better unseen. It was an internal matter and foreign organizations would be discouraged. Richard was sad it had come to this.

Tbilisi was hot and hot. Half the population had fled to Tskineti or to the coast. Only the flies were left. For some reason I had no inclination to try to sell my inside titbit of Halo Trust/FSB allegations scandal to a paper. I felt bad for Richard and for Alman in a detention camp. Perhaps I was not a journalist after all, I thought. But then, what was I? I laughed at myself; at the evidence: I was voluntarily sipping Borjomi, salty Georgian mineral water, hating the Russians and sitting about doing nothing. Perhaps I was becoming a Georgian.

I resumed my seat on the balcony and read the paper. There was a budget crisis. There was always a budget crisis. Lawyer Dato called by to ask me if I wanted to come up to Tskineti and go swimming in his friend's pond. He was tired of sweating through the gridlock in Parliament.

'No taxes are paid,' he explained.

'It's always the same.'

'There are some revenues, but –'

'No customs revenues.'

'Exactly. There are no customs revenues.'

Someone, an American, had told me unofficially that the Americans had given the Georgians three months:

'Three months to show that they can produce something, anything. The State Department guy came down personally to tell them that we're not going to treat Georgia like a spoilt child any more. Three months and nothing, and we'll pull every aid package, every World Bank loan, every IMF bit of financing.'

'I thought the World Bank and the IMF were supposed to be independent organizations,' I replied.

'Yeah, well.'

I felt far too lazy to go up to Tskineti and drink cognac all afternoon. I pondered about who to go and see. Kakha was away, Lela was working. Sometimes I dropped in on Betsy. Betsy owned Betsy's guest-house and was the doyenne of the expat community. Entirely incongruous in Tbilisi: American, ballsy, bejewelled, blonde highlights and manicured pink fingernails. She had been in Tbilisi when Shevy was still biding his time in Moscow. She knew the turnover of the business community, the German who had sold a restaurant, some Brits who were running a couple of casinos – and she had all the gossip about who was sleeping with who at the American Embassy. She was smart and funny and sensible; Roland the manager told me she had left Tbilisi's summer and gone to Turkey for a month.

Sometimes I went to see Alex who was an academic who advised the President about foreign affairs. Alex had an office in a corridor filled with refugees from Abkhazia and he always poured me a sherry and we talked about football and Georgia. In the beginning I had asked him a lot of pertinent questions and he gave me insightful replies. Later we just bandied pessimism. Alex was more pessimistic than I was. He was in his fifties with a shock of thick white hair that made him look uncannily like an American actor. He knew a lot, understood more than most; he had become increasingly frustrated.

'They're all peasants! We are a nation of peasants! What can you expect from these idiots?'

But Alex was in Germany on a conference.

So I went to see Zaliko.

'It's too hot to work,' I told him. 'I just want to eat watermelon and read old copies of *National Geographic*.'

Zaliko chuckled.

'It's easy. Watermelon, we have it. I have some visitors coming, but you can stay, it's nothing important. Maybe they will be interesting for you.'

I ate watermelon and we watched the news on Rustavi 2. The budget crisis, the kidnap of two Red Cross women by ethnic Kists in the Pankisi Gorge. According to the news, the women were still alive and probably being held somewhere close by; they had not been taken across the border. The negotiations were, said a Georgian government spokesman, going well.

There was a story about a man who had hung himself from an electricity pylon because he could not find work. The footage showed his mother wailing beside his corpse, the camera panned across the corpse which still had the electrical cable tied around its neck.

'Too many who suicided themselves,' said Zaliko. 'There is nothing for them, they don't know what to do.'

Then there was the regular Chechnya feature about an attack on a Russian checkpoint in Grozny. The usual spurious official Russian figures: twenty Chechens killed, two Russians wounded.

'Those Chechens are all idiots,' said Zaliko. 'I am fed up with them. I am sorry for them, but I am fed up of them.'

Zaliko had just been in Svaneti with a group of mad Englishmen who were in the process of climbing the highest mountain in every European country. Appi and another guide had taken one of them up Shkhara in six days. He showed me the pictures. Snow, blue sky, crampons. From the summit of Shkhara they could see across the top of the Caucasus stretching far across the Russian border to the mighty Elbruz. I had teased Zaliko about a rumour in Tbilisi that he had been kidnapped in Svaneti.

'At least in Svaneti,' I said, 'you are protected by the blood-feud system. I knew you couldn't be kidnapped because you were with Appi and Appi has climbed Everest and is a local hero with bridges named after him.'

'It's true,' conceded Zaliko, 'they will never touch me in Svaneti. But they are still crazy! They rob the tourists. Svans are crazy people – really, Wendell, you went there only once! You don't know anything. Besso: who you stayed with? He shot two young men three months ago. He is stupid for what? He has a wife, children, his sister, her family live in his house and he will pull everything down?'

'I heard about the Japanese.'

'Pah! I know. It was funny!' Zaliko laughed and rubbed his beard. 'They took $10,000 from a group of Japanese.'

'What kind of morons would take ten grand in cash to Svaneti?' I wanted to know.

The poor Japanese, among the very few hardy tourists who braved Georgia, had a difficult summer. One group was robbed in Svaneti; another group was derailed on the vertical funicular railway that went up the Tbilisi mountain.

August the 11th was just one of those days. Odd things were happening, funny things, funny-peculiar things that we laughed at.

Parliamentary rumblings, artillery rumblings north of the Caucasus, news that went round, rumours. Zaliko and I sat talking. It was all farce: intricate, filigreed farce. I realized that there were a thousand things that I knew; a thousand stories, odd bits of strange juxtaposed fact and that it would be impossible to explain them. The retelling would stale the joke; simplification edit out the pathos.

There was, for example, the story of Eliava. Akaki Eliava was a Mingrelian Zviadist outlaw with a band of black Gore-Tex paramilitaries. He had been an army officer and had tried to overthrow Shevardnadze's government a couple of years before by stealing a tank and driving it into a tree on the way to 'seizing' Kutaisi. Afterwards he and his band of loyal followers were said to have fled into the impenetrable forests of Mingrelia. Said the Georgian security forces, who claimed they couldn't find him. Journalists, however, often conducted interviews with him in various restaurants in Zugdidi.

Eliava had been at large for more than two years. In July he and four colleagues, all dressed in their black uniforms, had their car stopped at a police checkpoint near Zestafoni. They were taken to the local police station where the police chief tried to explain to them that they were not allowed to carry guns. Eliava didn't want to surrender his gun so he took the police station hostage for the rest of the day. Negotiations went on for several hours and finally Eliava was given a verbal guarantee of safety. The National Reconciliation Act had come into force a week before, absolving Eliava of his previous misdemeanours; but by the terms of that Act he should not have been carrying a gun. Eliava and his four colleagues left the police station, apparently irritated, but unconcerned, and were promptly shot at by a Security Ministry unit. Eliava and his deputy were killed, the three remaining rebels surrendered.

Bizarrely, the whole encounter inside the police station had been video-taped by a cameraman who 'just happened' to be there. Eliava, white-haired, arrogant, waving his steel-shiny pistol in the face of the police chief. The main expression on Eliava's face was that of astonishment. Someone would dare to try to take his gun away? A *policeman*?

In Tbilisi, opposition politicians accused the government of 'assassinating a true Georgian patriot'. The media wanted to know why the security forces had waited until after the Reconciliation Act to kill him when he had been running around with impunity for two years. And in Mingrelia there was outrage. They said that Eliava had been deliberately lured into a trap. In protest, his family refused to bury him and for two weeks the neighbours all brought honey to pour into his open coffin to preserve the body in the July heat.

Finally they gave up and buried him in Senaki with a wailing choir of female relatives.

'Those Mingrelians!' said Zaliko. 'But it's interesting, honey is a good preservative.'

'Honey? That's the weirdest thing I ever heard.'

'I got some honey in Svaneti, it's a good one, I'll bring it.' Zaliko brought an enormous jar of brown-gold honey in from the kitchen. There was sticky comb floating on the top. He gave me a spoon.

'It's a sweet one,' said Zaliko, encouraging. 'Svans have good honey.'

The doorbell rang; it was Zaliko's visitor, Ruslan the Chechen who had brought me war footage the previous autumn. Zaliko had been helping him try to organize some kind of project with the Red Cross, but everything had gone bad; on hold, since the kidnapping in Pankisi. I said hello. Ruslan smiled weakly, he had lost an incisor since I had last seen him. He had come with his son, an eight-year-old boy, polite and intelligent, who Zaliko exhorted to have some Svan honey. The boy looked back at his father to see if that was all right.

'Go on, have some honey,' Ruslan told him and ruffled his hair.

He looked at his son with pent-up love, but his eyes were blank. He looked wasted. He tried to joke and be normal in front of me and Zaliko and his son. It was a small, wan effort. He smelled of alcohol and grime; there was something dull and wide-spaced in his eyes. His skin was stretched thinly and red and pale. I noticed several small burns on the inside of his arm, along the tender part close to the crook of his elbow. His old humour showed through his depression in worn patches. When he smiled it was not convincing.

'I want to go home,' he told me tiredly. I knew he didn't have any money. I knew that Zaliko couldn't give him any more.

'To Grozny?'

'To Grozny.'

'How is Grozny now?'

'Grozny is nothing.'

'How will you live there?' I asked him.

'I don't want to live,' he said, looking painfully over to his son.

Ruslan did not stay long. After he realized that Zaliko couldn't help him and that the Red Cross project was dead in the water, he left. The news was not good and not getting any better.

Zaliko agreed with me that he looked self-destructive, terrible.

'He has nothing,' Zaliko admitted, 'but he complains. Many times he has come here, I know he is not a bad man, but drunk, he is often drunk or on drugs – I don't know what he does with himself. But I don't like the complaining. He should have done something more with the Red Cross project. I told him how to do it, but he is lazy or he is busy; it is not right to come here. Just now, when I saw him out of the door, he asked me if he could ask you for money. It's not the right way. I don't like it.'

'I should go too.' I kissed Zaliko's beard. 'Thank you for the water melon, for the honey, for the tea and for the cigarettes.'

'It's a nothing.' Zaliko walked me down to the end of his street to where my car was parked. His street was too narrow for me to drive down.

'Next week I'm going to Karabakh to write for a month,' I told him, 'but I'll be back.'

It was about four in the afternoon. It was hot and the sun was shining. I had pleasantly idled the day away and now I decided to go to the swimming pool.

Laguna Vera was a big open-air Olympic pool, privatized and expensive to visit. It cost seven lari. Which meant that it was popu-lated by the richer new Georgians: beautiful girls in bikinis, hairy men and the speaker of Parliament, an intelligent political operator called Zurab Zhvania, who swam every lunchtime with a bodyguard at either end of his lane. In the summer the place was always full; mobile phones, tanning oil and bottles of Coke; a happy fleshy pick-up joint. The pool was blue but it wasn't very clean; I used to swim my laps with a mask on and you could see lumps of hairnet and bits floating about under the surface. But I didn't care; the water was cool after the foetid streets and as necessary in the summer as the *banya* was in the winter. I hired a plastic sunbed and lay down with my book.

Georgia was a funny place. Betsy and I had once tried to figure out why we liked it and why we had stayed so long. When nothing worked and the corruption was terrible and there was no electricity in the winter and nothing but heat in the summer. The cities were falling down and rusting, the countryside was scarred by the Soviets. Georgia was cut off from the world, poor and without much imagination. It did not like to go forward, it was happy enough wallowing in its traditions and wine. 'I think it's the quality of life,' I told her. It sounded absurd, but Betsy nodded, she knew what I was talking about. 'The little things, my neighbour bringing me *varenie* for the winter, strawberries that are soft and fresh and taste of real strawberries, being able to park right next to the post office, warm balcony evenings, friendliness, easiness. The pace of life is slower, it's more comfortable –'

'And it's free.'

'You can do whatever you want.'

'You can drive down a one-way street the wrong way, drive drunk, not pay your taxes – hell, you could kill someone if you wanted to. The bureaucracy is difficult, but there's always a way to get something done when you really need to, there's always someone who will help you or someone you can pay –'

'If you've got two hundred bucks in your pocket, you've got it made,' I said.

'That's true,' Betsy reinforced. 'If you're a Georgian in Georgia, you're screwed.'

My phone rang: it was Lado.

'I am in town. We're drinking tonight. At the Nali. Eight o'clock.'

'OK,' I said.

So I lay in the southern sun and browned my shoulders until a quarter to eight and then walked up the hill to Perovskaya through my special back way that terrified Lela because it went through someone's front yard with an enormous unchained barking dog.

*

Lado was a Georgian but he spoke acccentless American. He was one of Alex's protégés. Alex had been his professor at university and found him sponsorship to go to university in the States. Lado excelled, went to Harvard Business School and ended up working for a big European bank doing deals in Russia while fending off offers for him to come home and bring his expertise to Shevardnadze's young reforming part of the government. (The part that had no power and was always being frustrated by the old guard.) He was still under thirty. Lado liked to pretend he was a spiv. He ordered rounds of tequila shots and he and his friends, other Americanized Georgians with money in their pockets, recited passages from *The Godfather* to each other. There was always a big gang of people around Lado when he was in Tbilisi; we always ended up at the Beatles Club, trashed, dancing, more tequila and never home before four.

Lado borrowed loud from America, but he was Georgian and like a good Georgian he loved Georgia. Even though he understood pretty well what the reality was. He was looking for a bit of hope that things would get better. His hope was his patriotism but at the same time he could never fathom why I was so fond of the place.

'Wendell! Come and sit – what are you drinking? You've come straight from Laguna Vera, I can see your hair is still wet –'

I ordered vodka with three lemon slices in it.

'Lado, the wide-boy. Are you well? What brings you home? Surely not a deal?'

'No. No deals in Georgia; I'm trying to find something but –'

Lado seemed like a cash-flash wide-boy, but he wasn't really. It was just something he had picked up along with his American accent.

Later in the evening when we were drunker, I teased him that it was slipping. We were talking about books, about Georgia.

'Did you read Di Lampedusa's *The Leopard* as I suggested?' Lado asked me.

'Yes. I did. I read it in Istanbul. I liked it.'

'Sicily is the same as Georgia,' announced Lado, 'it's my new theory. Do you remember the passage that reads like it could have been written about Georgia?' I shook my head. I had been distracted with heartache when I had read the book. He pulled out a copy from his bag. 'Dato borrowed it from me. He agrees. I've just got it back from him. Listen. This is the part when the old Duke receives a young earnest official, a Chevalley. The Chevalley wants him to join the new progressive Republican government and the Duke refuses. The official doesn't understand why, so the Duke explains the Sicilian condition to him. Listen:

'Sleep, my dear Chevalley, sleep, that is what Sicilians want, and they will always hate anyone who tries to wake them, even in order to bring them the most wonderful of gifts: I must say, between ourselves, that I have strong doubts whether the new kingdom will have many gifts for us in its luggage. All Sicilian self-expression, even the most violent, is really wish-fulfilment; our sensuality is a hankering for oblivion, our shooting and knifing a hankering for death; our languor, our exotic ices, a hankering for voluptuous immobility, that is for death again; our meditative air is that of a void wanting to scrutinise the enigmas of Nirvana… that is the cause of the well-known time lag of a century in our artistic and intellectual life; novelties attract us only when they are dead, incapable of arousing vital currents; from that comes the extraordinary phenomenon of the constant formation of myths which

would be venerable if they were really ancient, but which are really nothing but sinister attempts to plunge us back into a past that attracts us only because it is dead...

... the Sicilians never want to improve for the simple reason that they think themselves perfect; their vanity is stronger than their misery; every invasion by outsiders, whether so by origin or, if Sicilian, by independence of spirit, upsets their illusion of achieved perfection, risks disturbing their satisfied waiting for nothing, having been trampled on by a dozen different peoples, they think they have an imperial past which gives them the right to a grand funeral...

'Oh my God,' I said, 'it's Georgia. It's exactly Georgia.'

'I know.' We were quiet for a moment while the crowd around us laughed and boomed. Lado continued, 'I mean there's actually a place out there that's equally fucked-up. Two weeks ago I went to Sicily. I wanted to see. It was the same! Fishermen, unshaven, with dirt under their fingernails, peasants handling the meat with bloody paper in the market, old women selling sunflower seeds, all the second-hand cars, the way the boys stood separately from the girls –'

'But Sicily is not as poor as Georgia?'

'No. Of course not. There's the hope. It's the same mentality, the same way of life, but things there work; there are hotels and investment. It showed me that it's possible to rack up the GDP just by virtue of being attached to something more civilized.'

'Like the Russians?'

'Georgia's too small to be alone.'

'Yeah, but the Russians?'

Lado gave me a stern look, 'No, not the fucking Russians. But Sicily gave me hope! It's possible... in thirty, forty, fifty years...'

Pankisi

AFTER NINE MONTHS OF silence, nine months of nothing, without news or communication between us, and just at the moment when I was over him, Thomas came back to Tbilisi on assignment. He asked me to come for a drink in the bar on Belinsky where the walls were covered in paintings. I was nervous, even a little afraid of him, but I did not want to refuse the meeting for fear of running away from something. He kissed me hello and then it was as if no time had passed at all and there had been no hurt between us. He was the same; dressed in layered-up layers of grey: T-shirt, shirt, canvas jacket, cotton scarf; bundles of film and light meters in webbing around his waist. He put his camera on the table. He looked back at me and I could see he did not understand what was in my eyes.

The main thing that had happened to Thomas was that he had got his break. He had been on the outskirts of Grozny when it fell in January, he had taken pictures of the retreating *boyeviki* and he had won prizes for these pictures.

'I felt guilty, awkward. I took a roll of film. It was dark. It was the most incredible thing I ever saw. The *boyeviki* were moving out of Grozny; they were moving silently, it was incredibly impressive, the silence. There were hundreds of them; their wounds were covered in black plastic bags. I tried to fit in, but I couldn't really. One nearly hit me because I took a picture of him trying to save his dying friend so I tried to help them load bodies on to a truck to look inconspicuous.' Teams of *boyeviki* mixed with civilians had slipped out of Grozny through frozen fields, clear corridors that had been paid for, in thousands of dollars of cash, to Russian commanders. 'Afterwards I didn't even think I had anything. I was completely miserable. It wasn't the suffering, I don't know. It was extraordinary. It was utterly dark. I honestly thought, I've ruined this – I wanted to throw the film away. I didn't even want to look at it. God, can you imagine how close I came to throwing it away?'

The following summer he had been invited to join the Magnum photographic agency. Ever since he was small Magnum had represented the very best he wanted to be. He could hardly believe he had arrived. He had been commissioned to take pictures for some French magazine illustrating the corruption in the south Caucasus – 'For God's sake, corruption, it isn't exactly photogenic – it's everywhere.' He sat across from me veering through scales of emotion – he was excited about Magnum, he was worried about being judged more thoroughly, he was sorry his freedom was curtailed, he had to work, but he wanted to work – he was trying to get some purchase on what was true. I had always loved him for these lurches; they were his special kind of confused honesty. He was happy with it all; he was thrilled; but he questioned it too – he was not someone who could be satisfied because other people were impressed. He hated a reply I gave him once when he asked, teasingly, why had I fallen for him? I had answered, flip, 'Because you're sexy and you've been to Chechnya.' He thought that was very base of me. His drive towards the truth in things was almost deracinating; he mistrusted any easy emotional reaction and that included success. It was hard to try to find the emotional truth in things in the Caucasus – especially in Chechnya – where one day there could be an incident of friendship that left you awestruck and humble and the next everything was jumbled, dangerous and covered in blood. It was easier, like me, just to be cynical and throw a stupid comment out like a punch-line. Thomas had spent most of his adult life in the Caucasus. It fed his soul. He had a rare gift to feel things keenly; his moods were up and down, like mountains; dense rock and eagle flight, but he had real despair and he had real joy; emotions that most of us denigrate with self-indulgence and pretence.

'It's good, Thomas,' I told him, 'it's great!' And he gave me a wan look that conceded the fact that he knew that.

'Yeah yeah, I know it's good –' he smiled in recognition. 'On the day I was going to find out whether or not I had been voted in, I was completely harassed. I could think about nothing else. I went outside and I dropped my door-keys on the ground. I never drop my keys usually – I looked and they had landed on a Magnum ice-cream wrapper. I couldn't believe it.'

'On a Magnum ice-cream wrapper?'

'Yeah.'

We caught each other's eyes and laughed. We laughed because we perfectly understood why the Magnum ice-cream wrapper was so funny, because it was so funny and because it was a wonderful thing to find ourselves laughing together again.

Then he drew breath and looked at me with an expression I couldn't quite fathom.

'I'm no longer with Iceberg,' he said quietly.

I stared into my whisky. Thomas lit one of his sixty cigarettes of the day. I could not quite meet his eye.

'You have changed,' he said, watching me, 'you are stronger now.'

'Yeah, well.'

As he walked me home he admitted he wanted to borrow me and my car to take him to the Pankisi valley.

'Arbi's there, and I promised his wife I would see him. I can make it part of my corruption story. Don't you remember Arbi? He lived in my flat in Paris? When the phones were bugged and there were Chechen officials giving interviews in my kitchen. Arbi.'

'Pankisi, Thomas, it's bad in Pankisi, they kidnapped Red Cross expats this summer.'

'It'll be all right with Arbi; he's the local commander.'

'Thomas.'

'Honestly. It's not stupid.' Thomas flashed the old smile that I remembered, a sort of craziness mixed with love.

The Pankisi valley was at the end of Georgia, through Kakheti, past Akhmeta, almost to the mountains, across an invisible line. It was not Georgia any more. There was a man standing in the road watching cars drive in. He wore a mangy *shapka* on his head and a pair of camouflage trousers. He was not Georgian. His eyes narrowed as we drove past but he did not stop us.

Pankisi was uncomfortable, the atmosphere peculiar. There were four thousand Kisti in the valley in normal times. In the previous winter that number had been doubled by refugees, mostly the refugees that Kurtz and I had seen coming through Shatili. Now that the Russians had nominal control of Chechnya and the situation there had stabilized to a degree, many of these had left, back to Chechnya, to relatives in Azerbaijan, Kazakhstan, St Petersburg. Some families stayed, nowhere to go or waiting; it was a difficult time and the stories were difficult too. It was a small community, complicated by the extra tensions: the Russians accused the Georgians of harbouring *boyeviki* among the Kisti, local clans exerted control over the humanitarian aid that came through, there was an ambivalent 'business' relationship with the Georgians in neighbouring Akhmeta. The Red Cross kidnap.

It was October again and a heavy mist hung in the air. It had been raining on and off for days, everything was wet and clammy and muddy. Women collected water from standpipes, fetched bread from the bakery, the men sat around playing cards. Thomas stopped to take pictures of a crowd of kids playing in and out of the metal carcass of an abandoned car. A three-legged dog scuttled by, a boy on a donkey, a cart full of firewood. The kiosks sold Viceroy cigarettes and dried fish; a few cars went by – they were either very rickety Ladas, thirty years old, or gangster Nivas with blacked-out windows.

I walked up the road, out of sight of Thomas. A group of five or six young men, dressed in filthy camouflage, cigarettes cupped against the wind, loitered against a broken-down fence. They came around me, stopping me with a semicircle of raw Chechen faces. They did not smile or introduce themselves or say hello.

'Who are you with?' they asked, and then, 'What is your name? What are you doing? When did you arrive?'

I explained, fitfully. They were not friendly at all.

'Who are you with?'

And at that moment Arbi came striding up the road in search of me.

'Wendell – hello!' he gave me a welcome that was half bear-hug half handshake, 'Come!'

The young men saw him, backed off and mumbled OK.

We walked back down the road to the cars. Arbi had three men with him. One was big and burly with a thick neck and a round head that seemed too small for his body. One was sandy-haired and easy-going; this was Arbi's long-term bodyguard, he was normal-sized and friendly. The last was younger, in his early twenties with a strong, muscled, tough body; he cracked his knuckles almost constantly. His hair was shorn close to the scalp, his beard unshaven, his eyes were small, black and sunken beneath a heavy brow-bone; they seemed to twitch rat-like. He had a short thick scar near his left ear.

They took us to the house where they were living on the outskirts of the Pankisi villages; their neighbours were Georgian.

'The Georgians are a very hospitable nation,' said Ruslan who was the bodyguard, 'but they cannot understand it when you say you do not drink. They will put the glass right under your nose and they will hit you across the back and say again, drink! And when you explain again that we cannot because of our religion, they barely relent and say, "All right then, just a small glass" – !'

Arbi laughed a lot at this, we all laughed. Arbi had floppy brown hair, a big smile and kind eyes. He was careful and gentle. It was a strong aura.

I felt incredibly safe with him. He wore a pair of black waterproof salopettes, soft black trainers that came above his ankles and a large bulky warm grey jacket. On one hip was a mobile phone next to a Swiss army knife and on the other, in a holster, a steel Israeli pistol, a Jericho 941.

There was a Russian textbook lying on the table,

'What's this?' I asked, picking it up, reading the title, teasing them, incredulous. *'How to Prosecute War: For Beginners?'*

The big one laughed, shrugged his shoulders, 'I dunno, just interesting that's all. When those idiot Afghans turn up, we tell them, "Go home!" and they say, "But we want to fight the Russians, we know how to fight the Russians." So sometimes they stay, but they're useless, really. It's a different war.'

The conversation was Caucasian: kidnappings, battles, and dead people. Thomas and Arbi discussed the kidnap of a French journalist who had recently been released. They had their theories, ramifications, bits of information, but figuring out who had been originally responsible for it –

'It's impossible to get someone out when they've gone in. The hostage gets handed off to some other clan, maybe it's a commander that's ordered it, maybe it's one of his deputies –'

'Do you remember the Chechen Parliament?' Arbi was teasing Thomas. They were glad to see each other. Arbi kept cuffing Thomas on the shoulder. They were like old best friends and kept laughing at each other's jokes. 'Those nights when we sat up in your kitchen, drinking tea, in Paris with our friends. Oh, we made a lot of resolutions with our Chechen Parliament!'

'It was a real democracy – except when I got up to go to the toilet –' said Thomas.

'And you never washed up any teacups –'

'Tea,' said Ruslan, a deadpan lament. 'All we ever drink is tea.'

Islam, with his nasty face and the scar, sat playing solitaire on a laptop computer. His physiognomy was brutal, his face war-fucked: what he'd seen he had reacted to; his world was a simple reflex of reaction. He was not as clever as the others, he laughed at all the war jokes, the killing jokes, but he looked dimly into the middle distance when the conversation changed to more civilian topics like French visas or buying a car in the Tbilisi market or the cost of Turkish Air plane tickets. These things, regulations, forms to fill out, contracts, were not his world.

They had a lot of humour in them and they told a lot of bad black jokes. We sat and ate bowls of soup that were brought by the woman who lived in the next house who cooked for them. Islam and the big potato-shaped one breezed jokes back and forth for our benefit: 'It's a checkpoint, the Russian soldier asks, "Have you got anything illegal in this car?" "Yeah my nationality – I'm a Chechen."' When they asked me where I lived in Tbilisi and I told them Vera, they said, 'Ah, Vera, not a bad police station in Vera, we know it well.' They were always getting picked up in Tbilisi, but they had their protectors too (there were certain comments I caught, certain things they said) – a phone call to the Ministry usually sorted it out. In Georgia, Arbi was 'incognito' as he put it. Two fake Russian Federation passports, one identifying him as Ingush, and an expired French visa. 'Did you hear the one about the Chinese? Well. The Chinese wanted to have a war. They went to the Americans and asked, "Will you fight us?" But the Americans said, "We can't fight you this year, it's an election year. Why don't you try the Russians?" So they went to the Russians and they asked, "Will you fight us?" And the Russians said they couldn't because they didn't have enough money, but that if they were desperate, there were these people called Chechens they could call. So the Chinese called the Chechens and asked them. "How many people are you?" asked the Chechens. The Chinese replied, a bit embarrassed, "More than a billion." There was a big pause. The Chechens were conferring. Then one of them came back on the line and said, "OK, we'll do it. We were just worried about the numbers, but now I think we've figured out where to bury them all."'

Ha!

They told stories about Sharia courts in Grozny between the wars that couldn't carry out a sentence because no one had the right kind of stick to deliver forty lashes. And about all the times they'd fired at two parallel Russian checkpoints at night simultaneously and then ducked so that the Russians would think they were under attack and return fire at each other until the morning.

'It was always the same!' said the big potato one who had been Chechen *spetsnaz*, special forces, during the first war, in charge of weapons procurement. 'You'd go to the depot and do the deal with the Russian officer and they'd give you the guns, you'd give them the money and then they would say, "Don't fire this shit as us all right? Point it at those guys over there."'

I admired the fax/printer/scanner all-in-one machine lying on the floor.

'Electricity?' I asked.

'Generator,' said Arbi. 'Here there's no gas, no heat, no electricity at all, there's wood; we'll make a fire later. Are you cold? It's better living just out of Pankisi. These Kisti are bandits! Really. Six months already; I am going crazy.'

'Hey, Wendell,' said Islam across the table, tearing a piece of bread as he spoke, 'Thomas said we should kidnap you for him. He said forty days should be enough.'

I looked at Thomas and mouthed the word, 'Thanks.' Chechens with kidnap jokes; my favourite.

When we had eaten, Thomas and Ruslan the bodyguard and I drove into Douisi, the main Kisti village in the valley, to try to find a friend of Thomas. A refugee? I asked, a *boyevik*, a schoolteacher, an imam, a terrorist, a friend; what was he? Thomas nodded at me.

'All. Some of these things. And Chechen – Ah, Aslan-Beg!'

'Thomas!' Aslan had heard that Thomas was coming and he was waiting outside his house on the mud track. He had a beard, two gold front teeth and I could see immediately that he was a good man.

'Come, come!' he said, very friendly, and helped us up a series of rotten wooden steps to a room off someone else's upper veranda where his family lived. It was dark inside and dusk outside and his wife lit a kerosene lamp. There were two beds and a 50-kilo sack of sugar pushed up against the wall. Aslan indicated that I should sit on the bed, but I said, no, 'Here, the floor is better.' The floor was covered in thick felt and we all took our shoes off and sat about. Thomas and Aslan were catching up. Thomas had once stayed with Aslan-Beg at Itum Kale for several weeks during the early part of the first war; he wanted to know how everything was.

'And the house in Itum Kale?'

'The house! Bombed.' Aslan did not seem overly perturbed. 'They got the balcony and then the whole thing collapsed.'

'And Shamil?' Shamil was Aslan's brother.

'Ah, Shamil's gone to Moscow. But our father still lives in the village.'

'It was a beautiful house, I am sorry.'

Aslan shrugged. 'Everything was bombed. Rockets. And I sent my wife here.'

'Who was the commander in Itum Kale?' asked Thomas, trying to remember.

'In the village?'

'Yes, in the village – I've forgotten.'

'There have been several,' said Aslan. 'Which one do you mean?'

'I can't remember... the one with only one hand?'

'No, he's dead. Vacuum bomb.'

'And you stayed behind? You sent your wife out?'

'I came two months ago. Through the mountains.'

'It's not difficult?'

'It's difficult enough. It's difficult now, there is already snow on the passes. There's a group we're expecting, thirty people, they are coming through now and it's been difficult.'

His wife returned with a small baby heaved to her waist. She set the baby down in the care of a daughter and laid out mugs of tea, bread, and a plate of cheese on a low stool that served us as a table. Aslan took a mug and dipped it into the sack of sugar by the wall and shook it to indicate that we should use it.

'Nothing but the best humanitarian aid in this house,' he joked. It was for his wife's benefit; she was extremely embarrassed about the paucity of hospitality she had to offer. The baby crawled over to his father, alert, destructive, waving his fists at the sugar mug.

'Ah, hooligan! Our next generation!' Aslan picked up his son and tickled him and swung him high and then let him safely down into the curve of his lap.

'How many children have you now, Aslan?' asked Thomas. 'I remember three in Itum Kale, two girls and a boy.'

'Oh that was a long time ago.' Aslan smiled, 'I have five now.'

We sat around and talked and distracted the baby with spoons to grab and funny faces for a long time. They would probably go back, Aslan thought, but not yet, they needed money to rebuild the house and they had none. They were sustained by the kindness of strangers. 'Everything we have was given to us. The food, clothes for the children. They are very good people, the Kisti, tough, good. But it's not home.'

When we said goodbye, we said we'd meet again, in a free Chechnya, in a rebuilt Itum Kale, in a hundred years – that was the joke of the day. We laughed with them because the situation was beyond pity.

Thomas and I were allotted a room for the night. There weren't any light bulbs and there was no heat.

'It's the room of crosses!' said Arbi laughing and showing us, 'Look! He shone his torch around to reveal four walls that were covered in evenly spaced painted crosses, laid out in a grid. 'And the carpet!' The carpet was a tessellated cross-like pattern. 'You see! Fine decoration for a bunch of Wahhabis! Better for you Christians to sleep in here!'

It was cold in the room. I found a pile of seven blankets in the corner donated by a Saudi relief agency, got into bed fully clothed and piled them on top of me.

'Thomas,' I said, watching him take off his kit, 'you are the prodigal boyfriend.'

Thomas was, by birth if not by cultural inclination, German; his English was not perfect.

'Prodigal. What does that mean?' He stood up in the gloom tugging his trousers off, 'Does it mean ideal?'

'Not exactly.' He had taken his trousers off but it was cold enough to make him think twice about taking anything else off. He stood there, thinking for a moment. I explained to him; prodigal like the Bible, like the returning son.

'Oh, so it's a good thing, prodigal, it means you'll cook me dinner!'

I thought for a bit; I wasn't ever sure about that story. I just thought prodigal meant someone who had gone away and then come back; I had half forgotten that the point of the story was that the father was glad to have him back.

'Strange word; prodigal,' I said.

'I have to sleep here?' Thomas asked, pointing at the sofa. I looked at him.

'Yes, you sleep there,' I said. 'You can have some of the blankets.'

He came and sat on the edge of my bed. I lay under a great wad of blankets, fully dressed with all propriety. I had forgotten that I missed him. He was next to me and I still missed him. He started to flatten out, horizontal, as if he wanted to lie down and insinuate himself inside.

'You're not coming in,' I told him.

'OK,' he said, 'I'll just lie here for a couple of minutes.'

Thomas rolled on to his side so that he was facing me. His position made the crawl space between his chest and his arms that I had once longed to be inside. I did not move into it. Instead I lay there quiet, inert and afraid. I did not know what to feel.

'The room with crosses,' said Thomas, 'why do you think they painted the room with crosses?'

'Some kind of village art, religion, décor, a design passed on –'

'The crosses are slightly bulbous'

'They look like flowers.'

'They look a bit like Armenian crosses.'

'But less squirly.'

'Squirly?'

'Not so curly.'

'I like the Chechens,' said Thomas thoughtfully. 'I like the way they are cheerful, when there's no reason to be cheerful. I like the way they laugh at things. Aslan was smiling a lot this evening. He did not ask me for anything.'

'You are funny with them too,' I said, 'you know how to talk to them, they like all your stories and your news.'

'I don't know. Last October when I was in Chechnya I was scared shitless. I've never been so happy to get out of a place in my life. The French photographer was kidnapped just before I went. Arbi sent me to stay with the guy who probably ordered it. Before I went I thought better to be the guest of the big kidnap guy; then I got there and I thought if I was them *I* would kidnap *me* for the price of a Stinger missile. I couldn't really go out of the house, I had the feeling the commander didn't really want me there. When I got back through Shatili there was just relief; I had shit pictures. It wasn't worth it at all.' Thomas paused. I was happy listening to him.

'Thomas.'

There was a small silence, full of our thoughts. I don't know why I began to cry softly. Perhaps I thought, like you do in moments of revealing epiphany, that I finally understood everything. Perhaps I realized that I did not love him because he was sexy and he'd been to Chechnya, but because he was honest enough to say that it had been miserable and scary.

'Thomas,' I said, hesitant, unsure, 'I don't know. I am confused. I am over you and I love you. What do you want me to do?'

Thomas kissed the top of my head. 'Marry me,' he whispered.

I cried; Thomas cried, just as Lela said he would. There was a kind of hope between us but everything was absurd as usual.

'So,' said Thomas, as he took some blankets and retreated to the sofa, 'has anyone ever proposed to you before in a *boyevik* hideout in Pankisi in a room with crosses all over the walls?'

*

The next day was the same mud rain and mist draped in a veil over the hills, hooked in snags on the treetops. The car was muddy, my hands were cold, and I kept losing my pencil. Thomas wanted to take pictures and we stopped at a narrow dirt cross-roads and he took pictures of the things around it: a tiled roof with pumpkins growing on it, a mosque, newly built with Arab money (revealed Arbi reluctantly), in the local style out of red-brick and grey river stones stacked in a herringbone pattern. A brand-new gold crescent stood on top of the minaret. Each house was built behind a compound wall; the village lanes were walled and graffiti-chalked: verses from the Koran in Arabic and other scrawlings half in the Cyrillic alphabet, half in the Georgian alphabet, but in the Russian language, *Magomed loves Maka*.

We drove further up the narrowing valley. Every so often there was a new grand house, built with money, next to falling-down houses held up with rotten wooden balconies, unplastered breeze-block walls and blue plastic UNHCR sheeting. The lanes were very bad, rock tracks, potholes, and full of overflowing water from the standpipes and dirty, ragged kids wearing rubber boots. There was a stillness in the damp air. The forest on either side was quiet. Further along there was a graveyard and four old men in mismatched grey suits and embroidered Turkish caps on their heads stood in a line murmuring: it was the day after. There had been a funeral yesterday, but soon they would perform the *zikr*. They invited us.

Thomas and I followed them a short way up a sticky mud track and off along a stream that ran through a green gully covered in beech trees. A little further there was a clearing with a house, a yard and an oak tree. The men sat in the yard on rough benches, assembling around the fire. The women and I sat in the women's part of the house, the kitchen. The woman who had died had been a refugee from Grozny; she had died of cancer. She had a grown daughter, Khadijat. Khadijat had a long face and eyes that drooped; her face was pale but strong. I felt intrusive, but when we began to talk, I could see that she was happy to see someone who was not from the village. It was a sad day, but also a relief, I think, and she did not seem so sad, in fact she was voluble and funny and smart. It turned out, for example, that she and Thomas knew all the same people from Grozny.

Presently eight men came into the house and gathered in a room that had been cleared of furniture to perform the *zikhr*. The women stood and watched, prayed, incanted responses when necessary. The men were old and wizened; one had no arms. They wore an assortment of hats: a Turkish cap sewn with green sequins, a white linen Turkish cap, a *pappakha*, a trilby, a *shapka*, a felt Svan hat. They took off their shoes and a mullah standing by called to Allah in a throaty voice. They thumped in a circle, foot-thump round in the circular drum rhythm of the heartbeat, faster, faster; the thumping noise went through us. The women watched, their palms held upwards in supplication. The old men moved faster, banging their stocking feet on the wood floorboards, faster; their breath ragged, until it was a flow of feeling and the women wiped their palms down their faces in cleansing and it was done.

Khadijat and I went and sat in a small room off the kitchen and she watched me while I drank a mugful of bouillon and ate a plate of liver.

'It was beautiful,' I told her, 'I have never seen a *zikr* before.'

'Yesterday it was the women, we did it ourselves – it was better.' Khadijat was smiling.

'Where will you go now?' I asked her.

'I don't know. I will stay here for a while; the family we have been living with, they are very kind, but sometimes it's boring, really there's nothing to do in Pankisi; there isn't even a café.'

'Will you stay through the winter?'

'The winter? No, I hope not! I have a brother in St Petersburg. I will go there.'

'Georgia in winter! God it's terrible,' I agreed, 'even in Tbilisi there's no heat and no electricity. Everyone just goes to bed.'

'Are you married?' she asked me, suddenly.

'No,' I replied. 'But last night Thomas asked me to marry him and I said no.'

Khadijat put her hand to her mouth. I don't know why I told her this, but she understood immediately.

'Why did you say no?'

'Because he's too much like me.'

Khadijat laughed. 'But even so –'

At which point Thomas came in from taking pictures and we both broke off, looked up at him, and like eternal sisters, giggled.

'Wendell – we should go,' he said, 'Arbi is waiting for us.'

I had two crystal bracelets around my wrist. My mother had given them to me for my birthday. When we were leaving and saying goodbye I took one off my wrist and gave it to Khadijat. She was embarrassed; she had nothing to give me in return. I was embarrassed to have intruded on the day after her mother had been buried.

Arbi was waiting for us in the car.

'What did you find?'

'A funeral,' I told him.

'Oh, a funeral; Thomas's favourite! He's always taking pictures of funerals.'

I felt a bit guilty that Arbi the commander was acting as our chauffeur. He drove my Niva, and Ruslan the bodyguard drove behind us, in convoy.

'It's OK,' said Arbi, 'I am not so busy now. At the beginning when I came there was a lot to do and organize, but now it's just problems to sort out.'

We drove back and stopped at the market. It was a muddy, ragged small market, set up on rickety stalls beneath tarpaulin. A bit of everyday Pankisi was here. Women buying packets of detergent and soap. Old men, dressed in old, greasy suits, their faces, weather-burnt, creased with age and unshaven. I saw two men in smart clean camouflage uniforms, both with fuzzy black beards. There were a few cars parked about and people doing business from them. An old woman with a thick face like a rhino saw Thomas taking pictures and began to intone a list of woes, loudly: 'I come from Itum Kale. Everything is bombed. Everything is burnt. The Russians bombed and then the Wahhabis came. All our clothes were burnt, our furniture. Our children were killed. Everything was burnt. Everything was levelled. Everything was destroyed.' It was impossible to listen to; I walked away. Harangue of bitter loss; grim, dull and awkward. To be honest, in that place, where many people had lost something and many people everything, her outrage seemed a little mad.

A man came up and asked Arbi if he could talk to him. Arbi got out of the car and went to listen to him. The man was middle-aged and poor; I couldn't tell if he was local or a refugee. They bent their heads together in a serious, private conversation, the man had clasped his hands in front of him, circumspect, gesticulation held in deferential check. Arbi listened to him politely, staring at the ground because there was probably nothing he could do to help.

Thomas was having an altercation with a man in a tracksuit who had objected to finding himself in the background of a photograph. He hauled Thomas to the side of the road, pointed at his camera, demanded his film, flapped opened his jacket to indicate a pistol.

Thomas put out his hands, non-threatening, 'I'm sorry. I was just taking general pictures. I don't mean anything by it, it's nothing. I wasn't aiming at you.'

Thomas had the presence of mind to walk backwards towards Arbi and when Arbi waved at him the *boyevik* became less hostile; he began apologizing, laughing at his own reaction,

'OK, it's OK. You should forgive me. I have only just come down from the fighting. I have only been in Pankisi three days; it's difficult to adjust to being in a civilian environment! It's OK.' And he pressed his hand into Thomas's to show friendship and walked off with a stiff limp.

Two men sat on upturned crates with a chessboard balanced on a crate between them. A cow urinated in the sloppy mud in the middle of the market. A man sat in a chair to which was tied a white-painted board; he was having his photograph taken for documents. Arbi fiddled with my glove box, looking for a new cassette, and pulled out the large silver shiny plastic gun that I had bought in the market in Spitak because it was funny at the time.

'It looks like mine!' he said, pulling his out to compare, 'it's almost identical!' and he gave me a waggish look of reproach. A BMW went past and splashed an old woman dragging several kilos of potatoes behind her in a cart. I bought a kilo of hazelnuts. Thomas found a clock. It was a wall clock, cheap and plastic; in the middle of its face a picture of snow-capped mountains and the Chechen flag had been pasted together with the word (in Turkish) Çeçenistan. The numbers ran counter-clockwise and the hands ran backwards.

'It's a Chechen clock!' said the man who was trying to sell it to Thomas for $30. 'It goes in the wrong direction. Time goes backwards into the past. You see, it is clever! It's necessary! We have to erase the last seventy years!' Thomas was completely delighted with this piece of Chechen ingenuity and got the man down to $20.

Arbi laughed indulgently, 'Thomas! Only Thomas!'

And Thomas turned around, all innocent, and said, 'What? – What?'

Arbi's authority was quiet and strong. He did not need to bang his fists. He was a trustworthy man and a good fighter. This is what people knew about him, and this was respected. Most things I didn't know and could not presume to guess. He had probably done bad war things, but it was impossible to see this in his face, which was always open, friendly, and full of gentle smiles and good childish laughter. He was incredibly kind.

'Wendell, I would be very glad to be able to help you, if you need anything, information or anything,' he told me. He was sincere. It was not necessarily an easy thing for him to say; there were many people, his own people, who he could not help.

I did not particularly care if he had killed Russians. The Russians had behaved in Chechnya as racist bullies: bomb it, shoot it, kill it, burn it. But the politics were entangled. The Chechens were nasty too: proud, unbending, brutish, thieving, vengeful, cruel, divided amongst themselves, at the same time honourable and treacherous, as hard as it is possible to be: the best guerrillas in the world. It was a war about freedom and it was internecine; things were complicated. Arbi and I did not talk about politics. I did not know why Arbi continued to fight (or to organize logistics or whatever the hell he was doing in Pankisi with his three henchmen). He had been a sector commander in the first war and seen a lot and had thought about what he had seen and understood it properly. It was his own choice.

Sitting in the passenger seat, shaking over potholes, Arbi asked me when I would leave the Caucasus and go back to England.

'Leave the Caucasus?' I said, mock incredulous. 'I'll never leave the Caucasus.' He understood that I was half joking, saw my irony and smiled in recognition. 'I don't think I can go back to England,' I continued. 'There are very strange people there. You know, they are completely inhospitable and the policemen refuse to take bribes!' He turned sideways and laughed. I began to muse, 'Sometimes, though, I think about Italy and a little stone house with a garden and some chickens.'

'Italy eh?'

'Warm sun, wine, bureaucratic chaos.'

'Yes, I see,' said Arbi, indulging my vision and understanding the truth of it. 'I would also like to live somewhere warm and easy. What kind of a place will Chechnya be when this is all over? I was thinking about going to Greece.'

'Greece?'

'Well, it's only a winter dream,' Arbi seemed a bit sheepish to be caught dreaming. 'For when your feet are cold.'

Roses

ON 6 OCTOBER IT was my birthday, a year since we'd been in Gorbachev's dacha. I was exhausted. The doorbell rang at 7 a.m. It kept ringing. Very reluctantly, cursing, I swung my legs out of bed, put on my kimono and answered it.

A man was standing outside my door holding a large bucket full of red roses. He beamed expectantly at me. I told him he could come in. He came in and put his bucket down in the hall. He was immediately followed by a second man climbing the stairs with another large bucket full of red roses. He was smiling too – it was a great surprise! For ten minutes the two of them went up and down the stairs, unloading a small flat-bed truck laden with buckets full of red roses. They filled the hall, they filled the living room, I had two buckets on my bedside tables and the place smelled like a harem.

'How many are there?' I asked the first man, who looked like the elder brother of the two.

'One thousand!' he said proudly.

I looked at the line of buckets, each full of flowers, a dense carpet of roses – I began to cry gently.

'Don't cry, unless they are tears of happiness,' said the younger brother, who seemed gratified to have produced such a reaction.

'I've been in this business fifteen years,' the elder brother whispered to me conspiratorially, 'and I've never seen anything like it. A thousand roses! It's like Pirosmani!'

The door closed. Perhaps I made myself a cup of tea, I don't remember. I stood there for a long time, looking at the enormity of what he'd done, stroking the wet velvet petals and catching my fingertips on the thorns, my head frozen in a kind of warm terror. Hundreds and hundreds – red velvet expensive, a sort of monstrous thing, Thomas's great crazy love, a thousand roses that would have paid my rent for months – and every petal was beautiful, soft and curved, cool, opaque velvet red, the most delicate thing to hold in your hand, admiring its belly and the way your tears splashed into its hollow.

I felt the tight pathos around my heart dissolve into a Cheshire cat grin. Ha! Ha! Ha! A thousand roses! This was gratification indeed; and I momentarily remembered how I had cried silently at the Opera in Baku, and that I must not be bought easily; but I confess this did not last long. I ran a bath. The water flowed through the gas heater and did not choke like it sometimes did. I decapitated roses and threw the petals in to the water, counting as I dissected: I love him; I love him not; I love him; I love him not.

The story of the thousand roses. The whole street had seen them being delivered, Venera came rushing over, banging on the back door, before I had even got out of the tub.

'Wendell! Esma told me! One thousand! Oh!' she was breathless. I opened the door dripping wet. Venera paid no attention, 'Was it Thomas?'

I snuffled at her, 'Of course he is a fool bastard. One thousand! Like Pirosmani –'

And then she caught sight of them, 'Oh my God! They're beautiful!' Venera began to caress the blooms lovingly.

'Venera, my dear,' I said, pre-emptive, 'of course you can borrow some.'

Lela called. Kate called. Kakha called. Levan called. They had all known.

'So you've got them!' said Kakha.

'Yeah, I've got them,' I replied ruefully.

'Jees, I was up all night with Thomas; it took the man three days to collect all the roses – he was driving around Kakheti for three days just collecting them and then all the flower dealers in Tbilisi were furious – have you noticed you cannot buy a single rose in Tbilisi for the last two days? Thomas bought them all – the flower dealers were all furious about it, they thought that it was some Mafia plot to corner the market.'

'Kakha –'

'So they put it all on a truck – you know we had to get Levan to organize the truck for God's sake – and then the truck got stopped on Rustaveli Avenue because trucks are not allowed on Rustaveli Avenue, but when the police heard why there was a truckful of red roses – they were laughing. "Just get out of here," they said; they didn't even want any money! – So they really look good eh?'

'Kakha. There are a thousand of them.'

Lela said, 'He was pacing around all night. He wouldn't sleep. It's like Pirosmani.'

According to legend, Pirosmani, Georgia's most famous artist, a naïve painter who died penniless before the Revolution, had once sold his house to fill a square with roses for an actress he had fallen in love with from afar. There was a song, some pop croon from the Soviet days, '*A Million Scarlet Roses*'...

Lela and I had planned to go to the *banya* in the afternoon to recuperate and talk. The weather was fine and sunny, Indian summer. I was in the car, the radio was playing Abba, 'The Winner Takes It All'. I was as high as a kite, faintly hysterical, crying and laughing at the same time; glad of life and its funny sharp edges and glad of the sun and happy that I was in Tbilisi, where such things, it seemed, such rank happiness, were possible. The traffic ahead congested hesitantly. I looked up; the electricity cuts had begun and people were often confused about whether or not to stop at dead traffic lights. These lights, however, were more confusing than usual. They were simultaneously flashing red and green. Stop Go. Stop Go. Decide. I began to laugh hysterically. At everything all at once and mostly at Tbilisi, warm, indulgent and mad.

'Even God is confused,' Lela said half an hour later, sloshing in the *banya*, 'even God doesn't know which sign to give you.'

A few days later Thomas told me he'd been on a *marshrutka* going along Chavchavadze Avenue. He'd got talking to a man sitting next to him.

'Ah, you're German,' said the man, 'but it's only a Georgian who knows how to woo a woman properly. It's part of the Georgian romantic soul. It's in here.' And the man tapped his chest. 'I don't know, though. Apparently some of the foreigners are catching on. I heard that one foreigner ordered a thousand roses for a woman! Now that's really something.'

'I didn't know whether to be proud or ashamed,' Thomas told me, relating the story.

'Thomas,' I told him slowly, retreating from the great warm glow of his gesture and remembering how much he had hurt, 'you are crazy.'

Thomas cocked his head and smiled winningly, doing his best impression of a lost thing that needed to be found,

'Yes, I know,' he said, 'but it's the Caucasus.'

Afterword

I WROTE MOST OF this book in Karabakh one autumn. Karabakh was a good place to write because it was so boring. Perhaps places that have been ethnically cleansed tend to be boring, certainly quiet; half the population has gone and taken with it their diversity, their kids playing in the street, their different way of cooking, their different noses, language, slang and wedding ceremonies, the alternative smell of coffee or tea. Everything left behind is all the same.

Karabakh and its capital, Stepanakert, was a rump population. Within the last ten years there had been a war which the Armenian Karabakhis won. They threw out all the Azeris and afterwards rebuilt their own homes with bricks taken from ruined Azeri homes. The Stepanakert I lived in was a generous, wide-spaced town, with more individual houses than blocks, green trees and good views. It had a newish, unfinished concrete atmosphere; some smashed-up walls had not yet been torn down, municipal buildings had only just been rebuilt, clean and sharp; there were still shrapnel holes across some façades, fresh paint on others. Life on the streets was fairly sparse. There were few cars, there were a few kids in falling-apart hand-me-down shoes, there were some chickens and patches of overgrowing blackberry bushes on the derelict sites.

There was not much to do. An Italian called Giuseppe who worked for Médecins Sans Frontières had built his own pizza oven and when he had finished his contract he had given it to Armen, the MSF local manager, who smartly opened a pizza restaurant. The pizza was good although Armen had a penchant for adding canned peas to the topping. There were also a couple of bars where you could drink beer and listen to Russki pop, there was one disco called the Blue Room because it was blue and in a basement, and there was a casino where we persuaded the manager to let us play for one buck a game instead of the usual minimum $5. When it got colder I started to do jigsaw puzzles. On Saturday nights some of us would get together and play Monopoly.

There was a peace process, but as usual it was stagnant. Jan Koehler was working for the OSCE who were trying to shepherd negotiations, and he used to come and share my pea pizza and tell me that nothing was happening. I had no particular desire to interview the President who still limped from an assassination attempt the previous spring, or the Defence Minister who had lost a leg during the war when the tank he was driving exploded. I could have toured the Armenian monasteries and walked the hills (which were beautiful), but on previous trips I had done a bit of this. That autumn I was just stuck in bed writing.

Next to my bed was a window and through the window I could see a single presidential guard pacing outside the President's residence across the street. There was always one there, twenty-four hours a day: neat camouflage uniform, scarlet beret and Kalashnikov. Every morning at seven, in the dark pre-dawn, a contingent of troops would march past tramping along the road and wake me up. Stepanakert was a military town. Soldiers in barracks, soldiers and minefields along the cease-fire line and a khaki atmosphere. There were tanks parked as monuments along the main road, commemorating things like the Fall of Shushi and the Surrender of Aghdam. The Armenians had fought the Azeris in almost every field, and left behind, lying about, were mines, submunitions and unfired missiles (UXO – unexploded ordnance in Halo Trust parlance) scattered next to burnt-out APCs and flails of wire from shot-up power lines.

Every five or six days the Internet connection would work long enough to download a page of email, which took about thirty minutes. News from Tbilisi leaked through: *shuki* demonstrations, several foreigners had been beaten up in a series of nasty muggings, two Spanish businessmen were kidnapped near the airport, the Russians had instituted a visa regime against Georgians in retaliation for all Shevy's NATO talk and Chechen *boyevik* activity in Pankisi. Kakha wrote despairing words. Everybody was tired and cold and it would never change. Nanuli, Shevardnadze's wife, was pruriently rumoured to be in some kind of mental sanitorium in Germany; well that made us laugh a bit.

This is my last paragraph but I can form no conclusions: the Caucasus, Georgia, would make a fool out of anyone with the temerity of prediction. I can say though that things do not always get better and that sometimes they get worse and most often they just stay the same. It is depressing and true and universal: there is nothing to be done about it. The best we can do is to respect our family, love our friends, open a bottle of wine, drink it, and then open another one.

❈

Ethnic Glossary

Abkhazia and Abkhaz

The great chronicle of Abkhazia over the last century is a book called *Sandro of Chegem* by Fazil Iskander. Sandro is the very model of an Abkhaz hero, a dashing man from a mountain village, whose life is a series of great adventures involving ravishing Svan princesses, duelling with Bolsheviks and Mensheviks, meeting Stalin (known as 'the Great Moustache') no less than three times and becoming a wise and respected *tamada* with a callus on his neck from drinking so often and so much.

In the foreword to *Sandro of Chegem*, Iskander grapples with 'the ethnic question'; which is 'the Abkhaz question', which might as well be the question of the whole Caucasus:

> *Every people perceives its own way of life as the greatest one of all. This perception seems to reflect a nation's instinct for self preservation: why should I imitate another people's way of life if mine is the greatest? Hence ethnic prejudice; it is inevitable, for the time being. To pretend that it did not exist would be cowardly and vulgar. Ironic mockery of another people's way of life is the most peaceful form of ethnic prejudice...*

The Abkhaz and the Georgians don't like each other. They don't like each other childishly, in the way that cousins who know each other well but don't like each other bitch and backbite and fight.

The Abkhaz and the Georgians are different; the Abkhaz are a north Caucasian tribe, have their own north Caucasian language, and are more likely to be Muslim than the Georgians (although there are plenty of churches in Abkhazia and no actual mosques...). Less clear is the question: what is Abkhazia? A territory, a nation, someone else's province? Soviet histographs on the subject invariably begin: 'In the eight millennia before Christ the civilization that lived on the Colchis shore of the Black Sea...' As if anyone can remember back that far; as if there is any archaeological proof about who was there when, as if it's remotely relevant to a war which happened last week six years ago. It is the endless finger-pointing: who was there first?

The fact is that Abkhazia was always mixed between Abkhaz and Mingrelians, Armenians, Jews, Greeks (left over from the Byzantine Empire), Russians (who moved south for the weather, the ice-cream beaches and the slackness) and the usual assortment of lost Tartars. Sukhumi was a port; there was trade and later tourists, people came and went and some of them stayed longer than others.

Along with the mellow inter-living of the Brezhnev era (40 per cent of Mingrelians and Abkhaz married each other; there were Abkhaz schools, Georgian schools, Russian schools; there were statues of Abkhaz cultural heroes and Georgians side by side in the parks; there was a disproportionate number of Abkhaz invested in the local government) lay, latently, the grievances: Stalin had awarded Abkhazia to the Autonomous Republic of Georgia in 1931; Beria, head of the Soviet security apparatus, encouraged Mingrelian immigration into Abkhazia through the early fifties. There were always fights between Georgians and Abkhaz in bars in the summer months; the Georgians swanned about the place as if they owned it, the Abkhaz felt marginal...

The Soviet Union collapsed. Abrasive nationalism. Georgia fractured into civil war; there were bandit attacks on the railways, there was ethnic fighting in South Ossetia between Ossetians and gangs of Georgians. The Abkhaz were frightened, proud, defensive and bolstered by promises of help from the Russians. And then one day, 14 August 1992, Kitovani sent his Georgian National Guard into Sukhumi with tanks and started a war.

The war was fought badly and nasty. There were civilian atrocities, small massacres, burnt villages, rape. Eventually the fighting coalesced around a front line along the Gumista River, on the northern edge of Sukhumi. The Georgians dug in with minefields and the Abkhaz stared at them from the other side. The Russians gave the Abkhaz a couple of planes to drop bombs with, communications equipment, some guns. The Abkhaz retook Sukhumi in the late summer of 1993. Shevardnadze remained in the city until the final moments.

The Georgian population fled along the M27 into neighbouring Mingrelia. The retreating Georgian army blew the road bridges along the way. A quarter of a million refugees fled to Georgia. A few months later the Abkhaz pushed out the final pocket of Mingrelians from Gali. It was autumn and they were forced into the mountains to escape through Svaneti. The mountains were high and there was snow; many people, especially old people, died along the way and had to be left behind by their families.

Afterwards there was a cease-fire but no peace. The Russians maintained a peacekeeping force of a little over a thousand men, sand-

bagged in checkpoints in Gali and along the M27, with their headquarters in Sukhumi and bases in Eshera and Gudauta. Georgia, in
frustration, maintained a blockade against Abkhazia which was ironi-
cally enforced by the Russians. From time to time Georgians and
Abkhaz met in Istanbul and refused to agree on anything. Abkhazia
became cut off and forgotten, an unrecognized state, without banks or
an Internet connection, without much petrol or passports. People sold
scrap metal to the Turks and mandarin oranges across the border to
the Russians and cigarettes to each other to survive.

I interviewed the Abkhaz President, Vladislav Ardzinba, in 1999.
He was a former academic nationalist, like they often were in the
Caucasus in the early nineties, trying to create a government out of
nothing. I found him dapper and articulate, but his logic went round
in circles and never arrived. He was stuck in his own rhetoric.

'It's not necessary to have recognition,' he told me, 'recognition
needs to be made by the people and secondly by the international
community. Look at Eritrea, fighting thirty years for recognition. Look
at America – I do not think that England easily recognized America.
Our people consider that they are living in an independent state. No
one tries to understand our situation. They only label us as separatists.
We are not separatists. We are not a part of Georgia seceding from
Georgia. For twelve centuries we had our own state until the Soviet
1931 treaty when our status within Georgia was imposed upon us.
We are talking about a neighbour state trying to capture territory that
does not belong to them. The very fact of the collapse of the Soviet
Union means that borders are broken, so why don't we have the same
rights to build an independent state as Georgia?'

Gali

The region just across the Enguri River in Abkhazia, populated exclusively by Mingrelians; there were never any Abkhaz there (or Armenians or Russians) – at least not that anyone can remember. The land is fertile and lush, and they grow hazelnuts which fetch a good price in Batumi. The Abkhaz are unsure what to do with them and an uneasy truce exists between the reduced and cowed Mingrelian population and the Abkhaz administration in the area.

The Enguri River separates Mingrelia from Abkhazia. It's now also the official cease-fire line; a demilitarized zone exists for fifteen kilometres either side of it, patrolled by the Russians and the UN.

There is one intact bridge over the Enguri, torn tarmac and flanked with Abkhaz, Georgian and Russian sandbagged bunkers. Mingrelians walk across between the market in Zugdidi and their homes and relatives in Gali, pushing handcarts full of produce and shopping. In the summer it's hot and they wear straw hats and walk slowly. There are many, unofficial crossings. These pathways are important when the Abkhaz become more threatening to the Mingrelian population in Gali. When the Abkhaz came through and burned everything again in 1998, casualties among the Mingrelians were almost non-existent; they all gathered their few belongings and ran over their little bridges to the other side.

Adjara and Adjarians

Adjara is on the Turkish border and beautiful, but not as beautiful as Abkhazia. For large parts of its history it was occupied by the Turks, Ottoman and earlier, and the capital, Batumi, reflects this. There are mosques next to churches, baklava, Turkish coffee; on the coast there are villages of fishermen, unlike anywhere else in Georgia, where fish is considered an insipid alternative to pork. Adjarians in Tbilisi like to tease their friends and pretend they are infidel Muslim, but really they are Georgians, like the rest.

Armenia and Armenians

A conversation in Stepanakert in Nagorno-Karabakh in the summer of 1990:

> *'Our question,' says one of those present, 'is, How do we survive? It has been weighing on Armenians for hundreds of years. For centuries we have had our own culture, our own language and alphabet. For seventeen centuries the Christian religion has been the national religion of Armenians. But our culture has a passive character, it is the culture of the ghetto, of a defensive fortification. We have never imposed our customs, our way of life upon others. A sense of mission or a desire to rule are foreign to us. But we find ourselves surrounded by people who, brandishing the banner of the Prophet, have always wanted to conquer this part of the world. In their eye, we are a poisoned thorn in the healthy body of Islam. They are thinking about how to remove this thorn, meaning, how to efface us from the surface of the earth.'*

> – Ryszard Kapuscinski, *Imperium*, 1993

The main thing about the Armenians is that no one much likes them. In the Caucasus they are used to occupying the position that the Jews once occupied in Central and Eastern Europe. They were the outsiders among islets of Armenian ghettos, pogroms, *unassimilation*. They were the traders, the money-men, the perceived rip-off merchants. They have their scars too; their own genocide – 1.5 million Armenians were killed by the Turks in 1915 – but no one seems to take much notice and the Turks remain unapologetic. Greater Armenia was once a great kingdom that stretched far into what is now eastern Turkey. But the thousands of churches that they built there are gone, razed along with the population in the genocide. Lake Van has been lost and Ararat, towering peak and symbol of the Armenian nation, dominates the skyline of Yerevan, but is cruelly cut off by a closed Turkish border.

Yerevan is an ugly city, built by the Soviets out of pink tufa stone which is the colour of boiled flesh. It is modern and dirty. The surrounding land is high, dry, rock-swept, covered in veins of pink tufa and black obsidian; few trees. It's easy to see why the Armenians are proud, embittered. Their existence has always been hardscrabble, persecuted and massacred for centuries by the Muslim hordes on either side of them, Persian and Turk. And yet they were the first Christian nation, they wrote their own alphabet while the Europeans were covered in wode and superstition. God, it seems, didn't like them either; with divine spite he gave the fertile land and the best grapes to the lazy Georgians next door.

Between 1988 and 1994 Armenia supported a war of independence fought by ethnic Armenians in an enclave of Azerbaijan called Nagorno-Karabakh. The Armenians won this war, the Azeris fled their homes and their villages and towns were razed to the ground. Aghdam, which once housed 40,000 Azeris, is now utterly empty and in ruins, not a roof left, few remaining walls higher than my shoulder.

Karabakh now has an independent government, a well-defended cease-fire line and no peace settlement. It is a cut-off cul-de-sac, beautiful, mountainous, scarred by war, dotted with brand-new Armenian churches built on promontories, like monuments of conquest. For

Armenians, winning back Karabakh has gone some way to redress the ancient historical imbalance of lost land.

Azerbaijan and Azeris

Before the Russians came Azerbaijan was a series of Khanates on the edge of the Persian Empire. Its incarnation as an independent nation is as recent as 1991, although more ethnic Azeris live in what is now northern Iran than in Azerbaijan. Azeris are Muslim; Azeri is a Turkic language. Bakuvians are cosmopolitan, Russified, speak Russian, drink vodka and eat Turkish kebabs.

Their President, Heydar Aliev, is a Soviet dinosaur of the Politburo, much like Shevardnadze, but with a nastier streak of authoritarianism. He does not encourage political pluralism or a free press; his police are drunk, mean and dangerously corrupt. The economy is a pyramid built of oil and caviar monopolies which are controlled by his son Ilham. Azerbaijan is ground zero for pipeline politics because Caspian oil is the future of European supply; Aliev treads his geopolitical fault line between the Americans and the Russians carefully.

Chechnya and Chechens

'And have you been long in the Chechen region?'

'Yes, I was stationed there for about ten years with my company in a fort near Kamenny Brod [Stone Ford]. Know the place?'

'I've heard of it.'

'Well, my good sir, we did get tired of those cut-throats. Nowadays, thank goodness, things have quietened down, but the way it used to be – you just walked a hundred paces beyond the rampart, and there was

258

bound to be some shaggy devil sitting and watching you: one second off guard, and it would happen: either a lariat would be around your neck or there would be a bullet in the back of your head. But what brave fellows!...'

– The narrator gets talking to a veteran of the Caucasian wars in Lermontov's story 'Bela' from *A Hero of Our Time*, first published in St Petersburg, 1840

The enmity between the Chechens and the Russians is old. The Chechens fought the Russians for more than thirty years during the Murid Wars of the mid-nineteenth century. Almost alone among the Caucasians, the Chechens resisted Russian imperialism. They were galvanized by a warrior imam, Shamil, the Lion of Dagestan, who fought guerrilla tactics from mountain eyries against the Russians. Eventually the Russians chopped down the forests which gave the rebels cover and paid off enough of Shamil's commanders and Chechnya was subdued.

But Stalin remained wary. In 1944, as the Germans advanced towards the Caucasus, he deported the entire Chechen nation to Kazakhstan, fearing they would support the invaders. Thousands of Chechens died in cattle trucks on the way, thousands more died in the cold Kazakh winters that followed. In the fifties, after Stalin died, they were allowed home and the rest of the Soviet period saw Chechnya become Russified: Grozny became home to a sizeable Russian population; vodka and tower blocks proliferated.

The President, Jokhar Dudayev, once a Soviet air force general, declared Chechen independence in the nationalist mêlée of the early nineties. In 1994, Yeltsin sent in troops to regain control. For two years the Chechens lost territory and ground but in 1996, incredibly, bloodily, against the odds, they retook the bombed ruins of Grozny, ambushing Russian armoured columns in the rubble-strewn streets and firing randomly at checkpoints. The Russians sued for peace and left the Chechens to their own devices.

Dudayev had been killed during the first war and his successor, Maskhadov, had little control over the victorious warlords. Bandit rule, kidnapping, pockets of Islamic fundamentalism flared. The Russians invaded Chechnya again in October 1999, advancing to their old cordon on the Terek River. The Chechen civilians, women and children, fled the artillery assault on Grozny. Most of them went west to their cousins the Ingush in North Ossetia, to refugee camps, tents, railway cars, mud, or joined the lines of refugee cars that clogged the border for kilometres. Others fled south across the mountains into Georgia.

The war fought since then has been horrendous. As usual the Chechen fighters were pushed back into the mountains. The Russians do not often allow Western journalists in, the Red Cross and other aid agencies are also routinely denied access. The Chechens continue to kill Russians in ambushes and small massacres; the Russians have retaliated with summary executions, mass graves and detention centres. The rest of the world turns a blind eye.

Khevsureti and Khevsurs

The Khevsurs are a good Caucasian tribe; tough highlanders, grey-eyed, red-cheeked, poor; their land is vertical and treeless. They are hospitable, but not as overwhelming or quite as dangerous as the Svans. They have always been Georgians; they speak Georgian, they were the special bodyguards of the Kartli kings, they are not Muslims. They are not exactly Christian either: there are no churches on the north side of Khevsureti; instead there are ancient crosses and spirals carved into the old abandoned slate towns that cling to weathered hill-sides, lichen-covered burial grounds on high promontories and caches of rock and prayer trees that stand as shrines, surmounted by the skulls of mountain goats. The Khevsurs have their own traditions: poetry, everyday epics, mountain vodka, family, clan, village, a long isolating winter, a few hardy cows and not much else. According to travellers' accounts of the early twentieth century, the Khevsurs were chiefly known for two things: wearing chainmail, which encouraged the myth that they were descendants of a lost party of Crusaders, and sending their women alone into stone huts to give birth on a pile of straw. In the early twenties Odette Keun wrote: '*When the mother's cries tell that the confinement is a difficult one, the husband, who usually wanders around the hut, but may on no pretext whatever rejoin his wife, encourages the sufferer by firing shots from his gun.*'

Kisti

The Kisti are not a separate tribe as such; they are Chechens who settled in the Pankisi valley in the middle of the nineteenth century, refugees from the Murid Wars. The Pankisi valley lies forty moun-tainous kilometres from the border with Chechnya and the same distance from the high passes above Omalo that were always trod back and forth between local Khevsurs, Kisti and Chechen villagers on the other side. The Kisti learned Georgian, wrote their dialect in the Georgian alphabet and added the Georgian suffix, *shvili*, to their surnames. After the break-up of the Soviet Union they applied for Georgian passports. They never interacted much with their Georgian neighbours, but relations were cordial. The Kisti retained Chechen customs; their tombstones were written in Georgian script and adorned with a Muslim crescent and star, the women wore head-scarves. When I first went there just after the start of the second Chechen war in 1999 I talked to a village elder in a room decorated with pictures of Dudayev, the former President, killed by a Russian helicopter gunship ambush.

There were never very many Kisti; they were poor and they kept to themselves. The Georgians seemed surprisingly sympathetic to them. During the second Chechen war the Russians accused the Georgians of treating wounded *boyeviki* in Tbilisi hospitals, of har-bouring Chechen 'terrorist commanders', of allowing a supply route through the mountains, of tolerating Chechen training camps in Pankisi. But the Georgians stuck up for the Chechens and denied all these things publicly despite the fact that they were mostly true. There wasn't much the Russians could do about it, but still, they dropped a couple of aerial bombs on Shatili and on Pankisi 'by accident' and thumped their fists on the table.

Mingrelia and Mingrelians

Mingrelians are Georgian, but like the Svans, a different kind of Georgian. They speak Mingrelian, like the Svans speak Svan, a sepa-rate language within the Georgian family, although most of them speak Georgian as well to get around with. Often you can hear an indecipherable mixture of Mingrelian-Georgian-Russian being used in jumbled phrases.

Mingrelia is in the west of Georgia, where the botany shifts from temperate forest to subtropical and palm trees begin to grow in front yards. They live next to Abkhazia and over the years many have gone to live in Abkhazia. It is said (by the Abkhaz, of course) that Beria was a Mingrelian and that he encouraged Mingrelian immigration into

Abkhazia to dilute the local population. Certainly half of Abkhazia, even now, even after the Abkhaz threw out all the 'Georgians', has Mingrelian surnames that end in *ia* as opposed to an Abkhaz surname that usually ends in *ba* if it has not been Russified to *ov*. But all attempts by tribes in the Caucasus to define themselves in terms of territory are tenuous. For centuries groups were either arriving, leaving, building or rebuilding after a period of ethnic tension, moving in and out among each other, populations shifting and migrating, intermarrying.

Ossetia and Ossetians

The strange thing about the Ossetians is that they speak an Indo-European language; unlike anyone else in the vicinity. And they are unfortunate enough to have their homeland divided between Georgia and Russia into South Ossetia and North Ossetia.

The South Ossetians fought the Georgians in the early nineties when the Georgians ran amok and nationalist. Like the Abkhaz, they won; the capital Tskinvali got smashed up by rockets on one edge. The Ossetians, however, seem gentler than the Abkhaz, the hatred is not acute. For a while things were difficult between Ossetian villages and Georgian villages, neighbours and intermarried couples, but proximity takes away a lot of the fear. Tskinvali is only twenty minutes up the road from Gori. After a couple of years Georgian cars with Georgian plates were driving up to Tskinvali to buy contraband coming through the tunnel from Vladikavkaz on the other side of the Russian border. Tskinvali doesn't have much; very little electricity, no money, not very many people; but it does have a huge bazaar selling petrol stolen from pipelines, bags of cement, raw alcohol, Viceroy cigarettes and lurid Russian soda pop – in other words, all the basics.

There was always a rumour that Stalin wasn't entirely Georgian; that given the fact that his birthplace, Gori, is next to Ossetia, his father, at best an obscure character, may well have been Ossetian. Perhaps this is moot. But the Ossetians, hemmed in by the Georgians, mistrustful of their Ingush neighbours in North Ossetia, always retained a special brand of pro-Russia. The main road in Tskinvali is still called *Ulitsa Stalina*; in the fly-blown schools, they still polish the old Komsomol cups and there are cases full of fading photographs, head shots of soldiers and tank commanders: heroes of the Afghan war of the 1980s.

Svaneti and Svans

The Svans live in Svaneti, in the very high western Caucasus – the most beautiful place on earth. The towering peaks of Shkhara and Ushba rise above valleys which tumble gently down along forests and meadows, cliffs cut by rushing rivers, pine and ash, wildflowers, children running alongside wooden fences, wells of mineral water, enormous glass jars of gold honey... I remember the village of Becho, lying in Besso's orchard counting apples idly, watching the women make meat pies with bread dough in the beetle-black oven, stoking the wood, drinking tea, eating pancakes with apples, the children watching me closely. A police colonel came to talk to Besso. There had been an incident – something, someone shot, a horse stolen – the colonel was wearing his best uniform, a pair of riding breeches stretched over his thighs, gold braid looping his shoulders, a big-brimmed hat covered in more gold braid and red stars. He was followed by a group of remonstrators, men from the village. They stacked their rifles by the door as the colonel asked them to. Besso, who had been chopping wood, threw a shirt over his vast hairy shoulders and, fulfilling his office as headman of the village, went to sort it out.

There was a big *supra* that night and we drank. The Svans are legendary among Georgians for drinking, for their blood feuds, for their craziness, their inbred banditry and for being a bit thick. We drank *chacha* and mountain vodka out of huge goat horns. I have a dim recollection of standing on the table to make a toast. In the morning I was very ill indeed and I watched Besso drink four tumblers of vodka with his bread-and-cheese breakfast, laughing at my incapacity.

In the villages of Svaneti there are eleventh-century towers; families still live in these, defences against attack and avalanches. The Svans always kept their gold and icons in families for safety; they never had churches that could be plundered for museums by the Soviets. They, among all Georgians, were never invaded. Svaneti was too far, too high, too easily defended, rich, fertile and full of heavily armed men. Their creed was only ever half decipherable to ethnographers. Even Zaliko would scratch his head: they had a something, but they were mad too. Some said they were the closest to the original Georgians.

Bibliography

W. E. D. Allen, *A History of the Georgian People*, London, 1932

   Allen admits that when he began to write the book he was 'impressed by the lack of accessible work on Georgian history, either in English or indeed any West European language'. It is still the main source work and it stops when the Russians arrive in 1801.

Neal Ascherson, *Black Sea*, London, 1995

John F. Baddeley, *The Russian Conquest of the Caucasus*, London, 1908

C. E. Bechhofer, *In Denikin's Russia and the Caucasus 1919–1920*, London, 1921

Andrei Bitov, *A Captive of the Caucasus, Moscow, 1969*, translated by Susan Brownsberger, New York, 1992

Lesley Blanche, *The Sabres of Paradise*, New York, 1960

   Great towers of purple prose; apart from Odette Keun, Lesley Blanche was my favourite female Caucasus traveller.

Stephen Brook, *Claws of the Crab: Georgia and Armenia in Crisis*, London, 1992

G. Poulett Cameron, Esq (Lieutenant-Colonel, lately employed on a special service in Persia), *Personal Adventures and Excursions in Georgia, Circassia and Russia*, 2 vols., London, 1845

Sir John Chardin, *Travels into Persia, and the East Indies through the Black Sea, and the Countrey of Colchis, describing Mingrelia, Imiretta, Georgia and several other Countries unknown to these parts of Europe*, London, 1686

Chardin was a roguish, libidinous adventurer, rollicking across the Caucasus to sell European jewels to the Persian Tsar. He was always on the lookout for a tasty slave girl (indeed, on occasion, describing their 'exemplary nipples'), he was always getting rid of two-faced servants conspiring to rob him and dodging bandit bullets – he seems to have travelled rather heavy, with large quantities of ox-carts etc. His energetic descriptions are wide-ranging: feasts (and he seems to have endured quite a few of these), how the Georgians and Armenians always lived in separated villages and were on bad terms, various bouts of dysentery, Ararat and Armenian myths about its summit, Erivan (Yerevan) and weddings, the drunken antics of the Shah or a self-made French ambassador at the Persian court. He was commissioned by the Shah to get jewellery for him in Europe. A great swashbuckler.

Here's an extract:

> *Almost all Mingrelians, both men and women, even the most noble and wealthy, never have but one shirt, and one pair of breeches at a time; which lasts 'em at least a year: In all which time they never wash 'em above three times: only once or twice a week they shake 'em over the fire, for the vermin to drop off, with which they are mightily haunted; and indeed I cannot say I ever saw any thing so nasty and loathsome. Which is the reason that the Mingrelian ladies carry a very bad scent about 'em. I always accoasted 'em, extreamly taken with their beauty; but I had not been a minute in their company, but the rank whiffs from their skins quite stifl'd all my amorous thoughts.*

Ilya Chavchavadze, *Collected Works*, originally written in the mid-nineteenth century and translated in the late-nineteenth century by Oliver and Marjorie Wardrop. My edition published in Tbilisi, 1987

Robert Conquest, *Stalin: Breaker of Nations*, London, 1991

Thomas de Waal, *Black Garden: Armenia and Azerbaijan through Peace and War*, New York University Press, 2002

Tom's new book about the Karabakh war is the only sensible work that has been written on the subject. Ever diligent, compassionate, thorough, Tom was always worrying that his efforts at producing a balanced account of this nasty ethnic conflict would only succeed in antagonizing both sides as they read between the lines for each other's propaganda. I used to tell him not to worry: that he could never hope to satisfy every enflamed opinion. In fact he would only know that it was a real success, that he had come close to the truth, when both sides equally vilified him for lies and distortion.

Thomas de Waal and Carlotta Gall, *Chechnya: Calamity in the Caucasus*, New York, 1998

This is an excellent book.

Giuseppe Tomasi di Lampedusa, *The Leopard*, Everyman edition translated by Archibald Colquhoun, New York, 1991

Alexandre Dumas, *Adventures in Caucasia*, Paris, 1859

> *Dumas (who had put on Caucasian dress with a gigantic dagger, sword, and revolver on the very day of his arrival) astounded Georgian writers by his – even to the natives – amazing capacity for filling himself up with unheard-of quantities of wine.*
>
> Essad Bey, *Twelve Secrets of the Caucasus*, London, 1931

George Ellis, *Memoir of a Map of the Countries Comprehended between the Black Sea and the Caspian*, London, 1788

Essad Bey, *Twelve Secrets of the Caucasus*, London, 1931

Trevor Fishlock, *Out of Red Darkness*, London, 1992

Monsieur and Madame Freygan, *Letters from the Caucasus and Georgia*, translated from the French, London, 1823

Zviad Gamsakhurdia, *The Spiritual Mission of Georgia*, translated by Arrian Tchanturia, Tbilisi, 1991

Suzanne Goldenberg, *Pride of Small Nations: The Caucasus and Post-Soviet Disorder*, London, 1994

Bibliography

Darra Goldstein, *The Georgian Feast: The Vibrant Culture and Savory Food of the Republic of Georgia*, Berkeley, CA/London, 1999

Thomas Goltz, *Azerbaijan Diary*, London/New York, 1998

> The best post-Soviet Caucasus chaos book ever. The *New York Times* reviewed it: '*Goltz's account of six years as a freelance journalist in a volatile region where oil men, spies, Islamic militants, mercenaries and corrupt politicians jockey for power reads like a combination of John le Carré and Hunter S. Thompson*'.

Agnes Herbert, *Casuals in the Caucasus: The Diary of a Sporting Holiday*, London, 1912

George Hewitt, *The Abkhazians: A Handbook*, London 1999

Peter Hopkirk, *The Great Game: On Secret Service in High Asia*, Oxford, 1990

Fazil Iskander, *The Thirteenth Labour of Hercules and Other Stories*, translated by Robert Daglish and K. M. Cook, USSR, 1978

——*Sandro of Chegem*, translated by Susan Brownsberger, New York, 1983

Ryszard Kapuscinski, *Imperium*, Warsaw, 1993

Odette Keun, *In the Land of the Golden Fleece*, translated by Helen Jessiman, London,1924

> During her travels, Odette, saucy French bourgeois socialist adventuress and free lover, was somewhat smitten with the Georgians, particularly the male variety. She was particularly impressed with the Khevsur men she met: '*Above all things they are male: upstanding, intolerant and independent, their muscles hardened by marching, hunting and carrying of loads, everything about them is virile or rugged and they have the imposing, arresting carriage that comes of conscious courage and unquestioned liberty.*'
>
> Odette's romanticism was not only theoretical. Her first guide, a twenty-year-old boy of good family ('*tall, slender, graceful... full of braggadocio and irresponsibility*') shot himself with her revolver with the shame of losing her money playing cards all night in Telavi; her second, a nobleman with socialist politics, declared undying love and ravished her

in a house in Svaneti while under siege from a band of Bolshevik brigands (*'And suddenly Grisha took me in his arms, kissing my shoulders –'*). As it turns out, the book is dedicated to a certain Captain Prince George Gregory Tsereteli...

Oleg V. Khlevniuk, *In Stalin's Shadow: The Career of 'Sergo' Ordzhonikidze*, published in Russia 1993, translated by David J. Nordlander, New York, 1995

David Marshall Lang, *A Modern History of Georgia*, London, 1962

John le Carré *Single & Single*, London, 1999

Mariam Lordkipanidze, *Georgia in the 11th–12th centuries*, Tbilisi, 1987
——*Essays on Georgian History*, Tbilisi, 1994

Fitzroy Maclean, *Eastern Approaches*, London, 1949
——*To Caucasus: The End of All the Earth*, London, 1976

I often came across people in Tbilisi who knew Fitzroy Maclean. They were always beautiful women of a certain age and breeding; often they had visited him at his house in Scotland. After all his Central Asian adventures and his months in war-time Yugoslavia, Fitzroy Maclean ended up a devoted Georgophile. He went to Georgia several times in the seventies, wrote *To Caucasus*, took some wonderful pictures (all landscapes, no people though), kept contacts, friendships, lectured on Georgia at the Royal Geographical Society in his eighties. When, in September 1991, demonstrating crowds were solidifying between Gamsakhurdia in the Parliament and Kitovani (head of the National Guard) and other yelling 'democrats' at the TV station, Maclean interviewed the President who looked spooky and heavy like a KGB king, avoided eye contact and gave a lot of guff about difficult times and young countries and no specifics at all about anything.

Andrei Makine, *Once Upon the River of Love*, Paris, 1994, translated by Geoffrey Strachan, London, 1998

This book is very very fine. It is one of my favourites and this bit of the

Soviet experience, the shut-in boredom of the sixties and seventies, is seldom explored.

Osip Mandelstam, *Journey to Armenia*, Moscow, 1933

> *At once travel narrative, an allegorical journey, a withering comment on state building, a humanist philosophy of life, a preparation for death and a prophecy of resurrection (both for Armenia and for himself), this breathtaking, elliptical prose first appeared in the Soviet magazine* Zvezda *in 1933. It was the last piece Mandelstam saw published.*
>
> –Bruce Chatwin in his introduction to
> Clarence Brown's translation, London, 1989

Mandelstam wrote a nasty funny poem about Stalin, 'The Kremlin Mountaineer', with fat grubs for fingers and cockroach eyebrows, who flung horseshoes into groins, and recited it to a few friends – six or seven, maybe. He was arrested and died in a transit camp on the way to the gulag, probably in 1938. I have always asked myself if it is a reasonable thing to swap your life for a poem. 'The Kremlin Mountaineer' is one of the few pieces of truth to survive from the time of the Terror, and it survives to make us smile awfully. I don't know; Mandelstam was a marked man; probably he would not have survived even without the evidence of the poem.

——*Selected Poems*, translated by James Greene, London, 1989

Nadezhda Mandelstam, *Hope Against Hope*, translated by Max Hayward, London, 1971

Philip Marsden, *The Crossing Place*, London, 1994
——*The Spirit-Wrestlers*, London, 1998

Carolyn McGiffert Ekedahl and Melvin A. Goodman, *The Wars of Eduard Shevardnadze*, London, 1997

Avtandil Menteshashvili, *Trouble in the Caucasus*, New York, 1995

Eskander Beg Monshi, *History of Shah Abbas the Great*, Persia, early seventeenth century

Peter Nasmyth, *Georgia: A Rebel in the Caucasus*, London, 1992

——*Georgia: In the Mountains of Poetry*, New York, 1998

    I first met Nasmyth at the Aitar compound in Sukhumi. He was up there taking pictures of the old bombed, decaying art nouveau seaside architecture. He told me he'd been going to Georgia for years. He had pictures of Sukhumi from the old days when there were still tourists walking along the promenade eating ice-cream. He had pictures from the Tbilisi civil war, he had stories; he'd been all over – in the back of taxis and NGO vehicles, sometimes as a journalist, more recently as a photographer/NGO unto himself. In Tbilisi with an American partner, Nasmyth, opened an English bookshop with really good coffee. He was the eternal Englishman abroad, never learned the language but probably knew more about odd bits of it than any local. I once described his footwear as execrable in print and he has never let me hear the end of it. 'What do you mean, *execrable?*' he said, pointing at his leatherette basket-weave lace-ups, 'I got these in the market for 5 lari!'

Guram Odisharia, *The Pass of the Persecuted*, translated by Elene Pagava and Ia Iashvili, Tbisili, 2001

Soulkhan-Saba Orbeliani, *The Book of Wisdom and Fiction*, first published in Tbilisi at the turn of the seventeenth century. My edition translated by J. Mchedlishvili and I. Petrova, Tbilisi, 1978

Boris Pasternak, *Letters to Georgian Friends*, London, 1968

Michael Pereira, *Across the Caucasus*, London, 1973

Pushkin, *Complete Prose Tales*, translated by Gillon R. Aitken, London, 1966

Donald Rayfield, *The Literature of Georgia*, Oxford, 1994

John Reed, *I Saw The New World Born*, an anthology published in English, Moscow, 1976

Roger Rosen, *Odyssey Guide: Georgia, A Sovereign Country of the Caucasus*, Homg Kong, 1999

Friar William of Rubruck, *His Journey to the Court of the Great Khan Mongke*,

1253–1255, translated by Peter Jackson, London, 1990

Mary Russell, *Please Don't Call it Soviet Georgia*, London, 1991

Eduard Shevardnadze, *The Future Belongs to Freedom*, translated by Catherine A. Fitzpatrick, London, 1991

Self-propagandic and not remotely interesting.

Mikhail Sholokhov, *And Quiet Flows the Don*. First published in 1934, translated by Stephen Garry, London, 1957

——*Fierce and Gentle Warriors*, translated by Miriam Morton, New York, 1967

John Simpson, *A Mad World, My Masters*, London, 2000

Henry M. Stanley, *My Early Adventures in America and Asia*, London, 1895

John Steinbeck, *A Russian Journal*, 1948, illustrated by Robert Capa

I thought it almost impossible to find this book any more, but apparently it has been recently reprinted. Thomas gave me a copy for my birthday, photocopied, samizdat, gleaned from the archives of Magnum in Paris. There is no story here, but very precise, meticulously described observations. Capa's pictures are almost all of bombed cities. I loved this book because it's like always: they start off in Russia a little stifled between red tape and fear and formal vodka banquets and then they arrive in Georgia and discover the whole population bending the rules with a wink, slapping them on the back and pouring wine down each other's throats.

Strabo, *Geography*, Rome, 7 BC (or a bit later), 8 vols., London/New York, 1917–32

Ronald Grigor Suny, *The Making of the Georgian Nation*, London, 1988

Apart from Allen, this is really the only book about Georgian history in English. Unfortunately, it's completely unreadable and full of chapters about the social structure of medieval Georgia. Academese. Also he does not even mention Giorgi Saakadze.

——(ed.) *Transcaucasia: Nationalism and Social Change: Essays in the History of Armenia, Azerbaijan and Georgia*, Michigan, 1996

Stories I Stole

Tolstoy, *Master and Man, and Other Stories* including 'Hadji Murat', translated by Paul Foote, London, 1977

—*The Cossacks*, Everyman edition, translated by Louise and Aylmer Maude, London, 1994

Dato Turashvili, *Stories, Short Stories and Very Short Stories Written in Kathmandu*, Tbilisi, 1999

When Dato was younger he used to stand on soapboxes and shout freedom at riot police. Now he writes stories (in pencil, in notebooks) and goes on television, pronouncing whatever comes into his head: being Georgian, living in Georgia, the greatness of being Georgian, the greatness of Georgian wine and whether the cross of St George should appear on the national flag. I find Dato's nationalism a bit didactic: for example, he has a Georgian cross tattooed on his bicep.

Julius von Klaproth, *Travels in the Caucasus and Georgia performed in the years 1807 and 1808*, London, 1814

Christopher J. Walker (ed.), *Visions of Ararat: Writings on Armenia*, London, 1997

John Oliver Wardrop, *The Kingdom of Georgia*, London, 1888

Thirty years after he wrote this competent, but a bit bland and unadventurous sort of travelogue, Oliver Wardrop became Her Majesty's first and (for seventy years) only Ambassador. He arrived in Menshevik Georgia perhaps a bit bemused by the goings-on: British troops in Batumi to secure Georgia against the Turks who were in the process of having their territory stripped from them at Versailles, Bolsheviks in the cities, Whites in the countryside; the fall-out chaos of the combined fall of the Ottoman Empire and the Russian civil war. Wardrop was a big Georgophile but his sister, Marjory, was even better prepared for his posting than he, having spent the previous decade learning the Georgian language in an English village.

The Georgians loved the Wardrops, but they loved Marjory best of all. She threw her arms open to the place and spent her time translating

Georgian poetry, including the whole of Shota Rustaveli's epic poem *The Knight in the Panther's Skin*. Everywhere she went crowds thronged railway stations, affection was heaped by the indolent and doomed aristocracy and the indolent and doomed intelligentsia alike.

Wardrop's embassy did not last long; the Bolsheviks arrived in 1921. The Bodleian Library in Oxford now houses the collection of manuscripts, translations and photographs that the Wardrops collected in Georgia.

A. N. Wilson, *Tolstoy*, London, 1988

Acknowledgments

THANK YOU, PEOPLE WHO fed me, who told me things and taught me things who don't appear as themselves in the narrative – in no particular order:

Aunty Tina (the best *matsoni* soup), Kunchulias, especially Esma (*aladiki*), Amany Radwan (dinners on boats in the middle of Cairo), Ashraf Ezz (lunches with servants and a DVD player for post-lunch recovery), Scott Macleod (best barbecued chicken with view of the Pyramids), Hussein Sherif Gohar (seafood in Alexandria), Dato Kajaia (brains on Sunday morning at Nikusha's), Giorgi and Irina Topuria (tea and cake and excellent news reports on the Web), Dali Tolordava (Christmas tea with soft-boiled eggs and cake), Peter Boit and Renna Effendi (caviar for breakfast in Baku), Sabina (birthday party feast in Baku), Tim Jones (gin and tonics at the Ambassador's residence in Yerevan), Iosef Adamian and his wife (home-made *tutovka* in Stepanakert), Armine Alexian (Spanish tortilla in Stepanakert), Heather and Jurg and Patrick (Turkey and trimmings at Thanksgiving at the ICRC house in Stepanakert – sorry for bringing the grenade), Milla (*blinchiki* in bed at the Halo House with *kisil varenie*), Piers Lewis (air-conditioning and *borjomi* when I had dysentery), Maka Antidze and Nana (coffee and cigarettes at Reuters), Amy Spurling and Bdzina (seriously good potato pancakes and Bloody Marys), Teona (lemon tea when I was weak and pathetic), Lika Basilaia (herb tea and bread and butter in Khevsureti – but dashing man!), Akaki Gogichaishvili (always too busy to stay for dinner...), Onnik Krikorian (*horovats* in *tone*), Kate Whyte and Gia (beer and *chipsi* on the Tbilisi Sea), Marion Staszewski (Monica Lewinsky chocolate bars for my birthday in Sukhumi), Mikho Abramishvili (a diet of requests for articles), Ted Jonas (summer dinner in Tskineti), Lawrence Sheets and Magdalena Fricova (strawberry chicken), Tamriko Machavaviani (*pirogi* for tea), Dato Koguashvili (drinks at the Beatles Club), Chris Lockwood (*chacha* and LAOS), Andrew Barnard (*pelmeni*), Zviad Mukbaniani (*kinkhali* when I was sick), Goga (extra Internet time at the office), Sukho (tea and Turandot – courtesy of Lasha), Tura (beer at Gircha), Dato Janelidze (vodka and chocolate in the kitchen), Sveta and Tengiz (*varenie* – don't remind me!), Lela and Guram (large amounts of fab chocolate cake), Vatta Gorgikia (shashlik in Mtskheta), Elena Gabedava (champagne with Jaba), Gio Dartismelia (*lobio* when the lights went out), Dato Shengelia (well I was supposed to feed you, I know), Lali Barkaya and Gogola (*tsatsivi*), Lia Bagrationi and Temur (*khajapouri* and football).

Also thank you to SMSP, although you are an idiot: you were the first to read it, and you said that you liked it.

R U S

C a u c a s u s

Pitsunda

Gudauta

Sukhumi ABKHAZIA

SVANETI

GALI

Gali

Zugdidi

MINGRELIA

Black Sea

Poti

Kutaisi

Rioni

M27

GURIA

IMERETI

Batumi

AJARA

TURKEY

Separatist regions

International boundary

Autonomous boundary

M27 Highway

Georgian Military Highway

Rivers

0   10   20   30   40   50 Miles

0   20   40   60   80 Km